Early English Poetic Culture and Meter

FESTSCHRIFTEN, OCCASIONAL PAPERS, AND LECTURES

Volume XXV

Medieval Institute Publications is a program of
The Medieval Institute, College of Arts and Sciences

WESTERN MICHIGAN UNIVERSITY

Early English Poetic Culture and Meter

The Influence of G. R. Russom

Edited by

M. J. Toswell and Lindy Brady

Festschriften, Occasional Papers, and Lectures

MEDIEVAL INSTITUTE PUBLICATIONS

Western Michigan University

Kalamazoo

Library of Congress Cataloging-in-Publication Data

Names: Toswell, M. J., editor. | Brady, Lindy, editor.
Title: Early English poetic culture and meter : the influence of G. R. Russom / Edited By M. J. Toswell and Lindy Brady.
Description: Kalamazoo : Medieval Institute Publications, Western Michigan University, 2016. | Series: Studies in medieval and early modern culture | Includes bibliographical references and index.
Identifiers: LCCN 2016032463| ISBN 9781580442428 (paperbound : alk. paper) | ISBN 9781580442435 (eISBN)
Subjects: LCSH: English poetry--Old English, ca. 450-1100--History and criticism. | English poetry--Old English, ca. 450-1100--Versification. | Russom, Geoffrey.
Classification: LCC PR203 .E37 2016 | DDC 829/.1009--dc23
LC record available at https://lccn.loc.gov/2016032463

ISBN: 9781580442428
eISBN: 9781580442435

Printed and bound in the United States of America

Geoffrey Richard Russom

Contents

Foreword

Thomas Cable
University of Texas at Austin

THE TITLE OF GEOFFREY RUSSOM'S first book, *Old English Meter and Linguistic Theory* (Cambridge University Press, 1987), stated the double goal that has guided his scholarly career. There was a time in medieval studies when the aim of conjoining poetics and linguistics would have seemed unremarkable, indeed natural and necessary. The world was that way when Rick was a graduate student. In the decades since, departmental and disciplinary drift have made it necessary for couriers to travel back and forth between the territories. Eventually, as islands split off and communication became increasingly difficult, bridges had to be built, and simple couriers found that they had to acquire the knowledge and wisdom of emissaries. To the benefit of the profession and of areas across boundaries, Rick has been an exemplary bridge-builder and emissary.

His "word-foot" theory of Old English—and eventually Old Germanic—meter has proved elegant and capable of covering the facts. Equally important, it has proved capable of *not* covering facts that turn out not to be facts. The construction of this kind of filtering template can be learned from many empirical disciplines, but it has been an especially explicit and recurring tenet of theoretical linguistics since the mid-twentieth century.

There are medievalists for whom the most basic kind of metrical notation seems as alien as a chemistry formula. Even the clarifying reduction of Sievers's Five Types can be off-putting to those eager to get back to their studies of the Benedictine reform or the hero on the beach. The far more abstract rules of generative metrics, one of Rick's main intellectual resources, are simply hopeless. Out of these competing abstractions, Rick has offered something tangible: think of a verse of Old English poetry as a combination of two words in the various shapes that words could take at that stage of the language. Words are things anyone can deal with: any Anglo-Saxonist has spent countless hours looking them up in glossaries and dictionaries. Because even the least linguistically oriented medievalist has to deal with words, it is a simple step to think of a verse of Old English poetry as a combination of two words. Leave it at that and let the prosodists fuss over the details.

For example, the much-discussed Kaluza's law has presented a problem for some interpreters dealing with weak verbs of the second class. If a past-tense form like *þrēatedon* is assumed to receive secondary stress on its middle syllable, *-te-,* then that syllable, though short, should not "resolve" by Kaluza's law, because it is followed by a "long" syllable, *–don.* Yet in a verse like *þrēatedon þearle* "suspension of resolution" would result in the unmetrical sequence / \ x / x, disallowed by all serious theories of meter. Russom's solution elaborates on R. D. Fulk's questioning of secondary stress on this morphological category, which had been assumed since Eduard Sievers in 1885. The word-foot theory, by recognizing words with the pattern / x x *(þrēatedon)* as perfectly natural, provides an additional way of getting to the conclusion that Fulk reached (the verse having the ordinary shape / x x / x). This is contrary to assumptions by Sievers and introductory Old English grammars and readers for the past century but compatible with recent findings. In fact, much of Russom's work aims to show the fit of his system with other systems, including competing ones. It's a refreshing attitude in the contentious field of metrics—of any period—where scorched-earth tactics often accompany the announcement of "a new theory."

Russom does something similar with another set of generalizations for which the word "law" is attached: Hans Kuhn's famous prescriptions of 1933, which involve both syntax and meter. Kuhn's taxonomy of stressed words, particles, and proclitics does quite a bit of work, even if expert metrists usually have to look up the hierarchy constantly to remind themselves of what's what. Russom's word-foot approach makes it easier for everyone: he suggests that the distinction between particles and proclitics is a distinction between more and less *wordlike* constituents. Particles are more wordlike than clitics; unstressed prefixes are less wordlike than other clitics. With this rational start, the details are more manageable. Russom of course does not ignore the details, because in addition to an eye for simplicity, he has a knowledge of the corpus, a corpus that often seems anything but simple.

Those who have had the chance to exchange ideas with Rick over the years at Kalamazoo and at lesser conferences with better wine know that the relevant parts of the corpus—that's to say, specific lines—always seem within easy reach of the indexing part of his brain. This could be embarrassing for a panelist who has just seen their eighteen-minute solution fall apart. However, Rick's genial manner has a way of offering an alternative idea through his word-foot theory without insisting on it, maybe even downplaying it as one of several paths. This lack of dogmatism leaves the presenter a chance to return to the drawing board with new knowledge gained in the give and take, a way to salvage the argument without abandoning its core.

In his scholarship and his presence at scholarly conferences, Rick Russom has nurtured the international community that thrives on difficult linguistic subjects from the Middle Ages. Those of us who have not had the pleasure of knowing him on his home ground, Brown University, are not at all surprised by the trust and confidence his colleagues have placed in him. Clearly, his achievements in teaching and administrative patience have been appreciated not only over the course of his career but also since retirement. He continues to be called back to teach his History of English course and to contribute to the team-taught course for the concentration in Medieval Studies. Meanwhile, his scholarly work is a point of reference for many, as the essays in this volume show. More important than a retrospective, however, is the likelihood that Geoffrey Russom relieved of duties—chair of the Medieval Studies Program, chair of the English department, and all the rest—will make discoveries about the early stages of the English language that will surprise even him.

Introduction

Lindy Brady and M. J. Toswell

GEOFFREY RUSSOM'S RARE GIFT to elucidate—and to value—both the metrical abilities and artistic accomplishments of Old English poets defines his scholarship. His comments on *Beowulf* in Milman Parry's *Festschrift* encapsulate this generous and intelligent approach, which scintillates in all of his work, both scholarly and pedagogic. Noting that "the study of *Beowulf* has suffered from an unfortunate polarization of opinion," Russom concludes, "to me the *Beowulf*-poet's refinement of language and loyalty to oral tradition seem equally remarkable."[1] He finds a way to bring what are generally opposing forces together, pointing out the synergies and connections, arguing that the *Beowulf* poet was both sophisticated in language use, and aware of the tradition of storytelling and oral material available for use. As Thomas Cable's foreword to this volume makes clear, few scholars have done more to illuminate the intricacies of Old English poetic meter than has Russom; however, the essays in this collection are a testament to the fact that Russom's work will long be remembered not only for his achievements in demystifying the inner workings of Old English (and Germanic) meter, but also for his rare ability to appreciate both sides of the poetic coin simultaneously: technical skill and art, logic and beauty, order and aesthetic pleasure.

Russom's *œuvre* returns Old English poems to their origin as the products of a metrical system whose inner workings were a natural reflection of the language patterns of native speakers. His gift to Anglo-Saxon studies has been to appreciate that system as one whose rules can indeed be deduced, and understood, centuries later. Russom's word-foot theory of Old English and Germanic meter reminds us of a fact often lost in the technical difficulties of parsing verse types: in order to be appreciated, any functional metrical system must have been immediately comprehensible by a poet's audience. Scansion, in other words, must occur at the speed of performance, and the clarifying simplicity of Russom's approach has been to argue that the building blocks of Old English verse correspond to "linguistic principles already internalized by the native speaker"—that is, the patterns inherent in native words.[2] Russom's theory—though so simple it can be reduced to just two rules (foot patterns correspond to word patterns, and verse patterns consist of two readily identifiable foot patterns)—accounts for the complexities of Old English verse while reminding us that such complexities "would not have to be learned by native speakers of Old English."[3] His approach allows for a more accurate classification of Old English verse types while facilitating appreciation of Old English poetry as an extension of natural language: in Russom's understanding, "the typical line of Old English verse is analogous to a musical cadence that progresses from aesthetic tension to aesthetic release."[4]

Yet as this last statement indicates, at the same time as he clarifies many technical difficulties of Old English meter, Russom pays equal attention to a given poem's artistry. While Old English meter was a system with identifiable patterns and rules, the many studies on *Beowulf* (in particular) and other Old English poems demonstrate the range of ways in which individual poets skillfully showcased their artistry within that system.[5] Russom's work shows that Anglo-Saxon poets, working within the structure of a metrical system originally inherited from oral tradition, nonetheless offered originality and artistry in that they "valued the richness of their tradition and exploited that richness systematically in their works."[6] A constant strength of Russom's work is a thoughtful evaluation of Old English poetry as a product of its place and time: a tradition inherited from an older oral system of verse and pre-Christian Germanic culture, yet enhanced by—rather than weakened by, or divorced from—its eventual contact with and emergence from the literate Christian intellectual milieu of Anglo-Saxon England. As Russom asks, "Why, exactly, is it so difficult to imagine brilliant epic poets with little or no ability to read, selective interest in the fruits of Christian scholarship, and sufficient authority to get thoughtful responses for their questions?"[7]

Indeed, as the essays in this volume make clear, Russom's work has been driven by a deep concern to approach not just Germanic poetry, but also Germanic culture as a whole, on its own terms. For Russom—despite his unifying theory of Old English meter—there is no unilateral category of 'Old English poetry.' The reader approaches each poem individually, with appreciation for both the inherited Germanic past and learned Christian present of Anglo-Saxon England. Thus, while one of Russom's articles might brilliantly illuminate the skillful Latinity of the author of Exeter Book Riddle 47,[8] while another demonstrates the Old Testament timescale of *Beowulf*,[9] Russom does not hesitate to ponder the lingering impact of pre-Christian Germanic culture in shaping Old English poetry either. Another of his studies finds in *Beowulf* the fingerprints of Norse mythological structure,[10] and likewise, his important studies on "The Drink of Death in Old English and Germanic Literature" and "A Germanic Concept of Nobility in *The Gifts of Men* and *Beowulf*" recover two key motifs in Old English and Old Norse literature—the 'drink of death' and the 'gifts of men'— for their original Germanic cultural origins, important discoveries that have helped us understand the full artistry of the literary works in which these motifs appear.[11]

Rick's body of work is substantial, and this brief sketch has only considered the highlights of his major articles and several books, without touching on his many contributions to the history of the English language (and pedagogical strategies to facilitate the teaching of this difficult course), the numerous book reviews which demonstrate his generosity to the field and kindness to his colleagues, his contributions to the serious study of the literary works of J. R. R. Tolkien, or indeed, his enormously significant studies of Middle English alliterative meter and the continuity of its progression from the Old English period. While no cursory survey can do Russom's body of work justice, the intellectual curiosity which continues to drive his career (with another book project arriving at completion) will, we hope, find a fitting tribute in this collection of essays on those topics to which his own work has contributed so much: Old English, and now also Middle English, meter and style.

In our first paper, Jun Terasawa tackles a tricky topic for metrists, who habitually begin their consideration of Old English texts with *Beowulf*: the poem has a number of short verses, verses which apparently have only three syllables. Moreover, some of these come in significant places in the poem, as they are epithets for the eponymous hero himself. As one might expect of a former Russom student, Terasawa first assembles all the evidence as to how major editors of the poem have treated this corpus, considering and weighing the emendations they propose and dispose, and analyzing their consistency of treatment of these short verses. Terasawa reaches a judicious and careful conclusion based on philological issues of grammar and semantics, and also adducing evidence from the alliteratively anomalous and quite late Old English poem, the *Battle of Maldon*. Basically, he identifies a constraint on Old English poets that seems to have held even stronger than did the requirement to produce alliteration: the four-syllable half-line. R. D. Fulk addresses another metrical conundrum, the verses which contain only particles that generally do not carry stress. He considers clause-initial particle verses in both Old English and Old Norse, that is, verses largely populated by finite verbs or pronouns in nominal function or some adverbs not usually taking stress. Clitics are also relevant, as Fulk investigates the differences in the way poets handle on-verse particle verses when they begin new clauses. He elucidates real differences in the way the *Beowulf* poet addresses these, with a verb placed finally in the verse being the most common pattern, rarely not followed and when not followed there is usually a good reason. This pattern of behavior demonstrable in the *Beowulf* poet's usage differs from the earlier *Guthlac A,* and from such texts as the *Meters of Boethius* and the metrical psalter, but is similar to the work of Cynewulf. Eddic particle verses differ in verb placement but are otherwise similar to *Beowulf.* Fulk here clarifies the standard patterns of usage for particle verses, and offers editors and students of Old English and Old Norse poetry a method for thinking about how to handle these common but often tricky verses.

Daniel Donoghue engages with the very common question of punctuation in Old English manuscripts, a question many have found tricky or downright tricksy. He approaches the issue from the perspective of linguistics—something our honorand frequently does in an effort to establish a *rapprochement* between historical linguistics, philology, and the study of Old English language and literature—and specifically using an insufficiently noticed book by Geoffrey Nunberg applying linguistic thinking to punctuation. Donoghue uses Nunberg's approach to rethink the whole issue of how punctuation marks off linguistic boundaries in Old English generally, and applies it specifically to a range of manuscripts of prose and poetry. His linguistic approach leads him to new and important thinking about how individual scribes approached their work and interpreted their texts. He finishes, in fact, where Fulk starts, with issues of verse syntax. Lindy Brady also has a tricky problem of interpretation to address in *Beowulf*: her question is whether the references to boars in the poem are of literary importance, or simply offer us a window on the material culture or the history of the relevant tribes and nations. She discovers both that the semiosis of the boar is significant in ways beyond the purely symbolic or the apotropaic, and that boars are associated with triumphant moments for the Geats, often in quite subtle and intriguing ways, and always in the first two-thirds of the poem. Her analysis spans Old English, onomastics, archaeology, issues of status and power, the possibility of shamanic usage, and the structure of the poem.

Beowulf is also the touchstone for Megan Hartman's application of Russom's most famous and useful metrical theory, the word-foot theory of Germanic meter, to stylistic analysis. She gets there by rethinking how the word-foot theory works in specific texts, beginning of course with *Beowulf* as the touchstone text, and comparing the work of the poets of the *Battle of Maldon* and the two *Maxims* poems. She investigates the stylistic choices of these poets, noting the greater frequency of unstressed syllables and words, and drawing conclusions about the choices made: thus, in *Maldon* the shift to a more analytic syntax changes the choice of verse types and the patterns of usage, whereas in *Maxims* a more obvious constraint is the proverbial language and its requirements for finite verbs and prepositions. Hartman notes that the poets here work out ways to handle the complexity of Old English verse structure, and to limit that complexity in ways different from those in *Beowulf*, but ways that allow the poets to accomplish their goals in verse that is recognizably using the same metrical system. That is, her poets have different priorities and turn the Old English verse structure to produce slightly different effects. Haruko Momma investigates the poet of the metrical psalter, another poet engaged in reworking the Old English verse structure; her approach, however, is by way of translation strategies and theories in order to investigate just how it is that the metrical psalms were acculturated in Anglo-Saxon England. For her approach she engages with translation theorists such as Eugene Nida and Laurence Venuti, and posits new ways of approaching the metrical psalms as a translation and as a text. For example, she points out that the different copies of this text do not demonstrate the freedom of linguistic variation that scribes offer for the handful of other poetic texts surviving in two or more copies from Anglo-Saxon England. The metrical psalter is also the focus for M. J. Toswell, who shifts away from the hegemony of *Beowulf* as the touchstone for Old English verse structure, and points out the ways in which polyptoton offers poets a mode of poetic engagement that allows them greater metrical and stylistic freedom. That is, for poets whose subject matter or approach or metrical ability required a different kind of thinking about how to create Old English verse, polyptoton offered an easy method of obtaining alliteration and metrical acceptability, as well as the rhetorical technique of repetition of the root of the word with some variation. Her examples include *Beowulf* but focus on the later verse, including especially the metrical psalter.

Thomas A. Bredehoft opens up a whole new way of thinking about Old English poetry and its structure, arguing for a completely new and original approach to the apprehension of what a poem might be, and how that apprehension actualizes itself in the resulting text. For his example he takes a manuscript addition to the Regius Psalter (British Library MS Royal 2.B.v), and argues that the text is axiomatically poetry. He presents an edition under the title *Confessio et oratio*, as in the manuscript, and then offers a detailed metrical and stylistic analysis of the 130 lines of text, noting particularly a remarkable number of parallels between the text and the writings of Ælfric.

The last paper in the volume shifts to the field in which Russom is now working, Middle English meter and its continuity or rupture from its Old English precedents. Eric Weiskott presents a critical edition of an unpublished late Middle English poem of political prophecy, which he entitles *The Vision of William Banastre*. Alliterative in its form, the poem offers a fascinating historical window into what Weiskott suggests were the 1470s in the north, and falls in a tradition of visions associated with Banaster and others in late Middle English. It appears here, however, because Weiskott uses the edition to reconsider the critical approaches to late alliterative meter, threading elegantly from Russom's argument for continuity from the early period to the late medieval period in England through the complications of the phonological and metrical arguments of Thomas Cable and Hoyt Duggan. Weiskott's metrical analysis concludes with an argument for the prohibition of final long dips in Middle English, as they would cause confusion; he rightly, and appropriately for the last paper in the volume, invokes Russom's principle of closure.

Together these papers celebrate the field in which Geoffrey Richard Russom publishes most frequently, the consideration of meter, metrical grammar, and stylistic effects in Old English (and to some extent Old Norse and other Germanic languages). He, of course, has supervised and taught many students in medieval English language and literature more generally, as well as Old Norse and those various other Germanic languages he keeps in his head. His students learn from him a rigorous but humble approach to their fields; they figure out what the facts are and then think about possible ways to explain those facts. Rick always has theories, but he also always makes them fit the facts rather than the reverse. We hope that in these papers we have done the same. Many of us have enjoyed the felicity of hailing Rick in a corridor at a conference, or ambling into a pub, only to hear a cogent and clear explanation of his latest linguistic discovery, or his latest theory and proof. We will be doing just that for many years to come.

NOTES

[1] "Verse Translations and the Question of Literacy in *Beowulf*," in John Miles Foley, ed., *Comparative Research on Oral Traditions: A Memorial for Milman Parry* (Columbus: Slavica, 1987), pp. 567–80 at p. 577.

[2] *Beowulf and Old Germanic Metre* (Cambridge: Cambridge University Press, 1998), p. 4.

[3] "Word and Foot in *Beowulf*," *Style* 21 (1987): 387–99 at p. 395.

[4] "On the Distribution of Verse Types in Old English Poetry," in Sally Crawford and Helena Hamerow, eds., *Form and Order in the Anglo-Saxon World* (Oxford: Oxford University School of Archaeology, 2009), pp. 108–118 at p. 108.

[5] Particularly relevant here are "Artful Avoidance of the Useful Phrase in *Beowulf, The Battle of Maldon,* and *Fates of the Apostles*," *Studies in Philology* 75 (1978): 371–90; "Verse Translations and the Question of Literacy in *Beowulf*," "Word and Foot in *Beowulf*," and "Aesthetic Criteria in Old English Heroic Style," in John Hill, ed., *On the Aesthetics of Beowulf and Other Old English Poems* (Toronto: University of Toronto Press, 2010), pp. 64–80.

[6] "Artful Avoidance of the Useful Phrase," p. 390.

[7] "Aesthetic Criteria in Old English Heroic Style," p. 79.

[8] "Exeter Riddle 47: A Moth Laid Waste to Fame," *Philological Quarterly* 56 (1977): 129–36.

[9] "History and Anachronism in *Beowulf*," in David Konstan and Kurt A. Raaflaub, eds., *Epic and History* (Oxford: Wiley-Blackwell, 2009), pp. 243–61.

[10] "At the Center of *Beowulf*," in Stephen Glosecki, ed., *Myth in Early Northwest Europe* (Tempe, AZ: Arizona University Press, 2007), pp. 225–40.

[11] "The Drink of Death in Old English and Germanic Literature," in Daniel G. Calder and T. Craig Christy, eds., *Germania: Comparative Studies in the Old Germanic Languages and Literatures* (Wolfeboro, NH: D. S. Brewer, 1988), 175–89, and "A Germanic Concept of Nobility in *The Gifts of Men* and *Beowulf*," *Speculum* 53 (1978): 1–15.

Secg betsta and *ðegn betstan*: A Reconsideration of the Short Verses in *Beowulf*

Jun Terasawa
University of Tokyo

FREDERICK KLAEBER'S THIRD EDITION of *Beowulf* had long been the standard edition for advanced scholars as well as for students.[1] In 2008, Klaeber's classic was revised and brought up to date by R. D. Fulk, Robert E. Bjork, and John D. Niles.[2] While following the basic form and organization of Klaeber's third edition, the new fourth edition (hereafter Fulk-Bjork-Niles) deviates from its predecessor in some respects. One of the divergences arises in the treatment of the following two epithets for Beowulf given below in the manuscript forms:

secg betsta (*Beo* 947a, 1759a)	[the best man]
ðegn betstan (*Beo* 1871b)	[the best thane]

Note first that these two verses are short, consisting of only three syllables. In his third edition, Klaeber leaves these short verses as they are in the manuscript, which results in violating a basic principle of Old English meter that each half-line must contain at least four syllables.[3] *Secg betsta* and *ðegn betstan* also pose a problem for Geoffrey Russom's word-foot theory since the verse pattern S/Sx (in his notations) would correspond to the foot pattern Ssx to violate a constraint that verse patterns may not overlap foot patterns.[4]

In the fourth edition, the editors make a change in these short verses; the mid vowel is recovered in the superlative *betsta(n)* to make rhythmically acceptable verses of Type D1.[5] Note that the initial syllable of *bet[e]sta(n)*, although short, can bear rhythmic stress alone as it is immediately preceded by another rhythmic stress:

```
 /    /  ×  ×
secg bet[e]sta

 /    /  ×   ×
ðegn bet[e]stan
```

The emendations adopted in the fourth edition go against a recent trend toward textual conservatism where a majority of the "post-Klaeber" editions have followed the third edition and retained the manuscript readings.[6] In the post-Klaeber era, there are only five editions (including Fulk-Bjork-Niles) that make emendations for MS. *secg betsta* and *ðegn betstan*: while Francis P. Magoun, Jr., Benjamin Slade, and Fulk basically adopt the conjectures followed by Fulk-Bjork-Niles, Ferdinand Holthausen reads *secg[a] betsta* (1759a) and *ðegn[a] betstan* (1871b).[7] As for 947a, Holthausen takes *mē* from the following off-verse to give *secg betsta, mē* with *mē* stressed. For the treatment of the above-mentioned two verses in the post-Klaeber editions of *Beowulf*, see Appendix 2.[8]

Although we have recently seen a more conservative attitude in the treatment of *secg betsta* and *ðegn betstan*, that was not the case with the "pre-Klaeber" editions—i.e., the editions published before the third edition. Particularly since Sievers proposed in his article of 1885 to add the genitive plural ending in *–a* to give metrically acceptable four-syllable verses,[9] the readings *secg[a] betsta* and *ðegn[a] betstan* formed a majority even including Klaeber's first and second editions, published in 1922 and 1928 respectively.[10] For the treatment of *secg betsta* and *ðegn betstan* in the pre-Klaeber editions of *Beowulf*, see Appendix 1.[11]

Some of the earliest editions of the epic also challenged the manuscript readings. In the *editio princeps* of *Beowulf*, Thorkelin divided the verses differently from most modern editions to read *þec secg betsta* (947a), *Leofa sæg betsta* (1759a), and *Scyldinga þegn betstan* (1871b).[12] I would imagine that Thorkelin, the very first editor of the epic, might have felt uncomfortable about the short verses and have attempted to fix the problems by transposing a word from the preceding verse.[13] Kemble's first and second editions followed Thorkelin in verse 947a to read *þec secg betsta*. In the first edition, Kemble added *guð-* in 1759a to give *guð-secg betsta*, which resulted in a legitimate four-syllable verse but spoiled the alliteration. In his second edition, however, he kept the manuscript reading, although the alternative reading (i.e. *secg[a] betsta*) was given in the footnote. As for 1871b, Kemble's first and second editions, while following the manuscript, provided *þegn[a]* as a possible emendation in the footnote. Heyne (in his 4th ed.) and Harrison-Sharp, who read *þec, secg betsta* in 947a, added the demonstrative *se* before *betsta* in 1759a and the mid vowel *–e–* in *þegn* to give *secg [se] betsta* and *þeg[e]n betstan* respectively. (The latter is, however, metrically of three syllables with *þegen* resolved.)

Thus we can see that Klaeber's third edition (first published in 1936) forms an important watershed in the treatment of *secg betsta* and *ðegn betstan*: while many of the pre-Klaeber editions do not hesitate to emend the short verses to avoid three-syllable verses, a majority of the post-Klaeber editions have followed the third edition and retained the manuscript readings since these verses do not pose any semantic or grammatical problems. In this connection, it is interesting to witness a change in the treatment of *secg betsta* and *ðegn betstan* among Heyne's successive editions published over a period of a hundred years: while various conjectures were made to fix the short verses until the fourteenth edition published in 1931, the fifteenth and later editions in the post-Klaeber era have kept the manuscript forms.

As has been noted above, the history of textual criticism concerning *secg betsta* and *ðegn betstan* in *Beowulf* offers a gradual shift towards using the manuscript forms. However, the Fulk-Bjork-Niles edition, returning to the liberal attitude towards emendation in the pre-Klaeber era, swims against the recent trend towards textual conservatism where metrical evidence alone is not considered as sufficient grounds for conjecture.

Although Klaeber's third edition and a majority of the post-Klaeber editions preserve the manuscript readings in *secg betsta* and *ðegn betstan*, they are not entirely consistent about the treatment of the other short verses. Consider the following half-line of three syllables in the epic:

gegnum fōr (*Beo* 1404b)
[(Grendel's mother) went straight]

While the manuscript reading is preserved by many of the post-Klaeber editions, quite a few editors attempt to emend this short verse to give a normal verse of four or more syllables even though this verse does not pose a semantic or grammatical problem any more than *secg betsta* and *ðegn betstan* do. While it sticks to the manuscript in the reading of *secg betsta* and *ðegn betstan*, for instance, Klaeber's third edition adds *swā* at the beginning of this verse:

[swā] gegnum fōr
[so (Grendel's mother) went straight]

This emendation is adopted by Magoun and Jack. Mitchell-Robinson and Fulk-Bjork-Niles begin the verse with *þǣr*:

[þǣr] gegnum fōr
[there (Grendel's mother) went straight]

Dobbie and Swanton supplement *þǣr hēo* at the beginning:

[þǣr hēo] gegnum fōr
[there she went straight]

Note that supplied words like *swā, þǣr,* and *þǣr hēo* are neither semantically nor grammatically indispensable. Trask replaces the monosyllabic *fōr* by the synonymous disyllabic verb *ferde*:

gegnum f[e]r[de]
[(Grendel's mother) went straight]

In *Beowulf*, there are attested some seventeen examples of short verses including the four verses discussed above, each of which Fulk-Bjork-Niles uniformly emend while other post-Klaeber editors are not always consistent in this respect.[14] In what follows, I will provide some interesting cases where the *Beowulf* poet skillfully avoids three or fewer syllable verses[15] and thereby suggest that short verses including *secg betsta* and *ðegn betstan* should be consistently emended in the epic, as Fulk-Bjork-Niles do. I conclude that the four-syllable principle is such a strong constraint in composing Old English verse as to call for possible emendation of other short verses.

Avoidance of Short Verses in *Beowulf*

In *Beowulf*, besides the commonly used *man(n)*, which is a masculine noun of a minor declension, the weak by-form *manna* appears six times exclusively in the accusative singular:

lēofne mannan (*Beo* 297b, 1943b, 2127a, 3108a)
[beloved man]

earmran mannon (*Beo* 577b)
[more wretched man]

ānne mannan (*Beo* 2774b)
[one man]

Why did the *Beowulf* poet choose the less common form of *man* in these verses? It is important to note that the use of the ordinary monosyllabic *man* (acc.sg.) would result in too short a verse of only three syllables, as **lēofne man*, **earmran man*, and **ānne man* (an asterisk denotes unmetrical verses). It would therefore appear that the *Beowulf* poet chose the alternative weak form of *man* primarily to satisfy the metrical requirement of at least four syllables per verse.

The *Beowulf* poet also seems to have avoided short verses in terms of choosing between morphological variants. When the agent-noun suffix *–end* is used in the nominative or accusative plural, there are chiefly two different forms available in verse texts, one in *-end* and the other in *-ende*, the latter being formed on the analogy of the strong adjective declension of present participles. In *Beowulf*, for instance, the compound *sǣlīðend* in the nominative plural occurs with and without final *-e*:

> sǣlīþende (*Beo* 377b)
> [seafarers]
>
> secgað sǣlīðend (*Beo* 411a)
> [seafarers say]
>
> Nū wē sǣlīðend (*Beo* 1818a)
> [Now we seafarers]
>
> þæt hit sǣlīðend (*Beo* 2806a)
> [so that seafarers (may call) it (Beowulf's barrow)]

The choice between *-end* and *-ende* is not free variation but it is rhythmically conditioned. In the first instance, the use of the nominative plural form in *-ende* is due to rhythmic reasons: without final *-e*, the verse would be too short, consisting of only three syllables (**sǣlīþend*). In the half-lines where *sǣlīþend* is used without *-e*, the compound is accompanied by one or two words to make the half-lines long enough to be normal verses.

Among fourteen other instances of words in *-ende* (nom./acc.pl.) attested in *Beowulf*, twelve are compounds occupying a whole verse of Type D1, reflecting the spelling in verse 377b above where the use of the shorter *-end* would result in too short a verse.[16]

There is another case where the choice between two morphological variants is due to metrical factors. In *Beowulf*, there appear eleven instances of *gēn* while the dissyllabic form with the suffix *-a* (i.e. *gēna*) is attested only twice:

> fremmað gēna (*Beo* 2800b)
> [attend further to (the people's need)]
>
> Cwico wæs þā gēna (*Beo* 3093b)
> [(he) was then still alive]

Note first that without *-a*, verse 2800b would consist of only three syllables (**fremmað gēn*). With the shorter *gēn*, although it consists of four syllables, verse 3093b would not belong to any of the five types or their subtypes:

> / × × /
> * Cwico wæs þā gēn

Conclusions for *Beowulf* and Old English Poetry

As we have seen, there are some interesting cases where the *Beowulf* poet resorts to less common variants to satisfy the requirement of at least four syllables per verse. In light of these facts, it would be hard to imagine that the poet, while avoiding half-lines of three or fewer syllables, left the short verses as they are. Concerning the verses *secg betsta* and *ðegn betstan*, I am in favor of emendation to give half-lines of four syllables. Following Fulk-Bjork-Niles, I take the original readings as *secg bet[e]sta* and *ðegn bet[e]stan* with *betsta(n)* preserving the mid vowel, which the scribe(s) would have transcribed with the later syncopated *betsta(n)*. Other conjectures favored in the pre-Klaeber editions, i.e. *secg[a] betsta* and *ðegn[a] betstan* are less plausible since it would be highly unlikely that the poet mistakenly dropped the genitive plural ending three times in different parts of the poem.

While many of the recent *Beowulf* editors are hesitant about emending short verses like *secg betsta* and *ðegn betstan*, they are ready to correct a manuscript reading that lacks alliteration. To provide alliteration in line 965, for instance, most of the *Beowulf* editions agree to replace the manuscript form *hand* by the synonymous *mund* even though the line makes perfect sense in the manuscript:

> þæt hē for *mu*ndgripe   mīnum scolde (*Beo* 965)
>
> [so that he (i.e. Grendel) should (lie struggling for life)
> because of my hand-grip]

Why have editors of *Beowulf* been much more reluctant to emend short verses than alliteration-free verses despite the fact that short verses occur less than half as often as lines lacking proper alliteration?[17] This undue favoritism towards alliteration could be ascribed to the fact that the number of syllables in a half-line would be a metrically less conspicuous feature than alliteration.

It is important to note here that the four-syllable principle is generally followed in late verse texts that show noticeable anomalies in the use of alliteration. In the *Battle of Maldon*, while the poet often deviates from the traditional rules of alliteration,[18] not a single instance of a short verse is attested. Moreover, there is evidence that the *Maldon* poet worked to avoid short verses. Consider the following verse from this late heroic poem:

> Gehȳrde ic þæt Ēadweard   ānne *slōge*
> swīðe mid his swurde,   swenges ne *wyrnde* (*Mald* 117–8)

[I heard that Eadweard fiercely struck one with his sword,
(he) did not withhold the stroke]

In the *þæt*-clause introduced by *gehȳrde* "heard," there occur two verbs with *slōge* "(would) strike" being unambiguously subjunctive and *wyrnde* "would withhold or withheld" being either subjunctive or indicative. Most editors of the *Maldon* take the latter as third singular indicative preterit since the verb *(ge)hȳran* usually requires the indicative in the object clause.[19] As Mitchell notes, the form *slōge* is the only unambiguous instance of the subjunctive after *(ge)hȳran* in the poetic corpus.[20] The anomalous use of subjunctive *slōge* here is probably due to metrical reasons: the indicative *slōg* (pret. 3 sg.) would make verse 117b too short (**anne slōg*).

The *Battle of Maldon* provides another piece of evidence that would also suggest the poet's concern to avoid a short verse. Compare the following similar verses:

ǣttrynne ord (*Maldon* 47a)
[a deadly point (of a spear)]

ǣtterne ord (*Maldon* 146a)

In 47a, the noun phrase is in the accusative singular with the strong adjective form in *–ne*. In 146a, on the other hand, the noun phrase is in the nominative singular, where instead of the strong adjective *ǣttern* we find the odd form *ǣtterne*. In their glossary, Pope-Fulk note that "*ǣterne* was perhaps influenced by *norðerne, sūðerne*, etc., or by some old poetic use of a weak form, *ǢTRENA*, metathesized as *ǢTERNA*."[21] But such archaism is not to be expected in a late poem like the *Maldon*. The use of the unusual adjectival form in 146a might be due to the fact that the regular strong form without final *–e* would produce too short a verse of three syllables, i.e. **ǣttern ord*.

If short verses are avoided in an alliteratively anomalous poem of the late Old English period, it would seem to follow that the four-syllable principle turns out to be a stronger constraint in the composition of Old English poetry than the alliterative requirement. This would lead us to reconsider short verses for possible emendation even if they do not show grammatical or semantic anomalies.

Appendix 1: Pre-Klaeber editions

- MS. indicates that the editions retain the manuscript readings.
- Letters or words added by the editors are enclosed in square brackets.
- Lacunae in a series of editions (e.g. Thorpe's 2nd edition) result from their inaccessibility.
- Sievers's article (1885) is added, which proposed the earlier influential readings, i.e. *secg[a] betsta* and *ðegn[a] betstan*.

	secg betsta 947a	**secg betsta 1759a**	**ðegn betstan 1871b**
Thorkelin (1815)	þec secg betsta	Leofa sæg betsta	Scyldinga þegn betstan
Kemble (1833)	þec secg betsta	[gúð]-secg betsta	MS. (fn. þegn[a])
Kemble (1835^{2})	þec secg betsta	MS. (fn. secg[a])	MS. (fn. þegn[a])
Thorpe (1855, 1889^{3})	þec secg betsta	MS.	MS.
Grundtvig (1861)	MS.	MS.	MS.
Heyne (1863)	MS.	MS.	MS.
Grein (1867)	MS.	MS.	MS.
Arnold (1876)	MS.	MS.	MS.
Heyne (1879^{4})	þec, secg betsta	secg [se] betsta	þeg[e]n betstan
Harrison-Sharp (1883, 1885^{2})	þec, secg betsta	secg [se] betsta	þeg[e]n betstan
Holder (1884)	MS.	MS.	MS.
Sievers (1885)	secg[a] betsta	secg[a] betsta	ðegn[a] betstan
Heyne-Socin (1888^{5})	þec, secg betsta	secg [se] betsta	þeg[e]n betstan
Wyatt (1894, 1898^{2})	MS.	MS.	MS.
Heyne-Socin (1903^{7})	secg[a] betsta	secg[a] betsta	þegn[a] betstan
Trautmann (1904)	secg[a] betsta	secg[a] betsta	ðegn[a] betstan
Holthausen (1905-6, 1908–9^{2}, 1912–13^{3}, 1914-19^{4}, 1921–29^{5}, 1929^{6})	secg[a] betsta	secg[a] betsta	ðegn[a] betstan
Heyne-Schücking (1908^{8})	secg[a] betsta	secg[a] betsta	þegn[a] betstan
Sedgefield (1910, 1913^{2})	secg[a] betsta	secg[a] betsta	ðegn[a] betstan
Wyatt-Chambers (1914)	secg[a] betsta	secg[a] betsta	ðegn[a] betstan
Heyne-Schücking (1918^{11,12})	secg[a] betsta	secg[a] betsta	þegn[a] betstan
Klaeber (1922, 1928^{2})	secg[a] betsta	secg[a] betsta	ðegn[a] betstan
Heyne-Schücking (1931^{14})	secg[a] betsta	secg[a] betsta	þegn[a] betstan
Sedgefield (1935^{3})	secg bet[o]sta	secg bet[o]sta	ðegn bet[o]stan

Appendix 2: Post-Klaeber editions

- MS. indicates that the editions retain the manuscript readings.
- Letters or words added by the editors are enclosed in square brackets.
- Lacunae in a series of editions (e.g. Heyne-Schaubert's 17th edition) result from their inaccessibility.

	secg betsta 947a	**secg betsta 1759a**	**ðegn betstan 1871b**
Klaeber (1936[3], 1941, 1950)	MS.	MS.	MS.
Holthausen (1938[7], 1948[8])	secg betsta, mē	secg[a] betsta	ðegn[a] betstan
Heyne-Schaubert (1940[15], 1946[16], 1963[18])	MS.	MS.	MS.
Dobbie (1953)	MS.	MS.	MS.
Magoun (1966)	secg bet[e]sta	secg bet[e]sta	þegn bet[e]stan
Nickel (1976–82)	MS.	MS.	MS.
Chickering (1977)	MS.	MS.	MS.
Swanton (1978, 1997 rev.)	MS.	MS.	MS.
Crépin (1991)	MS.	MS.	MS.
Jack (1994)	MS.	MS.	MS.
Wrenn-Bolton (1997[5])	MS.	MS.	MS.
Trask (1997)	MS.	MS.	MS.
Mitchell-Robinson (1998, 2006 rev.)	MS.	MS.	MS.
Kiernan (1999, 2011[3])	MS.	MS.	MS.
Alexander (2000 rev.)	MS.	MS.	MS.
Slade (2006)	secg bet[o]sta	secg bet[o]sta	ðegn bet[o]stan
Fulk-Bjork-Niles (2008)	secg bet[e]sta	secg bet[e]sta	ðegn bet[e]stan
Fulk (2010)	secg bet[e]sta	secg bet[e]sta	ðegn bet[e]stan

NOTES

[1] *Beowulf and the Fight at Finnsburg,* ed. Frederick Klaeber (London: Heath, 3rd ed., 1936; 3rd ed. with supplement, 1941; 3rd ed. with first and second supplements, 1950).

[2] *Klaeber's Beowulf and the Fight at Finnsburg,* eds. R. D. Fulk, Robert E. Bjork, and John D. Niles, 4th ed. (Toronto: University of Toronto Press, 2008).

[3] For the requirement of at least four syllables per verse, see, for instance, Eduard Sievers, *Altgermanische Metrik* (Halle: Max Niemeyer, 1893), §180, and Alan Bliss, *An Introduction to Old English Metre* (Oxford: Blackwell, 1962), §15.

[4] Geoffrey Russom, *Old English Meter and Linguistic Theory* (Cambridge: Cambridge University Press, 1987), pp. 26–27.

[5] This reading is first proposed by W. J. Sedgefield in *Beowulf,* 3rd ed. (Manchester: Manchester University Press, 1935), followed by John C. Pope in *The Rhythm of Beowulf,* rev. ed. (New Haven: Yale University Press, 1966), 320, 372, by Russom in *Old English Meter*, pp. 119–120, and by R. D. Fulk in *A History of Old English Meter* (Philadelphia: University of Pennsylvania Press, 1992), §205 and §276. The unsyncopated form *betost* is attested in *Beo* 3007.

[6] Although in their introduction Fulk-Bjork-Niles state that "[t]he editors have attempted to conform to the rational, conservative principles adhered to by Klaeber in regard to the establishment and presentation of the text" (p. clxxxix), they seem not to be hesitant about introducing quite a few emendations including *secg bet[e]sta* and *ðegn bet[e]stan*.

[7] *Beowulf and Judith,* ed. Francis P. Magoun, Jr., rev. Jess B. Bessinger, Jr. (Cambridge, MA: Department of English, Harvard University, 1966); *Beowulf on Steorarume* (*Beowulf in Cyberspace*), ed. Benjamin Slade. <http://www.heorot.dk>; *The Beowulf Manuscript: Complete Texts and The Fight at Finnsburg,* ed. and trans. R. D. Fulk (Dumbarton Oaks Medieval Library, Cambridge, MA: Harvard University Press, 2010); *Beowulf nebst dem Finnsburg-Bruchstück,* 2 parts, ed. Ferdinand Holthausen (Heidelberg: Carl Winter, 7th ed., 1938 [pt 1 only]; 8th ed., 1948 [pt 1 only]).

[8] Except for those already mentioned, the post-Klaeber editions to be consulted are: *Beowulf,* ed. Moritz Heyne, rev. by Else von Schaubert (Paderborn: F. Schöningh, 15th ed., 1940; 16th ed., 1946; 18th ed., 1963); *Beowulf and Judith,* ed. Elliott van Kirk Dobbie, The Anglo-Saxon Poetic Records, vol. 4 (New York: Columbia University Press, 1953); *Beowulf und die kleineren Denkmäler der altenglischen Heldensage Waldere und Finnsburg,* ed. Gerhard Nickel, 3 parts (Heidelberg: C. Winter, 1976–82); *Beowulf: A Dual-Language Edition,* ed. and trans. Howell D. Chickering Jr. (New York: Anchor Books, 1977); *Beowulf,* ed. Michael Swanton (Manchester: Manchester University Press, 1978; Rev. ed., 1997); *Beowulf,* ed. André Crépin, 2 vols. (Göppingen: Kümmerle, 1991); *Beowulf: A Student Edition,* ed. George Jack (Oxford: Clarendon Press, 1994); *Beowulf with the Finnesburg Fragment,* eds. C. L. Wrenn and W. F. Bolton, 5th ed. (Exeter: University of Exeter Press, 1997); *Beowulf and Judith: Two Heroes,* ed. Richard M.

Trask (Lanham: University Press of America, 1997); *Beowulf: An Edition,* eds. Bruce Mitchell and Fred C. Robinson (Oxford: Blackwell, 1998; rev. ed., 2006); *Electronic Beowulf,* ed. Kevin Kiernan. 2 CD-ROMs (The British Library and the University of Michigan Press, 1999; 3rd ed., 2011); *Beowulf: A Glossed Text,* ed. Michael Alexander, (Harmondsworth and New York: Penguin, 2000).

[9] Eduard Sievers, "Zur Rhythmik des germanischen Alliterationsverses," *Beiträge zur Geschichte der deutschen Sprache und Literatur* 10 (1885), 232, 312. The emendation to *ðegn[a] betstan* had, however, already been suggested by John M. Kemble in *The Anglo-Saxon Poems of Beowulf, the Travellers Song, and the Battle of Finnes-burh* (London: William Pickering, 1833; 2nd ed., Vol. I, 1835) and by Hermannus Schubert in *De Anglo-Saxonum Arte Metrica* (Berlin diss., 1870), p. 41. In the footnote to the second edition, Kemble suggested *secg[a] betsta* as a possible emendation for 1759a.

[10] In his third edition (1950:167), Klaeber still considers *secg[a] betsta* the most likely original reading.

[11] Except for those already mentioned, the pre-Klaeber editions to be consulted are: *De Danorum rebus gestis secul. III & IV, Poëma Danicum dialecto Anglosaxonica,* ed. Grímur Jónsson Thorkelin (Copenhagen: Typis T. E. Rangel, 1815); *The Anglo-Saxon Poems of Beowulf, the Travellers Song, and the Battle of Finnes-burh,* ed. John M. Kemble (London: William Pickering, 1833; 2nd ed: Vol. I, 1835, Vol. II, 1837); *The Anglo-Saxon Poems of Beowulf, the Scôp or Gleeman's Tale and the Fight at Finnesburg,* ed. Benjamin Thorpe (Oxford: J. H. Parker, 1855; 3rd ed., 1889); *Beowulfes Beorh eller Bjovulfs-Drapen,* ed. N. F. S. Grundtvig (Copenhagen: K. Schønberg, 1861); *Beowulf,* ed. Moritz Heyne (Paderborn: F. Schöningh, 1863; 4th ed., 1879; 5th ed., rev. Adolf Socin, 1888; 7th ed., 1903; 8th ed., rev. Levin L. Schücking, 1908; 11th ed. and 12th ed., 1918; 14th ed., 1931); *Beovulf nebst den Fragmenten Finnsburg und Valdere,* ed. Christian W. M. Grein (Göttingen: G. H. Wigand, 1867); *Beowulf: A Heroic Poem of the Eighth Century,* ed. Thomas Arnold (London: Longmans, 1876); *Beowulf: An Anglo-Saxon Poem; The Fight at Finnsburh: A Fragment,* ed. James A. Harrison and Robert Sharp (Boston: Ginn, 1883; 2nd ed., 1885); *Beowulf, II,* ed. Alfred Holder (Freiburg i.B.: J. C. B. Mohr, 1884); *Beowulf,* ed. Alfred J. Wyatt (Cambridge: Cambridge University Press, 1894; 2nd ed., 1898); *Das Beowulflied. Als Anhang das Finn-Bruchstück und die Waldhere-Bruchstücke,* ed. Moritz Trautmann (Bonn: Hanstein, 1904); *Beowulf nebst dem Finnsburg-Bruchstück,* ed. Ferdinand Holthausen, 2 parts (Heidelberg: Carl Winter, 1905–6; 2nd ed., 1908–9; 3rd ed., 1912–13; 4th ed., 1914–19; 5th ed., 1921–29; 6th ed., 1929 [pt 1 only]); *Beowulf,* ed. W. J. Sedgefield (Manchester: Manchester University Press, 1910; 2nd ed., 1913; 3rd ed., 1935); *Beowulf with the Finnsburg Fragment,* ed. R. W. Chambers, new ed. of A. J. Wyatt, rev. with introduction and notes (Cambridge: Cambridge University Press, 1914); *Beowulf and the Fight at Finnsburg,* ed. Frederick Klaeber (London: Heath, 1922; 2nd ed., 1928).

[12] Although we give line numbers according to modern editions, Thorkelin

starts a new line at the beginning of each verse, which causes discrepancies in line numbering.

[13] Thorkelin's divisions of the half-lines preceding and following the three verses 947a, 1759a, and 1871b are as follows (a slash stands for a caesura between verses): *Bearn gebyrod / Nu Ic Beowulf / þec secg betsta / Me for sunu wylle* (946–47); *Be beorh þe þone / Bealo niþ Beowulf / Leofa sæg betsta / And þe þæt selfe geceos* (1758–59); *Gecyste þu cyning / AEþelum god þeoden / Scydinga þegn betstan* (1870–71). Note that none of the verses above consists of three or fewer syllables.

[14] Besides the already mentioned 947a, 1404b, 1759a, and 1871b, short verses in *Beowulf* (including four-syllable verses that might be short as a result of resolution) occur in 149b, 652a, 1546a, 1889a, 2139a, 2299a, 2488a, 2525b, 2673a, 2714b, 3102b, 3171b, 3180b. Apparent exceptions are not included; these include verses such as *hēan hūses* (*Beo* 116a) and *dēaþwīc sēon* (*Beo* 1275b) where *hēan* and *sēon* were assumed to be uncontracted or disyllabic when the poem was originally composed.

[15] For the details, see Jun Terasawa, *Old English Metre: An Introduction* (Toronto: University of Toronto Press, 2011), §§ 5.2.1, 5.2.2, 6.1.3.

[16] *Beo* 51b, 245a, 255a, 568b, 1013b, 1346a, 1355a, 1798a, 1945a, 2022b, 2895a, 3113b.

[17] According to Fulk-Bjork-Niles (p. 335, "Textual Criticism," § 43), the manuscript of the epic contains some forty instances of non-alliterating lines.

[18] Alliterative irregularities are: alliteration on the second lift of an off-verse alone (see 45b, 75b, 288b); double alliterations in the off-verse (see 29b, 32b, 192b).

[19] In the *Maldon,* for instance, the indicative *segeð* (45) is used in the subordinate clause following *gehȳran.*

[20] Bruce Mitchell, *Old English Syntax*, 2 vols. (Oxford: Clarendon Press, 1985), § 2020.

[21] *Eight Old English Poems*, ed. John C. Pope, 3rd ed., rev. R. D. Fulk (New York and London: Norton, 2001), glossary, s.v. *ǣtren*.

Particle Verses in Old English and Eddic Poetry

R. D. Fulk
Indiana University, Bloomington

ALTHOUGH THE PRESENT VOLUME is designed to honor a great scholar in the field of English and Germanic linguistics, it is the contributors who doubtless feel most honored, having been invited to address him on topics to which he has introduced us with such insight and clarity of vision. His generosity to fellow scholars is unmatched.

Introduction

Speaking of the sea creatures that assailed him in the water during his swimming exploit with Breca, Beowulf explains that he prevented them from devouring him:

Næs hīe ðǣre fylle gefēan hæfdon,
mānfordǣdlan, þæt hīe mē þēgon,
symbel ymbsǣton sǣgrunde nēah ... (*Beo* 562–64)[1]

(By no means did they have the satisfaction of their fill, those evildoers, that they made a meal of me, sat around a banquet on the sea floor ...)

In line 563b, stress is to be assumed on the pronoun *mē*, as indicated by both the alliteration and the metrical requirements of the off-verse. Responding to the claim that this stress indicates rhetorical prominence afforded the pronoun, the comment on the verse in *Klaeber's Beowulf* explains why this need not be the case:

> No unusual rhetorical emphasis on mē need be assumed..., as in a verse that comprises only particles (and clitics) and ends in a finite verb, or even an infinitive, the last particle before the verb is in the majority of instances stressed even when not obliged (as in 317[b], 382[b], etc.) to bear stress under Kuhn's first law...: cf. 251[b], 417[b], 1482[b], 2490[b]; 15[a], 44[a], 56[b], etc. ...[2]

Although I have never doubted that the stress on *mē* can be explained as the result of the formal requirements of verse construction rather than an intent to highlight the word, even at the time I wrote this comment I felt some unease about it, wondering whether the explanation was hasty, and an account inspiring confidence could be offered only in consequence of a methodical study of verses in the poem which, like this one, lack words requiring stress regardless of their position within the clause. The present essay is an attempt at such a study, and the findings presented here confirm the larger point of the comment just cited and suggest that the reason offered in *Klaeber's Beowulf* is not wide of the mark.

Definitions, General Principles, and Aims

"Particle" is the term that will be used here to refer to parts of speech other than prepositions that variably may be stressed or unstressed, according to their position within the clause. (The terms "stressed" and "unstressed" are shorthand, indicating relatively high and low degrees of stress, as determined primarily by alliterative patterns in verse.) The chief particles are finite verbs, pronouns in nominal function, and some, mostly monomorphemic, adverbs, including *þā* "then," *oft* "often," and *hwæðere* "nonetheless," but not *eft* "in turn," *up* "up," or *ūt* "out," which are invariably stressed. "Clitic" is the term that will refer to parts of speech other than prepositions that normally do not receive any stress detectable by scansion. The chief clitics are conjunctions, preverbal negatives, and various pronouns used attributively, including demonstrative, possessive, and indefinite pronouns. Prepositions are a special category, normally behaving like clitics, but demanding stress under all circumstances if they do not stand directly in front of their object. Words other than particles and clitics are almost invariably stressed: these include nouns, adjectives, most adverbs, and non-finite verbs—that is, participles and infinitives, though the latter are occasionally treated metrically the way particles are treated.

A particle may fail to alliterate, and thus, presumably, receive relatively little stress, if it stands among the first sequence of low-stress elements in the clause (disregarding any anacrusis). This means that it may appear either before the first stressed element in the clause or, if the first element in the clause is stressed, after that element and before the next stressed element. For example, the finite verb *hȳrde* "heard" is unstressed in the first drop of the clause in the verse *ne hȳrde ic cȳmlicor* "I have not heard of (a ferry) more finely (decked)" (*Beo* 38a), where the alliteration is on *c*, whereas it is stressed in verses that are not clause-initial, such as *secgan hȳrde* "heard tell" (Beo 875b), where the infinitive *secgan* receives the first stress in the verse. Such variable treatment of finite verbs in regard to stress is paralleled in Modern English, where, for example, *heard* bears relatively little stress, in comparison to *noise*, in the sentence *She heard a noise*, whereas it is fully stressed at the end of a clause, as in *It's what she heard*. This account of particle stress is an interpretive reformulation of Kuhn's first law, and the terms "particle" and "clitic" are only roughly equivalent to the terms *Satzpartikel* and *Satzteilpartikel*, respectively, employed by Kuhn.[3]

Verses that contain only particles and, in some cases, clitics—verses that will here be referred to as "particle verses"—may appear in either the on-verse or the off-verse, but their behavior in the two is not identical, an asymmetry paralleled by other formal differences between the two halves of the line. A greater variety of metrical types may appear in the on-verse, in large part because light verses may appear in the on-verse but not the off-verse. For present purposes, a light verse is a verse without a stressed element in the first foot. This usually means that the verse contains just one stressed element, but verses like *forðon þū mē 'god eart* (*PPs* 58.9.2a),[4] with stress on the final two words, and which do not appear in classically composed poems like *Beowulf*, may also be regarded as light. For all practical purposes, then, it may be said that in the on-verse, in which there may be as few as two and as many as four metrical positions, the first stress in a particle verse may fall on any of those positions (though not with equal frequency), whereas in the off-verse, in which precisely four metrical positions are required, it must fall on the first or the second.

The aim of the present study is to determine what patterns emerge when a poet's choices as regards clausal stress are less constrained—that is, in particle verses. It therefore will be concerned chiefly with the on-verse, due to the greater freedom it affords in regard to where the poet may choose to place the first stress. For this reason, as well, only clause-initial particle verses will be examined, since the version of Kuhn's first law presented above predicts that verses appearing later in the clause will be highly constrained as regards stress on particles.

The Pattern in *Beowulf*

Beowulf plays an outsize role in the study of Old English metrics because it is perhaps the best example of a poem composed in the "classical" metrical style, without some of the peculiarities of apparently later compositions, some of which will be illustrated below. By my count there are 103 particle verses in the on-verse in *Beowulf*, for an average rate of 3.2 such verses per 100 on-verses. The incidence thus is not large, proportionately, but it is sufficient to allow some fairly firm generalizations about how stress is distributed in verses containing no obligatorily stressed elements.

A particularly salient feature of particle verses in *Beowulf* is that if the final syllable of the verse is stressed, it will be preceded by a lift plus a drop: examples are *swylce 'oft bemearn* (907a) and *hwæþer him 'ǣnig wæs* (1356a).[5] If, on the other hand, a lift at the end of the verse is resolvable, there may or may not appear a drop between it and the preceding lift: examples are, respectively, *Þanon 'eft gewiton* (853a) and *sē ðe 'eal fela* (869a).[6] There are no particle verses in *Beowulf* in which the only lift is the final position of the verse—that is, verses of the type that Eduard Sievers labeled B3 and A. J. Bliss e1.[7] Even in verses that do not contain only particles, the type is rare: Bliss finds just seven examples (e.g. *þenden hē wið 'wulf* 3027a and *Hwīlum hē on 'lufan* 1728a), and although he admits it as a valid type, he confesses doubt, because in all but one of the seven the lift is resolved. The honorand of this volume, to the contrary, regards the type as unmetrical (or unmetrical if resolved).[8] He is surely right, and the pattern encountered in particle verses supports his conclusion, since it is plain that if the *Beowulf* poet were free to stress only the final position in the verse, he would not in every instance, thirty-three in all, have avoided such a pattern in particle verses by ensuring that there were two lifts in the verse. It will be seen in the discussion below, as well, that when some other poets construct particle verses with final stress alone, they also construct in appreciable numbers other light verses of this type—that is, verses of Sievers' type B3 that end in a stressed element other than a particle—and so it is plain that, unlike the *Beowulf* poet, they found the type acceptable.

In the considerable majority of on-verse particle verses in the poem, the first lift appears in the penultimate position, and in this type the lift is nearly always a verb root: examples are *Hī hyne þā æt'bǣron* (28a) and *Þā gȳt hīe him ā'setton* (47a).[9] The pattern is so regular that even the copula may bear stress, as in *ond gē him 'syndon* (393a), despite the relatively low metrical salience of non-lexical verbs. In just one instance is the stressed element in such a verse something other than a verb root: *ðē wē 'ealle* (941a). The question thus arises whether verbs are favored in such a position because they tend to bear more stress than other particles—an assertion about lexical finite verbs and stress offered by B. R. Hutcheson on the basis of related observations about frequency of alliteration on verbs in relation to other particles[10]—or because the coda of the verse is a favored position for the placement of finite verbs. The two possibilities are not mutually exclusive, since it could be that in particle verses, at least, verbs tend to come last because of a greater degree of stress accorded them. In verses other than particle verses, however, it would appear that verbs are favored in final position for the opposite reason, that they bear relatively low stress,[11] and so any supposition about greater or lesser stress on verbs as the explanation for their placement must remain speculative. The example of 393a and other verses with a stressed copula also casts doubt on the supposition that a greater degree of stress on verbs is responsible for the prevalence of verses like *Hī hyne þā æt'bǣron*. It will be seen below that in the poetic *edda*, where final placement of the verb is less common than in *Beowulf*, patterns of stress in particle verses nonetheless closely resemble Old English ones. The discussion of particle verses in the off-verse, below, will shed some light on this question, as well.

There are relatively few violations of the rule that the verb occupies final position in the verse. In two instances the violation occurs because the construction is interrogative, and the subject must then follow the verb: *Hwæt 'syndon gē* (237a) and *Hwanon 'ferigeað gē* (333a). Another six instances have the particle *þā* "then" placed after the verb, as in *ā'lēdon þā* (34a).[12] In each of these verses the verb bears an unstressed prefix and begins the verse. This is a disfavored way to begin a verse, as it produces violations of Kuhn's second law, whereby a drop in clause-initial position must contain at least one particle.[13] The rationale for such a rule most likely is that an initial drop without a particle could be confused with anacrusis, and as the scholar whose life's work we celebrate with this volume has demonstrated repeatedly, Old English poets were inclined to avoid structural ambiguity in verse construction. One might suppose that the poet could readily have avoided such ambiguity by placing *þā* first, producing **þā ā'lēdon* rather than *ā'lēdon þā*. It is noteworthy, however, that there are no verses of the former type in *Beowulf*: there is always some element in addition to *þā* in the first drop, as with *Þā mē þæt ge'lǣrdon* (415a), *ond þā 'gyddode* (630a), and *Ðā hīe ge'truwedon* (1095a). The poet appears not to have been alone in avoiding the type: it does not occur in *Exodus* or *Daniel*, and the only instance in the signed works of Cynewulf involves an unprefixed verb (*Ðā 'reordode* Jul 66a), whereas the type appears to have been unstigmatized for the poet of *Genesis A*, with both prefixed and unprefixed verbs in evidence.[14] Haruko Momma has found that *þā* precedes pronouns and finite verbs when it can take the clause-initial position.[15] This might be taken to indicate a lower degree of salience, which in turn could explain why verses like **þā ā'lēdon* are avoided by some poets: the initial drop was perhaps considered too light.

Just three other verses in *Beowulf* violate the rule that in a verse with no obligatorily stressed elements, the verb is placed last. The placement of the pronoun in *Ðonne 'sægdon þæt* (377a) may be intended to emphasize it, since it serves as the antecedent of a clause of which the opening is delayed, and emphasis would thus reduce the possibility of confusion about the relation of the clause to the syntactic context:

> Ðonne sægdon þæt   sǣlīþende,
> þā ðe gifsceattas   Gēata fyredon
> þyder tō þance,   þæt hē þrītiges
> manna mægencræft   on his mundgripe
> heaþorōf hæbbe.   (*Beo* 377–81a)
>
> (Seafarers who ferried the gifts of the Geats here to our satisfaction used to say that he, brave in war, had the strength of thirty men in his hand-grip.)

In a language like Old English, as in Modern English, emphasis associated with the introduction of new information is effected by final placement of the emphasized element within a given domain, producing what is called "end focus." Likewise, final placement of the pronoun in *Ðonne 'wēne ic tō þē* "Then I expect for you" (525a) may be intended to emphasize it: here Unferth is tacitly comparing Beowulf to others who have tried to overcome Grendel, and he is predicting defeat for a man who, he says, was bested at swimming by Breca. The verse *ac hē ge'fēng hraðe* "but he quickly grabbed" (740a) is unusual inasmuch as normally *hraðe* would be placed before the verb, though this would require alliteration on *h*. The unexpected word order perhaps reinforces the monstrous sense of unexpectedness that the words convey: "The troublemaker had no mind to delay, but at the first opportunity he quickly grabbed a sleeping soldier and without hindrance split him, bit into the body, drank the arterial blood, swallowed huge mouthfuls; in no time he had devoured the lifeless man, feet, hands, and all" (*Beo* 739–45a).[16]

Particle verses which end in a trisyllabic verb with a heavy root syllable, like *Swā 'rīxode* (144a), are naturally of Sievers's type C, in accordance with the rule of the coda.[17] When a particle verse contains two verbs, they nearly always alliterate with each other, as with *'seomade ond syrede* (161a) and *'Wēn'ic þæt hē wille* (442a).[18] There are four exceptional verses, alliterating only on the second verb: *mynte þæt he ge'dǣlde* (731a), *cwæð þæt hyt 'hæfde* (2158a), *cwǣdon þæt hē 'wǣre* (3180a), *bæd þæt gē ge'worhton* (3096a). Exceptions are thus limited to those instances in which a new *þæt*-clause begins after the first verb. The verb *cweðan* "to speak" likewise fails to alliterate in such verses elsewhere in the poetic corpus, as discussed below. Finally, particle verses which contain no verb offer no surprises: the final word bears the first stress, as in *þæt hēo on 'ǣnigne* (627a) and *ðē wē 'ealle* (941a), unless this would result in a verse with stress on the final position only: compare *Hēo him 'eft hraþe* (1541a) and *þēah ðe 'ōðer his* (2481a).[19]

Particle Verses in Poems in the Classical Style

Conservative linguistic and metrical features mark the Old Testament narratives of the Junius Manuscript as early compositions, as they do *Guthlac A*, in the case of which there is also the poet's testimony that the events narrated in the poem were witnessed by persons still living,[20] and it is known that Guthlac died in the year 714. Three of these four poems closely resemble *Beowulf* in respect to the treatment of particle verses in the on-verse. In *Guthlac A* only *'Dōð efne swā* (592a) is a type not found in *Beowulf*: it will be remembered that in *Beowulf*, if otherwise the only stress in the verse would be on the final position, almost always the verb will stand last in the verse and the preceding particle will be stressed, whereas in this verse it is the first particle in the verse that is stressed. But this is plainly for syntactic reasons, since the verb is imperative and must come first in its clause. There do not happen to be any imperatives in particle verses in *Beowulf*, and so it cannot be known whether *'Dōð efne swā* is a pattern that the *Beowulf* poet would have used. In *Exodus* the only unusual particle verse in the on-verse is *siððan hie on 'bugon* (499a), which is like six of the seven verses of Bliss's type e1 in *Beowulf*, as discussed above. It should be expected, instead, that the first stress would fall on the particle preceding the verb. However, the verse is emended (the manuscript reads *on bogum* for *on bugon*), and it is inadmissible as emended, because if *on* follows its object *hīe* it must be stressed, spoiling the alliteration—and disqualifying this as a particle verse, since prepositions are not particles. In *Daniel* the verse *Ðā 'cwæð sē ðe wæs* (416a) is unusual, inasmuch as the stress falls on the former of two verbs. The verse *nalles þȳ hē wēnde* (529) is normal if the alliteration is on *w*, but the off-verse is *þæt hie hit wiston*, a light type that does not usually appear in the off-verse, and so alliteration on *h*, though less probable, cannot be ruled out.

The meter of *Genesis A* is in several respects unlike that of other poems in the classical style,[21] and it differs somewhat in regard to particle verses, as well. Verses in which the finite verb is not final are not uncommon, for example *Þū scealt 'ōðerne* (927a).[22] The verses *cwæð þæt hē 'wolde* (1279a) and *cwæð þæt him 'wǣre* (2028a) find parallels in *Beowulf* (731a, 2158a, 3096a, 3180a, as noted above), but not *'Tēmað nū ond wexað*, with alliteration on the first only of two verbs. The verse *Ic 'fela siððan* (2698a), without a verb, is unusual, since the final word does not alliterate.

The signed works of Cynewulf contain few particle verses in the on-verse without parallels in *Beowulf*. The verb is not final, and it does not alliterate, in *Ne þearft ðū swā 'swīðe* (El 939) and *Mōton þonne 'siðþan* (El 1315). In one verse without a verb, *Is nū 'feala siðþan* (El 636a), one would have expected the final word to bear the alliteration. The verse *Wolde ic þæt ðū 'funde* (El 1079a), however, with stress on the second only of two verbs, does have parallels in *Beowulf*. The only other unusual verse is *nē þū nǣfre ge'dēst* (Jul 138a), which is entirely unparalleled in the poems in the classical style surveyed for this study.

Particle Verses in Poems Showing Many Divergences from the Classical Style

For all its formal idiosyncrasies, the *Battle of Maldon* shows no particle verse types in the on-verse that are not also to be found in poems composed in the classical style. The only remarkable verses do not have the verb placed last: they are *Ne mihte hira 'ǣnig* (70a) and *hī woldon þā 'ealle* (207a).

Judgment Day II shows a greater variety of departures from Beowulfian norms. The verb is verse-internal in *Ic gemunde þis mid mē* (24a, with alliteration on *m*) and *Ic 'ācsige þē, lā* (65a), both of which represent violations of Kuhn's first law, since they contain unstressed particles in the second drop; and the stress is most peculiar in *'Ēac þonne cumað hider* (111a), though possibly the alliteration should be on *h*, making for a highly unusual off-verse, *ufon of heofone*. Even when the verb is final, the stress pattern may be unexpected, as in *eall 'swylce þū cwǣde* (12a); and the verse *and þonne þider cume* (158), with alliteration on *þ*, is prosodically knotty regardless of whether the first stress is on *þonne* or *þider*.[23] Only the first of two verbs in a coordinated construction alliterates in *and 'fēhþ and geblyssað* (275a).

Mark Griffith has conducted a magisterial survey of the distinctive features of the compositional techniques employed in the *Meters of Boethius*, and he has reached the conclusion that the *Meters*' departures from classical norms are chiefly a consequence of the influence of the prose source upon the verse.[24] This is indeed a possible explanation why the verb so frequently fails to appear last in particle verses in the on-verse.[25] In a verse like *'wēnað þonne* (19.46a), simple reversal of the word order would have produced a normal type, and **ðonne ðū 'siððan bist* for actual *ðonne bist ðū 'siððan* would also be a classical type. Even when the verb is final, it may not be the first stressed element, as in *'þā þā hē wolde* (11.15a).[26] Griffith finds that the *Meters* evince fourteen verses of Sievers's type B3, Bliss's type e1, three of which are particle verses: *Forðǣm þe nāne for'lēt* (10.66a), *þēah hē nū þæt 'eall* (16.19a), and *and forlǣte 'ān* (22.9a). The verse *sǣdon þæt hīo 'sceolde* (26.74a) is comparable to those in *Beowulf* like *cwǣdon þæt hē 'wǣre* (3180a), but the *Meters* also show an alliterative pattern in verses with two verbs unlike anything in *Beowulf*: compare *'hīt þonne hē wille* (29.70a)[27] and *'nimð þonne hē wille* (29.72a).

The psalms of the Paris Psalter show roughly the same sorts of divergences from classical patterns of verse construction as Griffith finds in the *Meters of Boethius*, but with greater frequency and, generally, in more obvious fashion. The relevant features include violations of Kuhn's laws, failure to confine light verses to clause openings, verses with fewer or greater than the canonical four metrical positions, over- and under-application of resolution, verses of Bliss's type e1 (e.g. *þonne hē his 'folc*, 52.7.3a) and his type a2 in which the final half-lift is a separate word (e.g., *forðon þū mē 'god eart*, 58.9.2a), unusual anacrusis or alliteration, and placement of verse types in the off-verse that are usually confined to the on-verse, among others. Particle verses in the on-verse likewise show a marked variety of divergences from classical norms. Verbs frequently do not come last in the verse, as in *Hwylc ge'lǣdeð mē* (59.8.1a) and *Noldan hī þā 'swīðe* (77.4.1a). Such is the case also in commands, whether the verb is imperative or subjunctive—examples are *Ge'hȳrað mē* (65.14.1a) and *ge'blētsige ūs* (66.6.2a), respectively—because in prose the verb usually comes first in such constructions, though it is notable that the poet usually, though inconsistently, stresses the verb in verses of this type. Even when the verb is final in the verse and eligible for alliteration, a preceding particle frequently takes precedence, as in *'Heonan ic cleopige* (56.2.1a) and *'hūru þū forlēosest* (72.22.3). Verses of Sievers's type B3 and Bliss's type e1, with or without resolution, are hardly uncommon, for example *Forþon ic ne on'geat*

(70.15.1a) and *Þū ūs tō'drife* (59.1.1a), respectively. It is unsurprising how relatively infrequent are verses of the classical type *and hī 'syððan ne bēoð* (58.12.6a), since these seem to be stressed to avoid the e1 type, whereas the e1 type appears not to have been disfavored by this poet. In verses containing two verbs, the first may be the sole alliterator even when the second is not in a subordinate clause, as in *'Cumað nū and gesēoð* (65.4.1) and *Ge'sēoð þæt and gefēoð* (68.32.1a). An example of Bliss's type a2 with a separate word for the final half-lift is *and ā'lȳs ūs* (78.9.2a). Examples of violations of Kuhn's second law are *ge'seoh on mē* (68.16.4a) and *Ā'gēot ofer hī* (68.24.1a); verses like *ne 'wīte mē þæt* (65.16.2a) and *Ne of'gif þū mē hūru* (70.11.1a) violate both laws. Although there is scholarly disagreement about the issue, I agree with M. J. Toswell that the evidence for the poet's reliance upon psalter glosses when he composed his translation is sparse.[28] If the poet did not rely heavily on a gloss or a prose version in composing his verses, that would mean that divergences from classical norms need not be due to such reliance, even though influence of that sort does seem to be largely responsible for the similar distinctive metrical and syntactic features of the *Meters of Boethius*.

Particle Verses in the Poetic *Edda*

Since *fornyrðislag* is the meter most closely resembling that of Old English normal verses, and it is generally believed to be descended directly from the same ancestral form out of which Old English meter evolved, the survey of particle verses in Old Icelandic will here be limited to poems in *fornyrðislag*. The representative sample surveyed was the first four poems in this meter in the poetic *edda*: they are *Vǫluspá* (*Vsp*), *Hymiskviða* (*Hym*), *Vǫlundarkviða* (*Vkv*), and *Helgakviða Hundingsbana hin fyrri* (*HH I*).

The alliterative patterns of particle verses in the eddic on-verse differ from their counterparts in Old English verse of the classical variety in some of the same ways that those in Old English poems in non-classical style do, but whereas the latter not infrequently convey the impression of more or less random assignment of stress, eddic particle verses instead seem simply to be constructed on different principles. For example, whereas in the psalms of the Paris Psalter verses of Sievers's type B3, Bliss's e1, seem to be regarded as normal, and to a lesser extent in the *Meters of Boethius*, particle verses of this type appear to be stigmatized in the *edda*. The general avoidance of the type among particle verses is remarkable because among verses other than those made up of particles the type is not uncommon. Seiichi Suzuki has shown that B3 verses in the *edda* comprise more than five percent of verses of type B, whereas in West Germanic the type is extremely rare. The discrepancy, he concludes, renders it probable that such verses in the *edda* do not belong to type B but represent a catalectic variety of type A—an assertion that is reasonable enough, given how many other verse types of fewer than four metrical positions in Old Icelandic are best explained as catalectic.[29] The disfavor accorded the type among particle verses supports Suzuki's claim, since particle verses cannot very intelligibly be analyzed as susceptible to catalexis,[30] and so the type ought not to occur among particle verses. Because type B3 is disfavored among particle verses, then, many verses of the familiar Old English pattern occur whereby a particle earlier in the verse is stressed to avoid placing stress on the final position alone: examples are *Enn 'ǫnnor gecc* (*Hym* 8.5) and *sá er 'oft hefir* (*HH I* 35.5).

As for the placement of verbs, in three of the four poems surveyed the verb is verse-final in fewer than half the particle verses; only *HH I* shows an unmistakable preference for the pattern that predominates in Old English. Unlike in *Beowulf*, where *þā* is the preferred verse-final element when the verb does not appear last, many different sorts of particles may come last in the *edda*, including personal pronouns (*Vsp* 28.5, *Hym* 11.7,14.1, 15.1, 18.1, etc.), reflexive pronouns (*Hym* 12.3), indefinite pronouns (*Vsp* 40.5, 47.5, *Hym* 33.7, etc), and adverbs (*Vsp* 16.5, 40.3, 61.1, *Vkv* 3.1, 27.1, etc.).

Aside from the difference in verb placement, eddic particle verses are strikingly similar to their Beowulfian counterparts. If the final word of the verse is bisyllabic and the root syllable is not light, or if the word is trisyllabic, it is stressed: examples are *þeir er 'sótto* (*Vsp* 14.5) and *oc hann 'vacnaði* (*Vkv* 11.3), respectively. Otherwise, the preceding particle is stressed, and the verse conforms to one of two patterns, resembling either *Hvers 'fregnit mic (Vsp* 28.5) or *sá er 'oft hefir* (*HH I* 35.5), depending on the structure of the final word. Eddic particle verses, like their Old English counterparts, are thus generally designed to avoid stress on the final position of the verse only. Aside from verses with double alliteration, the exceptions in the four poems sampled are these:

'seið hon, hvars hon kunni (*Vsp* 22.5)
'hræðaz allir (*Vsp* 47.5)
'Hvern léto þeir (*Hym* 15.1)
'Þess vænti ec (*Hym* 18.1)

'lucþi hann alla (*Vkv* 5.5)
'svá beið hann (*Vkv* 5.7)
'vilnomc ec þess nú (*Vkv* 31.7)

Plainly, then, the only significant departure from the usual stress pattern in particle verses with single alliteration is a type with stress on the initial word. In perhaps all these exceptional verses the stressed word is the most meaningful word in the verse. Commonly it is the verb that is most meaningful, but not consistently: in *'Hvern léto þeir* "they made each (bull shorter by a head)" the pronoun is at least as salient as the verb (which is often used as an auxiliary) in terms of conveying new information, and in *'Þess vænti ec* "this I expect, (that you will find it easy to procure bait in the form of an ox)," the pronoun serves as antecedent to the noun clause that is the point of the sentence. In *'svá beið hann* "thus he waited," the stress on the adverb relative to the verb may be judged by the English equivalent.[31]

Particle Verses in the Off-Verse

Because light verses are excluded from the off-verse, the first stress must fall on either the first or the second metrical position. In the off-verse in *Beowulf* the tendency to place the verb last is even stronger than in the on-verse. A final verb thus receives the first stress in the verse only if its root appears in the second metrical position, as in *þæt wē 'fundiaþ* (1819b), although a stressed verb may appear in initial position if the verse contains two verbs, as in *'brūc þenden þū mōte* (1177b). The usual pattern, however, is that the verb root will appear in the third or fourth metrical position and the first stress in the verse will fall on the second position, as in *syððan 'ǣrest wearð* (6b), *þanon 'eft gewāt* (123b), *þenden 'þǣr wunað* (284b), and *þæt ic 'þē sōhte* (417b). There are more than sixty-five off-verses of this kind in *Beowulf*.[32] The pattern is also conducive to initial stress in a verse like *'sōna hæfde* (743b), though initial stress may also be assigned when an initial particle bears greater meaning, as in *'fela þǣra wæs* (992b). It may thus be seen that whereas in the on-verse final placement of the verb results in very many verses in which the verb is the first stressed element, in the off-verse it results in a markedly robust tendency for some other element to receive the first stress. If the first stress in the on-verse is to be regarded as the strongest stressed position in the line and the final stress in the off-verse the weakest,[33] final placement of the verb results in diametrically opposed treatment of it in the on-verse and the off-verse in particle verses, suggesting that final placement of the verb is not prompted by any inherent salience or insalience of verbs as regards stress.

In *Beowulf*, exceptions to this pattern are relatively few. In the commonest sort of exception, the verb is followed by an adverb, most commonly *swā*, as in *ond þæt ge'æfndon swā* (538b), *hē ge'wræc syðdan* (2395b), and *gif ic 'wiste hū* (2519), or by *fela*, as in *Þanon 'wōc fela* (1265b).[34] In a few such instances verse-final *swā* is required by the syntax to preserve economy in the use of function words, as in *ðǣr hīe 'meahton swā* "wherever they could" (797b; cf. **swā hwǣr swā hīe meahton*). Once the verb is followed by a prepositional phrase: *Ðū þē 'lǣr be þon* (1722b). In a few instances, a particle other than the verb comes last, as in *'hēold hyne syðþan* (142b) and *ðonne is 'ēower sum* (248b).[35] Particle verses that contain no verb are stressed the same way as those containing a verb—that, is they are stressed as if the final particle were a verb, as in *Ic 'þē nūða* (426b) and *þæt 'syðþan nā* (567b).[36] Plainly, the normal pattern in the off-verse is for the verb to come last, and exceptions in *Beowulf* are infrequent.

Because stress patterns in the off-verse are more constrained than in the on-verse, there is less difference between *Beowulf* and late poems in regard to the off-verse. Nonetheless, there are discriminations to be made. In the verse psalms of the Paris Psalter, exceptions to final placement of the verb are commoner than verses that conform to the rule. These are of various sorts. Most commonly an adverb or a pronoun follows the verb, as in *and hī ge'hȳneð ēac* (54.18.1b), and *and 'hulpe mīn* (70.20.2). Elements following the verb may in fact be relatively heavy, as in *ne ge'wītað wē fram ðē* (79.16.4b), *þonne ic 'cleopode tō ðē* (85.6.2b), and *and þē ne 'sceaðeð ǣnig* (90.7.3b). The verb may fail to alliterate even when in a position to do so, as in *'fela gnorniað* (58.15.3b) and *'þæne blētsedan* (61.4.3b). The poet allows light verses, including Sievers's type B3, in the second half of the line, as in *ne sceal æt 'mē* (68.7.4b) and *þe hine 'sēceað* (84.7.4b). The differences between the psalms and *Beowulf*, then, seem more a matter of degree of hierarchical rigidity than of any fundamental difference in the treatment of particles.

In the *edda*, final placement of the verb is commoner in the off-verse than in the on-verse, and examples of non-final placement are few, most of them due to interrogative constructions, as in *'vitoð ér enn, eða hvat?* (*Vsp* 27.8; also 28.14, 33.8, 39.10, 41.8, 48.8, 62.8, 63.6) and *hví 'freistið mín?* (*Vsp* 28.6).[37] The verb is more commonly stressed than in Old English because the first stress may fall on the third metrical position, as in *oc mic 'bundo* (*Vkv* 12.4) and *þá er þér 'kunnið* (*Vkv* 33.12), though initial stress also occurs, as in *'nú mun hon søcqvaz* (*Vsp* 66.8) and *'mioc leiða sér* (*Hym* 8.2). More intriguing is the observation that clause-initial particle verses are relatively infrequent in the group of poems sampled, with the exception of *Vǫlundarkviða*, with thirteen examples, almost all with the verb in final position. This is the one poem in the sampled group based on legendary material from West Germanic, sometimes thought to show West Germanic metrical characteristics. By comparison, *Helgakviða Hundingsbana I* contains just one example. An increased sampling of poems in *fornyrðislag* would presumably reveal whether particle verses reliably distinguish native compositions from those thought to show foreign influence.

Conclusions

When the on-verse comprises only particles and clitics, so that the poet has considerable discretion as to where to place the first alliterating stave, one might have expected him to mold his verses in such a way that they would resemble verses of type A, like *'Wēn' ic þæt hē wille*. Such might be taken to be the prediction of the word-foot theory, since trochaic rhythms most closely emulate patterns of word stress in Old English; but it might be expected under any Sieversian analysis, as well, since A is the type most favored by the poets. As it turns out, however, particle verses like *'Wēn' ic þæt hē wille* are remarkably infrequent, the commonest patterns resembling light verses, followed by verses of types B and C. Yet a different sort of verisimilitude may explain the discrepancy. The first lift of the on-verse is the strongest position in the line, according to Russom.[38] To fill such a position with an undisplaced particle would be to lend a particle the sort of prominence that does not attach to words of this class in prose. Favoring light verses in the construction of particle verses is thus a way of minimizing mismatches between metrical pattern and the inherent prosody of the language, just as the word-foot theory predicts they should be minimized. That the first lift should appear in the coda of such verses is in accord with the universal principle "Minimize complexity toward the end of the line."[39] The frequency with which particle verses are of types B and C, rather than being light verses, is then due to the need to accommodate verse-final particles—chiefly verbs, since these are favored at verse end—that would place either a monosyllabic or a resolved lift in the final position of the verse, a pattern that the classical poets plainly avoided in both Old English and Old Icelandic.

To the question with which this study began—whether the stress on *mē* in the verse *þæt hīe mē þēgon* (Beo 563b) implies rhetorical emphasis—there is now plainly an answer. No such emphasis need be assumed, and the reason tendered in *Klaeber's Beowulf* is essentially correct. The verse simply conforms to what is by far the commonest pattern for particle verses in the off-verse in *Beowulf*, according to which the verb is placed last and the particle preceding it bears the alliterating stave.

NOTES

[1] All quotations from *Beowulf* derive from *Klaeber's Beowulf and the Fight at Finnsburg*, 4th ed., corrected reprint. Ed. R. D. Fulk, Robert E. Bjork, and John D. Niles (Toronto: University of Toronto Press, 2014), though most diacritics other than macrons have been omitted. Other Old English poems are cited from *The Anglo-Saxon Poetic Records*, ed. George Philip Krapp and Elliott Van Kirk Dobbie, 6 vols. (New York: Columbia University Press, 1931–1953), though macrons have been added. Short titles of Old English poems are those employed by Antonette diPaolo Healey, ed. *Dictionary of Old English Web Corpus* (Toronto: Dictionary of Old English Project, 2009). Citations from the Poetic Edda derive from Gustav Neckel and Hans Kuhn, eds, *Edda: Die Lieder der Codex Regius nebst verwandten Denkmälern*, 2 vols. Revised ed. (Heidelberg: Carl Winter, 1983). All translations are my own; translations from *Beowulf* derive from Fulk, ed. and trans., *The Beowulf Manuscript: Complete Texts and The Fight at Finnsburg* (Cambridge, MA: Harvard University Press, 2010).

[2] Fulk, Bjork, and Niles, *Klaeber's Beowulf*, p. 153.

[3] See Hans Kuhn, "Zur Wortstellung und -betonung im Altgermanischen," *Beiträge zur Geschichte der deutschen Sprache und Literatur* 57 (1933): 1–109. On the obstacles to presenting unaltered Kuhn's first law and what is meant by *Satzpartikeln* and *Satzteilpartikeln*, see Haruko Momma, *The Composition of Old English Poetry* (Cambridge: Cambridge University Press, 1997), pp. 28–54.

[4] In verse citations, an acute or prime symbol has been added immediately before the first stressed syllable in the verse, as determined by the alliteration (in the off-verse, in the case of on-verses).

[5] Others: 34a, 237a, 333a, 377a, 525a, 620a, 642a, 1356a, 1608a, 1787a, 1870a, 1875a, 2110a, 2157a, 2244a, 2345a, 2387a, 2481a, 2516a, 2848a, 3001a, 3116a, 3156a. On 658a, see below.

[6] Others of the latter type: 15a, 671a, 740a, 883a, 1541a. There are no others of the former type.

[7] Eduard Sievers, *Altgermanische Metrik* (Halle: Niemeyer, 1893), §16.2; A. J. Bliss, *The Metre of* Beowulf. Rev. ed. (Oxford: Blackwell, 1967), §§67, 73.

[8] Geoffrey R. Russom, *Old English Meter and Linguistic Theory* (Cambridge: Cambridge University Press, 1987), pp. 46, 132. It should be noted as well that

three of the seven verses involve the word *fæder* "father," which causes metrical difficulties elsewhere: see R. D. Fulk, *A History of Old English Meter* (Philadelphia: University of Pennsylvania Press, 1992), p. 181, for discussion and references.

[9] Others: 290a, 372a, 393a, 415a, 435a, 463a, 503a, 520a, 535a, 574a, 632a, 691a, 706a, 731a, 750a, 751a, 798a, 809a, 890a, 937a, 967a, 1082a, 1095a, 1130a, 1175a, 1270a, 1347a, 1392a, 1465a, 1497a, 1508a, 1578a, 1661a, 1671a, 1826a, 1846a, 1933a, 2036a, 2039a, 2124a, 2195a, 2634a, 2665a, 2797a, 2934a, 2976a, 3002a, 3038a, 3081a, 3096a, 3137a, 3180a; possibly also 175a, 1591a, 2158a, 2195a, 2204a, though these could have two lifts. Verses like *Him 'big stōdon* (3047a) are irrelevant because, as noted above, prepositions are not particles, and when displaced they must receive stress. Verses like *'mīn[n]e gehȳrað* (255b) are also excluded from consideration, since a possessive pronoun that does not stand directly before the word it modifies must be stressed, and thus an unavoidable constraint is placed on how the verse is stressed.

[10] B. R. Hutcheson, "Stress of Quantitative Adjectives and Some Common Adverbs in Old English Poetry: An Alternative to Kuhn's Law," *Leeds Studies in English* n.s. 24 (1993): 27–56, at p. 37.

[11] See Megan Hartman, "The Syntax of Old English Hypermetrics," *English Studies* 91 (2010): 477–91, at p. 483.

[12] Others: 620a, 1870a, 2345a, 2516a, 3156a.

[13] "Im Satzauftakt müssen Satzpartikeln stehen" (Kuhn, "Wortstellung," p. 43). For discussion, see Momma, *Composition*, pp. 65–75.

[14] *Genesis A* 92a, 126a, 192a, 206a, 1253a, 1598a, 2535a, 2674a.

[15] Momma, *Composition*, p. 144.

[16] The poet does treat *hraðe* as a particle: it is unstressed in 1294a, 1310a, and 1975a.

[17] Others: 630a, 1363a, 1944a, 2176a, 2933a, 2985a, 3178a. On the rule of the coda, see Fulk, *History*, pp. 197–235.

[18] Others: 600a, 658a, 1337a, 1604a, 2430a.

[19] Other verses without a verb: 869a, 883a, 1875a.

[20] See 93–4, 154–7, 401–2, and 753–4a.

[21] See Fulk, *History*, pp. 77 (n. 29), 88 (n. 49), 186 (n. 30), and 251.

[22] Others: 965a, 1110a, 1022a, 1175a, 1493a, 1697a, 2175a, 2253a, 2258a, 2462a, 2464a, 2600a, 2723a, 2727a, 2873a.

[23] If *þider* is stressed, the verse represents a violation of the rule that a short lift may not immediately follow a resolved lift.

[24] See Mark Griffith, "The Composition of the Metres," in *The Old English Boethius: An Edition of the Old English Versions of Boethius's De Consolatione Philosophiae*, eds. Malcolm Godden and Susan Irvine, 2 vols. (Oxford: Oxford University Press), I: 80–134.

[25] See 17.25a, 19.46a, 24.27a, 24.30a, 26.90a, 29.30a. The verse *and forlǣte 'ān* is an example if *ān* is regarded as a word rather than a separable prefix.

[26] Others: 20.103a, 20.195a, 28.7a, 28.35a.

[27] Here *hīt* is a form of *hȳðan*: see Denise Cavanaugh, "A Note on *Metre* 29 of the Old English *Metres of Boethius*," *Notes and Queries* 31 (1984): 293–96.

[28] See M. J. Toswell, "The Relationship of the Metrical Psalter to the Old English Glossed Psalters," *English Studies* 78 (1997): 297–315.

[29] Seiichi Suzuki, *The Meters of Old Norse Eddic Poetry* (Berlin: De Gruyter, 2014), pp. 82–83.

[30] Suzuki, *Meters*, p. 855 in his index of scansion, regards a verse like *'svá beið hann* (Vkv 5.7) as catalectic, but how this could be so in any concrete sense of the word is not plain to me.

[31] The remaining four of the seven exceptional verses listed mean 'she cast spells where she knew how' (Vsp 22.5), 'all are frightened' (Vsp 47.5), 'he bound all' (Vkv 5.5), and 'I wish this now' (Vkv 31.7). Similar conclusions may be drawn about these.

[32] Others: 44b, 251b, 296b, 400b, 444b, 445b, 450b, 543b, 563b, 598b, 680b, 691b, 743b, 831b, 881b, 900b, 913b, 944b, 956b, 996b, 1048b, 1058b, 1133b, 1134b, 1174b, 1185b, 1238b, 1252b, 1280b, 1338b, 1349b, 1381b, 1385b, 1404b, 1466b, 1476b, 1478b, 1482b, 1556b, 1587b, 1676b, 1815b, 1824b, 1858b, 1891b, 1901b, 1947b, 2005b, 2042b, 2071b, 2175b, 2217b, 2427b, 2459b, 2490b, 2713b, 2739b, 2787b, 2790b, 2859b, 3003b, 3070b, 3087b, 3167b.

[33] See Geoffrey R. Russom, Beowulf *and Old Germanic Metre* (Cambridge: Cambridge University Press, 1998), pp. 68–69.

[34] Others, with adverb: 762b, 797b, 1331b, 2091b, 2878b, 2990b; with *fela*: 2511b, 2738b, 3029b.

[35] Others: 1471b, 1525b, 1837b, 2442b, 2920b.

[36] Others: 932b (with *ǣnigra* for *ǣnige*?), 972b, 1182b, 1453b, 1772b.

[37] Final instances: Vsp 6.4, 21.10, 65.4, 66.8, Hym 18.2, 25.2, Vkv 4.6, 8.2, 8.4, 11.2, 12.2, 12.4, 21.4, 22.8, 23.8, 33.12, 34.2, HH I 40.4; non-final: Hym 8.2, 9.2, 38.2, Vkv 40.2, 41.2.

[38] *Beowulf*, pp. 68, 86.

[39] See Russom, *Beowulf*, p. 39.

Old English Verse Punctuation and Linguistic Theory

Daniel Donoghue
Harvard University

OUR HONORAND BREATHED NEW life into the study of Old English meter with his astute application of linguistic theory, drawing in particular from the ideas of Paul Kiparsky, first in his *Old English and Linguistic Theory* and again eleven years later with *Beowulf and Old Germanic Metre.*[1] A few years after the publication of Geoffrey Russom's first book, Geoffrey Nunberg published *The Linguistics of Punctuation*, which extended the principles of linguistic theory in yet another new direction.[2] Nunberg's book has fallen victim to disciplinary nearsightedness, because while it has been cited in studies in a number of other fields (e.g., computational linguistics, education) it has not so far as I know fallen under the appreciative gaze of literary or textual criticism.[3]

The following pages will introduce Nunberg's theoretical approach before extending its method to the punctuation found in medieval manuscripts—specifically Anglo-Saxon manuscripts. This turn represents an application that Nunberg explicitly discounts because of a mistaken assumption that punctation needed to await the arrival of printing before it could develop into a system. Work by Malcolm Parkes and others has moved independently, it seems, on a path parallel to Nunberg's theory in showing the systematic nature of punctuation within a robust system of textual representation. This study will use Nunberg's theory to explore parallels in the manuscript presentation of Latin verse, Old English prose, and, most tantalizingly, Old English poetry.

Punctuation as System

The systemic nature of punctuation may have an obviousness as an idea, which everyone trained in English or other modern-language writing conventions can intuitively grasp. Rules with varying rationalizations are laid out in well-known reference works like *The Chicago Manual of Style* and *Fowler's Modern English Usage.* Even without such guidebooks we know, to choose an obvious example, that a comma is not interchangeable with quotation marks and that each mark performs at least one function within a conventionalized system of textual representation, whether in print or in handwriting. Knowing the correct and incorrect use of punctuation is often taken as an index of "proper" literacy to a degree that seems (to many) far out of proportion with its pragmatic purpose—as if a misplaced apostrophe is a sign of the impending collapse of civilization.[4] Beyond the common-sense understanding of punctuation, how can we think of it as an independent system? What is its relation to spoken language? What is its relation to other graphic conventions such as spelling and word division?

Nunberg's *Linguistics of Punctuation* approaches the topic by considering punctuation as a subsystem within the larger linguistic system of written language. One of the book's goals is to move away from a contrastive approach to the topic, which Nunberg finds pervasive among linguists, "which requires that we characterize the features of the written language by reference to some analogous features of the spoken language."[5] According to this view, the purpose of punctuation is to compensate for what is lost in the transcription of speech. Yet as a compensatory device of written language, punctuation does a poor job of conveying intonation patterns and only a slightly better job of marking syntactic units. Because punctuation is widely taken as a poor substitute for the aural richness of spoken language, the attention it has attracted in the field of linguistics (which by convention privileges speech) is limited and often dismissive.

Once the focus shifts from language-as-speech to punctuation as a subsystem within the conventions of written language it becomes a more viable and interesting linguistic topic, because the question becomes "whether there is anything *more* to the written language than the features it shares with speech."[6] While some overlap with the spoken language certainly remains, that relation is incidental to the main function of punctuation within the written language. Some texts, especially some modern texts like an invoice or a bibliography, are not meant to be read aloud, and so it is meaningless (at least in these cases) to think of writing as a mere substitute for the rich auditory range of speech. Punctuation has arisen, writes Nunberg, "as a response to the particular communicative requirements of written language texts, and as an exploitation of the particular expressive resources that graphical presentation makes available."[7] For example, the modern colon and semi-colon "are virtually never used in transcription of ordinary spoken discourse"[8] because each of them serves a logical and syntactic function exclusively within a textual system of language. Other marks such as the hyphen add to the number of ways that modern English has morphological and syntactic features marked in written language that are not distinguished in speech.

Nunberg proposes the category "text grammar" (as distinguished from the "lexical grammar" familiar to linguistic investigations) for understanding the function of punctuation within a system in which "the basic units of text structure are the paragraph and the text-sentence."[9] There are smaller units as well, such as the dash-interpolation and the text clause. He formulates several rules, which are "interconstrained."[10] Promotion rules elevate, for example, a comma to a semi-colon. Linearization rules "map syntactic structures into linear sequences of alphanumeric and non-alphanumeric characters on which are realized all those features of font, face, case and size that are relevant to the identification of text-categories."[11] Pouring rules are projected onto the two-dimensional grid of a page and include features like line breaks, page breaks, and indentation. Absorption rules say that if a phrase-marking comma and a period, for example, logically coincide, the period absorbs the comma. Some marks can be cliticized.[12] And there are more rules, but for my purposes the details of Nunberg's system are less important than his success in offering a theoretical framework for understanding the punctuation as a textual subsystem. In this analysis the nine (or so) punctuation marks familiar to readers of modern English, which he usefully defines as the "set of non-alphanumeric characters that are used to provide information about structural relations among elements of a text,"[13] are absorbed into a larger category of textual representation that includes font changes, capitals, indentation, spacing, and other features identified by terms largely drawn from today's typographic conventions. Nunberg calls these graphic devices "*text-category indicators* of written language."[14]

Nunberg's interest is primarily with modern English, and he speculates that in earlier centuries the fit between intonational patterns and punctuation may have been closer. Yet his historical perspective is unfortunately limited. The kind of punctuation that excites his interest developed after the advent of printing: "[I]t is not until well after the introduction of print that there appears anything like the standardized, elaborated and autonomous system of punctuation that is found in the public uses of intellectualized written languages like English or French."[15] There is no reason to take Nunberg's historicizing pronouncements too seriously, because ultimately they are little more than a rhetorical convenience that allows him to focus his attention on English of the nineteenth and twentieth centuries, which is where his real interest lies. Medievalists recognize it as an unfortunately familiar move to consign centuries of texts to a netherworld of cultural darkness—in this case an imagined stage of writing that lacks system and reason.

In two respects, however, Nunberg is correct about earlier stages in the historical development of punctuation. First, neums and other early marks no doubt emerged as visible cues that facilitated the oral performance of written texts;[16] and second, it took time for scribes to arrive at a system that was "standardized, elaborated and autonomous," yet the process does not need to take as many centuries as Nunberg assumes. On the contrary, it was relatively rapid. Just to take one example, if the Carolingians could standardize a script with such success that it is still used today (you are reading a modified version in the lower-case letters here), and if they could standardize many dozens of Latin abbreviations, then they could certainly create and manipulate "text-category indicators of written language." The fact that these conventions were established in a scribal culture long before Gutenberg and Caxton undermines one of Nunberg's basic assumptions—an assumption that also begs the question of where writers in the era of print found and developed their conventions of punctuation in the first place. They did not make them up wholecloth.[17] Unfortunately, Nunberg's reading of history privileges the role of printing with little evidence in support of it.

Nunberg's glance to the past calls for a different way to historicize the question. At what point in the western scribal tradition did visible cues become incorporated into a textual grammar? How can we tell when that stage is reached? That is, how can we tell when the convention becomes "standardized, elaborated and autonomous"? The "autonomous" part might seem to be the most difficult to detect, because it is reached when the various graphic cues (of which punctuation marks are only a part) become incorporated into a closed self-referential "linguistic subsystem."[18] Yet the questions are not as daunting as they might be for one reason: the earliest systems were developed for Latin in circumstances when it was not spoken as a native language. In such an environment, the conventions of punctuation could move adeptly from marks guiding performance, to marks signaling syntactic constructions, to a fully elaborated textual grammar.

The Medieval Development of Punctuation

Working within the conventions of linguistics, Nunberg does not take advantage of the considerable work published on the history of punctuation. While Parkes's magisterial *Pause and Effect* (1993) did not come out until after Nunberg's *Linguistics of Punctuation* (1990), portions of it were published in articles dating back to 1978.[19] Moreover, as the bibliography of *Pause and Effect* copiously demonstrates, the number of studies that might have helped historicize Nunberg's project is not small. The most important corrective: as early as the seventh and eighth centuries, Irish (and later Anglo-Saxon) scribes developed a complex set of graphic conventions including word separation, abbreviations, and punctuation for their transcriptions of Latin texts. They were helped along by the fact that, as speakers of Celtic and Germanic vernaculars, they encountered Latin as an unfamiliar Romance language with its own extensive written tradition. For them, crucially, Latin writing was not a representation of uttered speech at one remove. In developing new graphic conventions, moreover, the Irish in particular were encouraged by the authority of Isidore of Seville (d. 636), who shifted away from the association of written words with spoken sounds, which was the view commonly held by late antique writers such as Augustine. Near the beginning of his *Etymologies* Isidore writes, "Indeed, letters are tokens of things, the signs of words, and they have so much force that the utterances of those who are absent speak to us without a voice."[20] The important distinction here is that Isidore does not say that written words are tokens of sounds, which are in turn tokens of the things held in thought; it is as though the middle term (utterances) drops out, and letters thus become silent signs (*sine uoce*) of their referents. Isidore's reformulation encouraged Irish scribes (and their successors in monasteries in England and on the continent) to give greater attention to the graphic presentation of Latin texts.[21]

Thus the reconceptualizing of writing as primarily textual (at some remove from spoken utterances) began at a relatively early stage in the history of medieval writing in the Latin West, centuries before the advent of the printing press. The process began in the seventh century with the Irish, who introduced word separation in the *scriptio continua* of the Latin texts that came to them; or more specifically, as Parkes puts it, "they set out the parts of speech by introducing spaces between words."[22]

Word separation and the consequent changes, observes Paul Saenger, "constitut[e] the great divide in the history of reading between antique cultures and those of the modern Occident."[23] It was the first step in introducing a complex of graphic conventions for written Latin that moved away from the older rhetorical understanding of the relation between writing and reading. With some early texts something as simple as a larger gap between words might signal a syntactic break, or a single mark might be used singly or in clusters of two or three to mark different kinds of syntactic units. Before long, however, different marks of punctuation were used as well as capitals (*litterae notabiliores*). "This complex of graphic conventions," writes Parkes,

> became the process by which the written medium of communication functions. A written text presupposes an indeterminate audience disseminated over distance or time, or both. A scribe had no immediate respondent to interact with, therefore he had to observe a kind of decorum in his copy to ensure that the message of the text was easily understood. This decorum—the rules governing the relationships between this complex of graphic conventions and the message of a text conveyed in the written medium—may be described as "the grammar of legibility."[24]

An eighth century manuscript of Bede's Commentary on Proverbs copied at Wearmouth-Jarrow illustrates these graphic conventions through its use of lineation, space, punctuation, and two different scripts.[25] Its presentation is clearly more for the eye than the ear in the way it visibly differentiates each verse of Proverbs from the following commentary. The most obvious distinction is a hierarchy of scripts: uncial for the biblical verses and insular minuscule for the commentary. A *littera notabilior* stands at the opening of each verse and each passage of commentary, and both blocks of text end with a terminal mark of punctuation. Two other marks of punctuation, a raised point called *punctus* and the *punctus elevatus* (see below), set off *sententiae* and phrasing within *sententiae* in the commentary. Even without an itemization of these features, and even without specific knowledge of the purpose of a commentary, the textual display of the folio is striking to the eye.

Among the earliest marks of punctuation were three *positurae* that emerged in the second half of the eighth century. These included "the *punctus versus*...used to indicate the end of a *sententia* containing a statement, the *punctus interrogativus*...used to indicate the end of a *sententia* containing a question, and the *punctus elevatus*...to indicate a major medial pause within a *sententia* where the *sensus* is complete but the *sententia* is not."[26] The three survive today (after modification of their shape and their function) as the semi-colon, the question mark, and the colon.

As the example of Bede's Commentary on Proverbs (MS Bodley 819) shows, by the eighth century the Anglo-Saxons had received this emergent "decorum" and "grammar of legibility" from the Irish and adapted it to their purposes. Aldhelm and Bede, for example, wrote explicitly about conventions governing marks of punctuation, and Alcuin urged Carolingian scribes to use marks of punctuation, which were at the time foreign to them.[27] If increasingly the written text was no longer conceived merely as a transcription of sounds, then punctuation was no longer confined to signaling rhetorical pauses (although it never lost that function altogether) and was free to signal syntactic units. In the ninth century, Carolingian efforts succeeded in standardizing a convention, and by the twelfth century the general repertory of what we might call either "the grammar of legibility" or "text-category indicators" was widespread in western Europe.[28]

The point of this excursus is less to call Nunberg to task for assuming that punctuation became codified in the age of print (and could become codified *only* then) than to emphasize how punctuation and other graphic conventions achieved a systematic stage at a relatively early date; already before the ninth century, they had become, in Nunberg's words, "standardized, elaborated and autonomous." This characterization applies to Latin texts, both poetry and prose; the use of systematic punctuation in vernacular texts was, as a rule, later in developing, in large part because it was intimately tied to their spoken language.

Having sketched out a broader historical context, I would like to point out some remarkable parallels between the two approaches, one historical, the other linguistic. Parkes's "grammar of legibility" has much in common with Nunberg's "text-category indicators of written language"—if the two are not identical—because each designates a set of graphic conventions that function in a closed textual system. Independently of one another Nunberg and Parkes have identified the following features that make up what each calls this "autonomous" system:

(1) different uses of space—gaps between words, gaps between sections of text, verse lineation, margins;

(2) capitals and font changes (for print) corresponding to *litterae notabiliores* and changes in script (for scribes);

(3) marks of punctuation.

Both Nunberg and Parkes identify the sentence/*sententia* and the paragraph as basic units of textual representation, with certain qualifications;

for example, a sentence need not be grammatically complete. Both recognize a tension between the oral and the visual; both see a historical progression in the display of text moving from the performative and rhetorical to the logical and syntactic. In many respects they pursue complementary approaches to the same phenomenon: Nunberg offers a largely synchronic study using theoretical linguistics and Parkes offers a diachronic survey based on detailed empirical examination of manuscripts.

Punctuation in Old English

The conventions guiding the copying of Latin verse were formalized at an early stage in Anglo-Saxon England, with each verse allotted a separate line, with capitals at the beginning and a mark of punctuation at the end.[29] Latin prose was more variable in its graphic presentation, but punctuation and capitals were employed with some regularity.

When we turn to Old English prose and verse, however, we find greater variability. In prose, for example, translations from the bible seem careful to mark off every verse. For example, the Old English illustrated *Hexateuch* and the Cambridge Corpus Christi manuscript of the West Saxon Gospels use *litterae notabiliores* to mark the beginning of each verse and include several marks of punctuation.[30] The manuscript copies of Ælfric's homilies have varying rates of punctuation, but the Royal manuscript and the Cambridge University Library Gg manuscript are punctuated so consistently (*punctus* and *punctus elevatus*) that the most recent editions forgo modern punctuation in favor of reproducing what the manuscript has.[31] Liuzza's edition of the West Saxon Gospels follows the same practice, which suggests that he, like Clemoes and Godden, found the manuscript punctuation to be elaborated and autonomous, if not also systematized. At the other end of the spectrum are prose manuscripts with sparse punctuation. These include both versions of the Old English Boethius and more than a few of the Blickling Homilies.[32] In general, however, it may be safe to say that as prose writing moved into the tenth century, a fuller graphic display became more common. This survey is necessarily superficial, but it suffices to show that when Anglo-Saxons turned from Latin to their vernacular, they had the choice of adopting the full array of graphic conventions used in writing out Latin. As Parkes suggests, the reason for this variable, nonstandard practice must have something to do with the inherent familiarity of their spoken language.

That familiarity would be even more pronounced with the Anglo-Saxons' vernacular poetry, which enjoyed a vigorous tradition extending back long before Old English prose was first written down.[33] Its antiquity, its native familiarity, its verse syntax, and its reliance on formulas create a fundamentally different context for its visual presentation in writing. The difference is striking, even if its familiarity to scholars has blunted its significance. In the most general terms, the punctuation of Old English poems in various manuscripts is sparse, and consists of a raised point; in *Beowulf*, for example, there are about five points per 100 lines.[34] A famous exception to this sparseness is the Junius Manuscript (Oxford, Bodleian Library, Junius 11), sometimes known as the Cædmon Manuscript, which contains *Genesis, Exodus, Daniel*, and *Christ and Satan*. The scribe who copied most of it inserted a point between half-lines with almost unerring accuracy.[35] With one possible exception, no Old English poem is lineated as verse; rather the lines are written out margin to margin.[36] The use of *litterae notabiliores* is generally limited to the opening of poems and section breaks in longer poems. So at first glance, the typical Old English poem copied in manuscript is sparing in Nunberg's text-category indicators: lineation and other uses of space, changes in scripts, and punctuation. It is almost as though when Anglo-Saxon scribes turned from writing Latin or Old English prose to writing their vernacular poems, they forgot about the text-category indicators at their disposal.

Yet as the discussion above suggests, the sparseness in the graphic display of most Old English poems can hardly be the result of a primitive state of the craft of writing. The *mise en page* of a typical folio of poetry calls for a different approach. Instead of examining it to see how it lines up with vernacular prose and Latin writing, or instead of looking for a threshold richness of graphic display that allows us to call a text "standardized, elaborated and autonomous," I propose the poems in their current state are adequate to the task of textual representation. After all, if the poems in written form called for more capitals or more punctuation, scribes had all the necessary tools at their disposal. This way of looking at the question turns it on its head, as it were, and assumes that for the practical purposes of reading, a Latin poem written with a hierarchy of scripts, verse lineation, and regular punctuation has no greater claim on text-category indicators than, for example, an Exeter Book riddle with no punctuation to break the flow of half-lines between the opening initial and the final *positurae*.

In advocating what may seem a counterintuitive approach, I am not reaching for the easy explanation that because their vernacular poems were such a familiar genre, Anglo-Saxon readers could do without punctuation altogether. There must be some truth in this generalization, but it leaves too much unexplained and even suggests that reading was a matter of effortless deciphering. Nor am I claiming that the bare-bones Exeter Book riddle, for example, becomes a script for some kind of non-textual reading, fundamentally different from an Anglo-Saxon's reading of a Latin poem or even your reading of this article. The strong version of the distinction I want to avoid is that in reading a poem like *Beowulf*, an Anglo-Saxon becomes the co-creator of meaning because so much is left to the reader's imagination; as if the written words provide a launch-point for a new poem on each performance.[37] Rather, in assuming a fundamental equivalence between a graphically rich Ælfric homily and a bare-bones Exeter Riddle, I am asking what allows the latter to be read much like the former. A related question asks how the punctuated poems in the Junius Manuscript *resemble* the most sparsely punctuated poems in other manuscripts, not how they differ.

No matter how rich the infusion of text-category indicators, they are never complete in conveying every syntactic nuance or every modulation of rhetoric. A familiar example of this is in the textual representation of dialect. In a humorous sketch that presents itself as nothing more than an extended conversation with a voluble young African American—the "Sociable Jimmy" of the title—Mark Twain uses some familiar typographic tricks to convey the features of Jimmy's particular speech habits. Twain claims, however improbably, "I took down what [Jimmy] had to say, just as he said it—without altering a word or adding one."[38] Here is an excerpt:

> We ain't got no cats heah, 'bout dis hotel. Bill he don't like 'em. He can't stan' a cat no way. Ef he was to ketch one he'd slam it outen de winder in a minute. Yes he would. Bill's down on cats. So is de gals—waiter gals. When dey ketches a cat bummin' aroun' heah, dey jis' *scoops* him —'deed dey do. Dey snake him into de cistern—dey's been cats drownded in dat water dat's in yo' pitcher. I seed a cat in dere yistiddy—all swelled up like a pudd'n. I bet you dem gals done dat. Ma says if dey was to drownd a cat for *her*, de fust one of 'em she ketched she'd jam her into de cistern 'long wid de cat. Ma wouldn't *do* dat, I don't reckon, but 'deed an' double, she *said* she would. I can't kill a chicken—well, I kin wring its neck off, cuz dat don't make 'em no sufferin' scacely; but I can't take and chop dey heads off, like some people kin.

Twain's writing highlights some phonological features of this dialect, such as simplification of consonant clusters, loss of final [ŋ], substitution of [d] for [θ, ð], dropping of postvocalic [r], raising of some vowels (e.g., *jis'*, *ketch*), etc. There are syntactic features like multiple negatives and non-standard usages like *seed, drownded,* and *done* as preterite. But even after admiring Twain's gift for conveying dialect this way, it is clear that his transcription does not—and cannot—capture every feature of Jimmy's speech; in fact the writing invites the reader to fill in many features that are not spelled out. For example, a general knowledge of American dialects—not necessarily Jimmy's in particular—would lead a reader to "hear" a nasalized vowel and a final glottal stop in *can't* despite its conventional spelling. And the phrase *yo' pitcher* shows a dropped [r] in the first word but not the second, where in Jimmy's dialect it almost certainly would be dropped: the reader intuitively makes up the difference.

The example of "Sociable Jimmy" shows that even at its richest, the graphic display of a text falls short of what a reader "reads." This falling short is hardly a sign of failure, because for its purpose Twain's pseudo-transcription is brilliantly successful. The modified spellings and typographic tricks (italics, apostrophes for a dropped sound, etc.) convey the illusion that we are reading something very much like a close phonetic transcription. This illusion is inseparable from the humor of the piece, because its humor begins with the pleasure of recognition. We laugh not because Jimmy is telling funny jokes (he isn't), but because in imagining his unselfconscious rapid-fire monologue we enjoy the illusion of hearing him speak. We have heard Jimmys before, even if we haven't.

I return now from the robust "Sociable Jimmy" to the comparatively anemic presentation of poems like *Andreas*, *Beowulf*, *Meters of Boethius*, and *Guthlac A*. It seems they could not be more different, and yet the manuscript presentation of the Old English texts must be as adequate to their intended readers as Twain's printed text was to his. If they were not, we would find more poems transcribed with ample text-category indicators. Anglo-Saxon scribes certainly had the means at their disposal.

How to explain this gap between the text-category indicators available to scribes and the comparatively spare manuscript presentation? The answer lies in features that poems inherently possess regardless of the presence of lineation, punctuation, or changes of script. I will discuss three of them, the first of which concerns formulas. We now know, from decades of extensive research, that a large percentage of half-lines and even full lines of Old English poems derives from formulaic systems.[39] Certainly an Anglo-Saxon reader would spot half-lines like *holdne hlaford*, *secgan wille*, and X *maþelode* as formulas, which would be an essential part of the task.

(Formulaic composition was also a feature of Latin verse in Anglo-Saxon England.)[40] Merely identifying half-lines, however, could not be sufficient for a reader to comprehend a poem of any length, because many if not most formulas are phrases that can appear anywhere in the word-order of a verse clause. Their contribution is more semantic than syntactic: valuable in its own way, but hardly enough to guide a reader from one clause to the next in a way that, for example, punctuation might do.

Meter is yet another characteristic of Old English poetry, which our honorand has studied with exemplary perceptiveness.[41] Russom's theory is especially pertinent in this regard because its first principle foregrounds the relation between the spoken language and the artifice of meter: "*Foot Patterns* correspond to native Old English word patterns. The foot patterns most easily perceived are those that correspond to the most common word patterns."[42] The familiarity of word-foot patterns in half-lines in turn made even complex metrical types discernible to Anglo-Saxon readers.

Between this correspondence to their spoken language and a lifetime of listening to poems in this tradition, the readers of poems in manuscript learned to intuit half-line boundaries with assurance. One indication of this skill is the fact that scribes who added points to manuscripts rarely made a mis-step. (Scribes, after all, were readers, too.) *Soul and Body*, for example, survives in two versions: one in the Exeter Book and the other in the Vercelli Book. They differ in many particulars, including the number and the location of punctuation, but each of them is consistent in pointing between half-lines, and not within a half-line. There are fewer points in the Exeter version, even allowing for its shorter length, 24 points in 121 lines (a rate of 20 per 100 lines), while there are 60 points in the 169 lines of Vercelli (a rate of 36 per 100 lines). Of these 84 points in total, only twelve coincide, appearing in the same location in each version of the poem, a variance that suggests a great deal of independence in how scribes punctuated this poem, and yet neither scribal program (if we can call it that) resulted in points falling within a half-line.[43] The following short passage from the Vercelli Book version has four lines with light verses in succession (Sievers type A3), three of which are preceded by a point, and one of which begins with a *littera notabilior*. I give them as they appear in manuscript except with modern lineation:

	ne synt þine æhta awihte •
þe ðu her on moldan	mannum eowdest •
Forðan þe wære selre	swiðe mycle
þonne þe wæron ealle	eorðan speda •

butan þu hie gedælde   dryhtne sylfum
þær ðu wurde æt frymðe fugel ... (*Soul and Body I*, 74b–79a)

[Those possessions of yours that you displayed before others here on earth amount to nothing. And so, rather than if you possessed all the earth's wealth (unless you shared it with the Lord himself!), it would have been better for you by far if, from the very beginning, you had been born a bird...]

It is a syntactically complex passage, which Jones's elegant translation navigates with disarming ease.[44] But would an Anglo-Saxon reader find it daunting? Probably not, because as Russom reminds us, "appreciative audiences have a remarkable ability to identify complex verses as variants of regular patterns."[45] Each of the words ending the on-verses in the four full lines (*moldan, selre, ealle, gedælde*) is the only word with metrical stress. Each of the four full lines is a complete clause. Three of the four are preceded by a manuscript point, as if the scribe responsible for adding the points was alert to a metrical boundary coinciding with a clause boundary. With one *littera notabilior* and three points, this short passage is more richly marked with text-category indicators than most passages, and yet it falls short of the conventional modern marks used in Jones's translation (to use a convenient comparison). The immediate point I wish to emphasize does not concern any particular passage or the difference between Exeter and Vercelli, but rather how each scribe's pointing presupposes a contemporary reader's ability to construe the metrical units of the poem, half-line by half-line. Our familiarity with half-line boundaries, thanks to modern editions and studies like Russom's two major books, may distract us from appreciating the sophisticated skills the first generations of readers used to navigate the words on the folio.

Because most poetic formulas constitute half-lines, there is considerable overlap in a reader's ability to recognize one and the other, and together they contributed greatly to comprehending the building blocks of a poem. They fall short, however, in one important respect. Because formulas and half-lines are metrically bounded, they reveal scarcely anything about larger units of discourse such as a clause.[46] For example, neither the scansion of *æðelinga helm* (SsxS) nor its semantic force as a formula signals where it might appear in a clause. It is here that a third feature unique to Old English verse (that is, not shared by Latin or by Old English prose) comes into play: verse syntax.[47]

The essential insight of verse syntax, the last of the three features characteristic of poetry, is that meter and word order are inextricably related. Certain categories of words will lack metrical stress in one position, while they gain it in another. A personal pronoun like *him*, for example, is usually found in an unstressed position at the beginning of a clause, but if it should migrate from that position it acquires metrical stress. The two following passages illustrate the general principle:

> Him þa ellenrof andswarode,
> wlanc Wedera leod, *Beo* 340
>
> Hroðgar maþelode him on ondsware *Beo* 1840

In the first, *Him* lacks metrical stress in a position that is (by far) the usual one for a personal pronoun. In the second the same pronoun is no longer in clause-initial dip and carries the alliteration of the line. This correlation between word categories and degrees of metrical stress was first formulated by Hans Kuhn in the 1933 article cited in the previous endnote, which has become the focal point of some animated critical discussion since about 1980. Recent studies have made it increasingly clear that Kuhn put his finger on a distinctive feature of Old English verse, even if some nuances are still uncertain.[48] Other features of verse syntax not directly tied to Kuhn's observations have been identified, such as the overwhelming tendency for metrically light auxiliaries like *mæg* and *sceal* to occur in the first half-line of a clause.[49] For a reader of Old English poems in manuscript such patterns are crucial in signaling where a verse clause begins and ends: if a half-line has the auxiliary *sceal* or an unstressed *him*, that half-line begins a clause.

The most extensive taxonomy of half-lines within the system of verse syntax is Calvin Kendall's *Metrical Grammar of 'Beowulf,'* which assigns each half-line type to one of three categories: clause-initial, non-clause-initial, and unrestricted.[50] For example, a reader coming across the half-line *him wearð selle lif* (*Phoenix* 417) would intuitively know that it begins a clause—just as surely as if it began with a clausal conjunction. It cannot be the second or a later half-line. Many half-lines fall into Kendall's "unrestricted" category. For example, *beahhordum leng* and *wyrm wohbogen* could, by Kendall's taxonomy, go anywhere in a clause. As it turns out they are the first and second in a passage from *Beowulf*:

> Beahhordum leng
> wyrm wohbogen wealdan ne moste 2824–5

The third half-line in this passage illustrates what Kendall calls non-clause-initial, which can appear anywhere except the beginning of a clause. Any half-line opening with a prepositional phrase like *ofer ealle men* (*Beow* 1717) is also non-clause-initial. Kendall's three categories are not airtight, and the third especially admits more than a few exceptions, but in this matter we are not aspiring to the neogrammarian ideal of exceptionless rules. When the focus shifts to the reader (rather than, say, the process of composition), Kendall's categories become functional and enabling, and the occasional exception emerges as little more than a temporary puzzle or an elegant deviation from the norm as the reader's eyes move along.

An Anglo-Saxon's intuitive grasp of formulaic expressions, the shape of metrical half-lines, and the principles of verse syntax obviated the need for a full system of punctuation, because such marks could only supplement what was already encoded in the words of the poem. The three features outlined here are not only interrelated but also (as Nunberg would put it) interconstrained. In this regard the vernacular verse was substantially different from Old English prose and Latin. I have argued elsewhere that the punctuation in *Beowulf* and other manuscripts is often sensitive to clause boundaries and metrical scansion.[51] For example, the passage quoted above from *Soul and Body I*, 74b –79a, shows three points that fall immediately before clause-initial half-lines (one of which also marks the clause opening with a *littera notabilior*). Here the punctuation supplements syntactic information already carried by the run of unstressed syllables before the first stressed word (e.g., *þe ðu her on móldan*). Even an expert reader might welcome an occasional mark of punctuation, but would not need it to place the half-line within the syntax of the larger passage. Parkes makes an equivalent observation from the perspective of medieval scribes and correctors, who "punctuate where confusion is likely to arise ... and do not always punctuate where confusion is not likely to arise."[52]

This brief survey of the state of punctuation across the Old English poetic corpus leads to two conclusions. The wide variance in the rate of pointing from one poem to the next is not terribly significant on its own. In the case of the Exeter Book, earlier scribes copied individual poems with different (perhaps idiosyncratic) principles for punctuation, which the Exeter scribe dutifully copied.[53] We should not be surprised that the punctuation of *Soul and Body* in the Vercelli Book differs so much from the version in the Exeter Book. We can expand the observation to all text-category indicators: they were not negligible—otherwise few scribes would bother to copy them—but neither were they essential. The second conclusion is that the Junius Manuscript, with almost every half-line marked by a raised point, is an outlier rather than a stage in the progression to a rich graphic display like that used for Latin poems.[54] Its heavy punctuation may be part of the same design motivating the lavish initals and the program of illustrations to create a visually striking display copy. By contrast, the line-ending punctuation for the late poem *Instructions for Christians* may reflect changed expectations regarding the intuitive knowledge that readers would bring to their reading.[55] By the time it was copied at about the middle of the second half of the twelfth century, readers may have welcomed verse paragraphs beginning with rubricated initials and points designating the end of the full line as an equivalent of verse lineation.

Concluding Thoughts

Like most good theories, Nunberg's *Linguistics of Punctuation* is useful to think with. If a text is required to show a threshold level (however that is measured) of text-category indicators before it reaches a state that Nunberg would call standardized, elaborated and autonomous, then most Old English poems would fall far short. On the other hand, Latin poems copied by Anglo-Saxon scribes and the more consistently punctuated Old English prose texts like the Royal manuscript of Ælfric's homilies are no less textual than the "Sociable Jimmy" printed in *The New York Times*. What is less clear is how much saturation of text-category indicators there needs to be. Nunberg says the text-grammar "is largely a matter of tacit knowledge."[56] What tacit knowledge can we assume in Anglo-Saxon England?

A recent compilation has identified more than a thousand scribes active from ca. 960 to ca. 1100, which is a salutary reminder of the complex environment for textual production at this time.[57] This scribal culture maintained in many cases a sophisticated grasp of graphic display, which many studies have made abundantly clear. Why should the copying of the scribes' vernacular poetry be qualitatively different? When the same scribe that copied the Exeter Book turned to copy Bede's and Augustine's Latin prose in Lambeth Palace 149, using *litterae notabiliores* and four marks of punctuation, did he shift from a non-textual to a textual mode of writing?[58] It seems unlikely. Because even the most sparsely punctuated Old English poem is the product of such an environment, it seems fair to ask *how* it utilizes a text-grammar, not *whether* it does. Uniquely among the kinds of writing surveyed here, Old English poems made use of verbal cues embedded in formulas, meter, and verse syntax, and because scribes could assume the manuscript's reader would know the conventions intimately, they could be sparing or expansive in the use of punctuation and other graphic cues. While *Christ II*, for example, has on average one point for every ten lines of verse, this sparseness by itself does not tell against a graphic display that is "standardized, elaborated and autonomous." Sparseness alone is less of an objection once one realizes that even the most fully marked-up form of writing can admit more text-category indicators, as the discussion of "Sociable Jimmy" earlier points out: *yo' pitcher* could be revised to indicate the loss of the second post-vocalic [r]; as it stands the reader intuitively supplies the lack. Old English poems are different only in the way the elements of this equation (words, reader, text-category indicators) coordinate with one another. The cues conveyed by the words themselves in verse syntax are "standardized, elaborated and autonomous." Anglo-Saxon scribes could assume that the readers of their vernacular poems had this "tacit knowledge," just as Twain could trust his readers to navigate his typographic clues. The very words constituting an Old English poem are supplemented by text-category indicators such as punctuation, which makes the scribal artifact as textual as any other form of writing in Anglo-Saxon England.

NOTES

[1] *Old English Meter and Linguistic Theory* (Cambridge: Cambridge University Press, 1987); and *Beowulf and Old Germanic Metre* (Cambridge: Cambridge University Press, 1998).

[2] *The Linguistics of Punctuation*, CSLI Lecture Notes 18 (Stanford: Center for the Study of Language and Information, 1990).

[3] According to a review of citations in August 2014 ("Web of Science").

[4] See, for example, Lynne Truss, *Eats, Shoots & Leaves: The Zero Tolerance Approach to Punctuation* (New York: Gotham Books, 2004), and the review by Louis Menand, "Bad Comma," *The New Yorker*, June 28, 2004. For a recent popular survey see David Crystal, *Making a Point: The Persnickety Story of English Punctuation* (New York: St. Martin's, 2015).

[5] Nunberg, *Linguistics of Punctuation*, p. 11.

[6] Nunberg, *Linguistics of Punctuation*, p. 4.

[7] Nunberg, *Linguistics of Punctuation*, p. 7.

[8] Nunberg, *Linguistics of Punctuation*, p. 14.

[9] Nunberg, *Linguistics of Punctuation*, p. 25.

[10] Nunberg, *Linguistics of Punctuation*, p. 23.

[11] Nunberg, *Linguistics of Punctuation*, p. 51.

[12] Nunberg, *Linguistics of Punctuation*, pp. 59, 73, 76.

[13] Nunberg, *Linguistics of Punctuation*, p. 17.

[14] Nunberg, *Linguistics of Punctuation*, p. 17.

[15] Nunberg, *Linguistics of Punctuation*, p. 10.

[16] See for example Bernhard Bischoff, *Latin Palaeography: Antiquity and the Middle Ages*, trans. Dábhí Ó Crónín and David Ganz (Cambridge: Cambridge University Press, 1990), p. 169. On the relation between musical neums and punctuation see Peter Clemoes, *Liturgical Influence on Punctuation in Late Old English and Early Middle English Manuscripts*, Old English Newsletter Subsidia; reprint of a 1952 pamphlet (Binghamton: CEMERS SUNY-Binghamton, 1980); and Jan Ziolkowski, *Nota Bene: Reading Classics and Writing Melodies in the Early Middle Ages*, Publications of the Journal of Medieval Latin 7 (Turnhout: Brepols, 2007), pp. 83–107.

[17] For a striking illustration see plate 68 in Malcolm B. Parkes, *Pause and Effect: Punctuation in the West* (Berkeley: University of California Press, 1993), which reproduces a page from the *editio princeps* of Augustine's *City of God* published in Italy, 1467. Parkes observes, "The punctuation in this edition follows that of the fifteenth-century Italian manuscript used as a copy" (285). See more generally the discussion on pp. 87–92.

[18] Nunberg, *Linguistics of Punctuation*, p. 6.

[19] See, for example, Parkes's "Punctuation, or Pause and Effect," in *Medieval Eloquence: Studies in the Theory and Practice of Medieval Rhetoric*, ed. James J. Murphy (Berkeley: University of California Press, 1978), pp. 127–42; and "Contributions of Insular Scribes of the Seventh and Eighth Centuries to the 'Grammar of Legibility,'" in *Grafia e Interpunzione del Latino nel Medioevo*, ed. Alfonso Maierù (Rome: Edizioni dell'Ateneo, 1987), pp. 15–30.

[20] *The Etymologies of Isidore of Seville*, trans. Stephen A. Barney, *et al* (Cambridge: Cambridge University Press, 2006). Parkes, *Pause and Effect*, p. 21 quotes and translates the Latin from *Isidori Hispalensis episcopi etymologiarum sive orginum libri xx*, ed. W. M. Lindsay (Oxford: Clarendon, 1911), I.iii.1: *litterae autem sunt indices rerum, signa uerborum, quibus uis est ut nobis dicta absentium sine uoce loquantur*.

[21] Parkes, *Pause and Effect*, p. 23.

[22] Parkes, "Contribution," p. 18; see also Parkes, *Pause and Effect*, pp. 23–25; Parkes "*Raedan, Areccan, Smeagan*: How the Anglo-Saxons Read," *Anglo Saxon England* 26 (1997): 1–22 at p. 5; and Paul H. Saenger, *Space Between Words: The Origins of Silent Reading* (Stanford: Stanford University Press, 1997), pp. 32 and 83. Parkes observes that the Irish derived their concept of Latin words as isolable linguistic units from grammars such as Donatus's *Ars maior* and Priscian's *Institution de nomine pronomina et verbo*.

[23] Saenger, *Space between Words*, p. 12. Saenger focuses on word separation, but the larger context of his argument assumes a broader set of changes; see for example, pp. 71–82. As Jan Ziolkowski memorably puts it, the introduction of

space between words "provided for the writing system what zero would do for the numerical system in the High Middle Ages," in *Nota Bene*, p. 87.

[24] Parkes "Contribution," p. 16.

[25] Oxford, Bodleian Library, MS Bodley 819. See the facsimile of folio 16 in Parkes, *Pause and Effect*, 180 (Plate 2) and the commentary on p. 181. An ancient mark of punctuation called the hedera [❧] reinforces the visible separation of the verses from Bede's commentary.

[26] Parkes, *Pause and Effect*, pp. 35–36. A fourth, the *punctus flexus*, used to mark a minor medial pause, appears in the tenth century.

[27] Saenger, *Space Between Words*, pp. 83–85; Parkes, *Pause and Effect*, p. 32.

[28] Parkes, *Pause and Effect*, p. 34.

[29] Katherine O'Brien O'Keeffe observes, "From the eighth century on, Latin poetry in England was copied in lines of verse," in *Visible Song: Transitional Literacy in Old English Verse* (Cambridge: Cambridge University Press, 1990), p. 26. Footnote 9 on the same page adds, "By the tenth century, English manuscripts of Latin verse are consistently formatted in lines of verse with redundant initial capitals and points at the ends of lines."

[30] The former is London British Library Cotton Claudius B. iv, which is dated by C. R. Dodwell and Peter Clemoes to the second quarter of the eleventh century in *The Late Old English Illustrated Hexateuch*, Early English Manuscripts in Facsimile 18 (Copenhagen: Rosenkilde and Bagger, 1974), p. 16; for the punctuation see Richard Marsden, *The Old English Heptateuch and, Ælfric's Libellus De Veteri Testamento Et Novo*, Early English Text Society 330 (Oxford: Oxford University Press for the Early English Text Society, 2008), p. xlvii. The latter is Cambridge Corpus Christi College 140, dated by N. R. Ker to the first half of the eleventh century in *Catalogue of Manuscripts containing Anglo-Saxon* (Oxford: Oxford University Press, 1957), §35. The gospels are edited by R. M. Liuzza, *The Old English Version of the Gospels*, Early English Text Society 304, 314 (Oxford: Published for the Early English Text Society by the Oxford University Press, 1994).

[31] London, British Library MS Royal 7 C. xii is the basis for Peter Clemoes's edition of *Ælfric's Catholic Homilies: The First Series Text* (Oxford: Oxford University Press, 1997); and Cambridge, Cambridge University Library MS Gg. 3. 28 is the basis for the M. R. Godden edition, *Ælfric's Catholic Homilies, the Second Series Text* (London: Oxford University Press, 1979).

[32] Oxford Bodleian Library, Bodley 180 contains the prose translation of Boethius; London British Library Cotton Otho A. vi has prose alternating with verse. See Malcolm Godden and Susan Irvine, *The Old English Boethius: An Edition of the Old English Versions of Boethius's De Consolatione Philosophiae* (Oxford: Oxford University Press, 2009), pp. 12 and 22. Rudolph Willard, *The Blickling Homilies,* Early English Manuscripts in Facsimile 10 (Copenhagen: Rosenkilde and Bagger, 1960), p. 36.

[33] For a masterful analysis of the workings of this tradition in early and

late poems, see Geoffrey R. Russom, "Artful Avoidance of the Useful Phrase in *Beowulf, The Battle of Maldon*, and *Fates of the Apostles*," *Studies in Philology* 75 (1978): 371–90.

[34] O'Brien O'Keeffe, *Visible Song*, 175; *Beowulf*'s rate is relatively sparse in comparison with, for example, *Widsith* and *Andreas*, but the difference is a matter of degree. For O'Brien O'Keeffe's survey of pointing in the major codices, see pp. 155–89.

[35] The pages with *Genesis, Exodus*, and *Daniel* were copied by a single hand; *Christ and Satan* was copied by two or three hands, and the metrical pointing is less consistent; see N. R. Ker, *Catalogue of Manuscripts Containing Anglo-Saxon* (Oxford: Clarendon Press, 1990), p. 408. For its punctuation see O'Brien O'Keeffe, *Visible Song*, pp. 179–86, who also lists several other manuscripts with metrical pointing. In his edition of *Exodus* P. J. Lucas notes that for this poem the scribe had an error rate of 2% in marking half-lines (London: Methuen, 1977), p. 22.

[36] The exception is the Leiden Riddle: "To some extent the Old English seems to be lineated as verse," observe Fred C. Robinson and E. G. Stanley in their facsimile edition, *Old English Verse Texts from Many Sources: A Comprehensive Collection*, Early English Manuscripts in Facsimile 23 (Copenhagen: Rosenkilde and Bagger, 1991), p. 20. But even this has been disputed: see Johan Gerritsen, "Leiden Revisited: Further Thoughts on the Text of the Leiden Riddle," *Medieval Studies Conference Aachen 1983*, ed. Wolf-Dietrich Bald and Horst Weinstock, Bamberger Beiträge zur englischen Sprachwissenschaft 15 (Frankfurt am Main: Peter Lang, 1984), pp. 51–59, and the studies cited there. A more remote possibility is the three-line *Gloria II*, but its "lineation according to verse-form may be accidental"; Robinson and Stanley, p. 26.

[37] This is not to deny the role of the reader in bringing meaning to the text, as reader-response theory has made abundantly clear. I am arguing that there is no difference *in kind* between the reading of the homily and the poem, even though one may be saturated with text-category indicators and the other apparently is not.

[38] First published in the *New York Times*, 29 November 1874, p. 7 col. 1. The appearance of a book in 1993 by Shelley Fisher Fishkin, *Was Huck Black?: Mark Twain and African-American Voices* (New York: Oxford University Press) generated much discussion about "Sociable Jimmy" because of her claim that Jimmy's (black) dialect was indistinguishable from Huck's (white) dialect.

[39] For a survey of the scholarly literature up to the early 1990s see Katherine O'Brien O'Keeffe, "Diction, Variation, the Formula," in *A Beowulf Handbook*, ed. Robert E. Bjork and John D. Niles (Lincoln: University of Nebraska Press, 1997), pp. 85–104. For a list of formulas in *Beowulf* see the second and third appendices in Andy Orchard, *A Critical Companion to Beowulf* (Woodbridge, Suffolk: Boydell and Brewer, 2003).

[40] Andy Orchard, "Old English and Latin Poetic Traditions," in *A Companion to Medieval Poetry*, ed. Corinne Saunders, Blackwell Companions to Literature and Culture 67 (Chichester, England: Wiley-Blackwell, 2010), pp. 65–82.

[41] See especially his two books, *Old English Meter and Linguistic Theory*; and *Beowulf and Old Germanic Metre*; to these may be added his many articles on meter.

[42] *Old English Meter and Linguistic Theory*, 2.

[43] On the punctuation of each version see Douglas Moffat, *The Old English Soul and Body* (Wolfeboro, NH: D. S. Brewer, 1990), p. 5.

[44] Christopher A. Jones, ed. and trans., *Old English Shorter Poems*, Dumbarton Oaks Medieval Library 15 (Cambridge: Harvard University Press, 2012), pp. 196–97.

[45] *Old English Meter and Linguistic Theory*, p. 149. Russom is speaking in particular about meter, but the observation holds for complex patterns of meter and syntax.

[46] This claim needs mild qualification, because a formula like *secgan wille* is rarely clause initial, while *X maþelode* consistently is clause initial. There is also a small number of full-line formulas.

[47] The literature on this topic is large, and it is variously known as metrical grammar (Kendall) and prosodical syntax (Momma). Some of the major studies include Hans Kuhn, "Zur Wortstellung und -betonung im Altgermanischen," *BGDSL* 57 (1933): 1–109; Daniel Donoghue, *Style in Old English Poetry: The Test of the Auxiliary*, Yale Studies in English 196 (New Haven: Yale University Press, 1987); Calvin B. Kendall, *The Metrical Grammar of 'Beowulf'*, Cambridge Studies in Anglo-Saxon England 5 (Cambridge: Cambridge University Press, 1991); and H. Momma, *The Composition of Old English Poetry*, Cambridge Studies in Anglo-Saxon England 20 (Cambridge: Cambridge University Press, 1997). For a re-evaluation of one of the central claims of verse syntax see Geoffrey Russom, "Purely Metrical Replacements for Kuhn's Laws" in *English Historical Metrics*, ed. C. McCully and J. Anderson (Cambridge: Cambridge University Press, 1996), pp. 30–41.

[48] One disputed area is the metrical status of clause-initial verbs in clauses like *Hwearf þa hrædlice, Beo* 356.

[49] See Donoghue, *Style*, pp. 9–11; auxiliaries in this regard are not merely modal auxiliaries but any finite verb that allows a second verb to be in non-finite form, either an uninflected infinitive (e.g., *ongan wyrcan*) or a past participle (*hæfde gefrunon*); "metrically light" includes monosyllables like *sceal*, resolvable two-syllable auxiliaries like *scyle*, and monosyllables with a prefix (*ongan*). For other characteristics of the opening of a clause, such as the fact that *wæs* is consistently found in the first half-line of a clause, see Mary Eva Blockley, *Aspects of Old English Poetic Syntax: Where Clauses Begin*, Illinois Medieval Studies (Urbana: University of Illinois Press, 2001).

[50] *Metrical Grammar*, pp. 32–42.

[51] Donoghue, "A Point Well Taken: Manuscript Punctuation and Old English Poems," in *Inside Old English: Essays in Honour of Bruce Mitchell*, ed. John Walmsley (Malden, MA: Blackwell, 2006), pp. 38–58; and Donoghue, "Reading

Old English Poems with Anglo-Saxon Eyes," *Studies in Medieval English Language and Literature* 27 (2012): 39–58.

[52] M. B. Parkes, "Punctuation, or Pause and Effect," in *Medieval Eloquence: Studies in the Theory and Practice of Medieval Rhetoric*, ed. James J. Murphy (Berkeley: University of California Press, 1978), pp. 127–42, at p. 138.

[53] For the Exeter Book see R. W. Chambers, *et al. The Exeter Book of Old English Poetry* (London: P. Lund Humphries, 1933), esp. pp. 61–62; N. R. Ker, "Review of *the Exeter Book of Old English Poetry*," *Medium Ævum* 2 (1933): 224–31; Bernard J. Muir, "A Preliminary Report on a New Edition of the Exeter Book," *Scriptorium* 43 (1989): 273–88; and Abdullah Alger, "The Verbal and Visual Rhetoric of Old English Poetry: An Analysis of the Punctuation and Formulaic Patterns in the Exeter Book (Exeter, Cathedral Library, MS 3501)" (University of Manchester, 2010).

[54] In this regard I differ from O'Brien O'Keeffe, who calls Junius 11 "modern" and "forward-looking" with a "system of metrical pointing independent of the specific poems it informs and elucidates" (pp. 182, 186). For more on the punctuation of the Junius Manuscript see Leslie Lockett, "An Integrated Re-Examination of the Dating of Oxford, Bodleian Library, Junius 11," *Anglo-Saxon England* 31 (2002): 141–73.

[55] James L. Rosier, "'Instructions for Christians': A Poem in Old English," *Anglia* 82 (1964): 4–22. See Ker §18 for the date; and for description Robinson and Stanley, p. 27.

[56] Nunberg, *Linguistics of Punctuation*, p. 23. It is not difficult to think of limit cases: is an Emily Dickinson lyric relying solely on dashes for punctuation or Molly Bloom's unpunctuated monologue at the end of James Joyce's *Ulysses* less textual than "Sociable Jimmy"?

[57] D. G. Scragg, *A Conspectus of Scribal Hands Writing English, 960–1100*, Publications of the Manchester Centre for Anglo-Saxon Studies 11 (Cambridge: D. S. Brewer, 2012). Peter Stokes surveys "somewhat less than five hundred scribal hands in around two hundred manuscripts" (3) from a shorter interval than Scragg in his *English Vernacular Minuscule from Æthelred to Cnut c. 990–c. 1035*, Publications of the Manchester Centre for Anglo-Saxon Studies 14 (Cambridge: D. S. Brewer, 2014); for a concise history of scribal hands see Stokes's first chapter, pp. 10–34.

[58] See Ker, *Catalogue* §275; David Ganz and Jane Roberts, ed. *Lambeth Palace Library and its Anglo-Saxon Manuscripts* (London: Lambeth Palace Library, 2007), pp. 36–38; Patrick W. Conner, *Anglo-Saxon Exeter: A Tenth-Century Cultural History*, Studies in Anglo-Saxon History 4 (Woodbridge, Suffolk, UK: Boydell Press, 1993), chapters 3 and 4; and Matthew T. Hussey, ed. *Anglo-Saxon Manuscripts in Microfiche Facsimile, Volume 22, Exeter Manuscripts* (Tempe, AR: Arizona Center for Medieval and Renaissance Studies, 2014), pp. 89–101.

Boars and the Geats in *Beowulf*

Lindy Brady
University of Mississippi

IN TRIBUTE TO OUR honorand's field-shaping scholarship on *Beowulf* and Germanic literature, this chapter argues that the seven passages in *Beowulf* which link *eofor* or *swin* to armor, weapons, or other war equipment have literary significance in the narrative structure of the poem.[1] These passages have been previously explored for their archaeological resonances, but they also share two curious (and unaddressed) features: they occur only in the first two-thirds of the poem, before Beowulf becomes king, and half of them take place at moments of defeat or tragedy.[2] It is the latter which complicates readings of the boar as a purely protective symbol on weapons and armor. In other words, while the memorable description of boar-helmets gleaming over Beowulf and his troop as they march towards Heorot does suggest that "the boar in the early Germanic world has fundamentally to do with protection and defence," the appearance of this symbolic image among the corpses on Hnæf's funeral pyre in the Finn digression evokes defeat.[3] I argue that these divergent images of boars in *Beowulf* create an internally consistent pattern in which boars are linked to victory only when worn by the Geats as warriors in their youth, while their association with any other tribe comes during scenes of tragedy. This resonance adds to the inevitability of Beowulf's triumphs at Heorot and explains the absence of boars from the poem's final section where—although boar armor would be expected against a serpentine dragon—Beowulf's death looms large.[4]

The symbolism of the boar figure in Germanic culture has been fruitfully studied. As A. T. Hatto and others have long noted, the descriptions of boar helmets within *Beowulf* match archaeological evidence of extant Anglo-Saxon and Germanic war helmets from the period.[5] The Sutton Hoo helmet and the Vendel helmet (of Grave 14) have boar figures on the eyebrow, nose, and cheek-plate guards, while the Benty Grange and Wollaston helmets have free-standing boar figures as crests on top.[6] The frequency with which boars are found on helmets in both the literature and archaeology of Anglo-Saxon England and other early Germanic cultures has led to the widely accepted conclusion that the boar was a symbol of protection and defense in the early Germanic world, though most are careful to note that whatever apotropaic properties the boar may have originally possessed, "qualities of this order survived in the conventions of early Germanic art and poetry at a time when their original function and meaning were either lost or only partly understood."[7] Yet while the connotations of the boar as a symbol of protection in *Beowulf* seem clear, its resonance with the Geats in their youth has structural significance within the poem, making this image more than an archaeological relic. Boars form a narrative chiastic structure in which scenes of Geatish victory bookend those of Danish tragedy. This imagery is evoked during Beowulf's confident arrival at Heorot and triumphant return to Hygelac's court, but also in the course of two Danish misfortunes—the Finn digression and Æschere's death—enveloped between these moments of Geatish success. The boar thus appears as a symbol with particular resonance for the Geats as warriors in their youth within this poem.

Seven passages in *Beowulf* link boars to war-equipment, and I will discuss them in narrative order. Boars appear when the Geats arrive at Heorot, during the Finn digression, in two passages surrounding the death of the Danish warrior Æschere, in two more passages during Beowulf's descent into Grendel's mere, and finally when Beowulf and his men return to Hygelac's court. My argument is primarily concerned with the material boars in this poem, which means that I will temporarily set aside the character Eofor, the Geatish warrior who kills Ongentheow at the battle of Ravenswood in the final third of the work. However, I will briefly conclude by suggesting some ways in which Eofor also fits this narrative pattern of a link between boars and the Geats as young warriors.

Boars first appear early in the poem after Beowulf and his men leave the Danish coast guard and continue their march toward Heorot. As they approach the hall of Hrothgar and his troops, the poem lingers over a description of their war-gear:

eoforlic scionon
ofer hleorbergan gehroden golde,
fah ond fyrheard (303b-305a)[8]

[Boar-figures shone over cheek-guards, ornamented
with gold, shining and fire-hardened.][9]

This image is introduced into the poem as the young Geatish warriors hasten towards Heorot, eager for the battle and glory that will come with Grendel's defeat. The boars on their helmets stand as both a protective symbol and an announcement of their arrival—there could hardly be a more natural emblem of a young, victorious troop, the standard interpretation of these lines.[10] While not all would go as far as Glosecki in arguing that "when it first appears in *Beowulf*, the boar crest clearly embodies a powerful animal guardian," it is clear that the poem consciously links boars and armor, drawing upon the visual symbolism of the boar's well-known ferocity in battle to call attention to the warriors' prowess if not actively offer apotropaic protection.[11]

The *Beowulf* poet's careful use of boar imagery in the first two-thirds of the poem means that boars are associated not just with the Geats as warriors but also particularly with them in their youth. Throughout *Beowulf*, the poet emphasizes the young age of the hero and his men during their time at Heorot. Of course, we know Beowulf was young when he fought Grendel, or he would not be able to say as an old king that *Ic ðas leode heold / fiftig wintra* (2732b–33a, "I ruled this people for fifty winters"). During his time at Heorot, Hrothgar and Wealhtheow both comment directly on Beowulf's youth. Wealhtheow calls him a *hyse* (1217a, "a young man") when speaking to him, and Hrothgar also tells him, *ne hyrde ic snotorlicor / on swa geongum feore guman þingian* (1842b–43, "I have never heard a man speak more wisely at such a young age"). As Beowulf's youth is emphasized so too is that of his troop. The poet makes clear that Beowulf is the oldest of the Geatish warriors: *him se yldesta* (258a, "he the eldest") answers the Danish coast guard upon their landing, and Wulfgar introduces him in this way to Hrothgar, reporting that *þone yldestan oretmecgas / Beowulf nemnað* (363–64a, "the eldest of these warriors is called Beowulf"). The Geatish warriors are also themselves described as young, as when Beowulf tells Hrothgar to watch over his *magoþegnum* (1480b, "young retainers") if he dies, or when the Geats are about to leave Denmark and *cwom þa to flode felamodigra, / hægstealdra* (1888–89a, "they came to the sea very high-spirited in youth"). The poem repeatedly emphasizes the youth of Beowulf and his men while they are at Heorot, and so the figure of the boar is linked to the Geats at the point in time when they are young warriors.

The clear link drawn between these boars and the young warriors in the passage above suggests that the boars in *Beowulf* are indeed a protective symbol. Yet this early association between boars and victory in battle makes a puzzle of subsequent lines. If boars symbolize armored protection, why do they next appear on the funeral pyre? During the Finn digression, boar helmets become a poignant synecdoche for loss, destruction, and a feud already spiraled out of control with yet more violence to come when envisioned on the joint funeral pyre of Hildeburh's son and brother, Hnæf:[12]

> Æt þæm ade wæs   eþgesyne
> swatfah syrce,   swyn eal gylden,
> eofer irenheard,   æþeling manig
> wundum awyrded;   sume on wæle crungon.   (1110–1113)

> [At the funeral pyre was easily seen a bloodstained
> mail-shirt, a golden boar, a beast hard as iron;
> many a noble destroyed by wounds;
> those who fell in slaughter.]

The boar here is a powerful symbol of the costs of vengeance, standing in as it does for the corpses of *þara ðe þær guð fornam / bega folces. Wæs hira blæd scacen* (1123b–24, "those who were destroyed in battle, there, of both peoples; their glory was departed").[13] As noted by the most recent editors of *Beowulf*, although both the Finn digression and the fragmentary *Fight at Finnsburg* provide an elusive and incomplete picture of the events alluded to, "a brief outline of the story as it is understood by the majority of scholars" would include what was probably a failed peaceweaving between the Danes and the Frisians: "Possibly there existed an old feud between the two peoples, and the Danish princess had been given in marriage to the Frisian chief in the hope of securing permanent peace, but with the same grievous result as in the case of Freawaru."[14] Yet whatever the cause of the feud between the Danes and the Frisians in this digression, its outcome is clear as Hildeburh mourns her son and brother side by side. The image of the boar on the funeral pyre is linked not to victory, but to loss and grief for those on either side of the battle.

A particularly Danish perspective imbues this tragedy. Though both Danes and Frisians perish in this battle, as Fulk, Bjork, and Niles note:

> The point of view is distinctly Danish. The valor and loyalty of Hnæf's retainers (in the Fragment), Hildeburh's sorrow, and Hengest's longing for vengeance (in the Episode) are central features of the narratives. It is not without significance, perhaps, that all the direct speech (in the Fragment) has been assigned to the Danes, whereas the utterances of the Frisians are reported as indirect discourse only.

> So, too, no concealment is made of the bad faith shown by those on the Frisian side of the conflict. The final attack on Finn and his men, culminating in the complete victory of the Danes, may be the salient point of the story in *Beowulf*, though the duplicity they show in breaking the treaty with Finn renders the victory less than glorious.[15]

The Finn digression in *Beowulf*, despite its enigmatic elements, is clearly linked to a Danish past. This is reinforced by the fact that the digression ends with Hildeburh's return to her native people and homeland. After the second battle and the Danish victory, *hie on sælade / drihtlice wif to Denum feredon, / læddon to leodum* (1157b–1159a, "they brought the noble woman on a sea-journey to the Danes, led her to her people"). The boar imagery in the Finn digression binds itself to memories of death, sorrow, and failed peaceweaving for the Danish people—hardly the protective, triumphant emblem gleaming over the heads of Beowulf and his men as they marched towards Heorot at the beginning of the poem.

Moments of significant grief and loss for the Danes link with the image of the boar in its next two appearances, two passages which come immediately before and after the second attack on Heorot and the Danish warrior Æschere's death at the hands of Grendel's mother.[16] The first is during her oft-discussed approach towards Heorot, when the terror is said to be less by as much as is a woman's strength in battle compared to that of an armed man:

> þonne heoru bunden, hamere geþruen,
> sweord swate fah swin ofer helme
> ecgum dyhttig andweard scireð. (1285–87)
>
> [when an ornamented blade, forged by a hammer,
> a sword stained with blood, its edges sharp, shears
> straight through the boar on top of a helmet]

It is worth noting Glosecki's comments on this passage: "extensive deposits of ruined gear suggest that warriors tried to 'kill' the boar in combat as well during the aftermath," and thus "the poet's reference to slashing at the boar implies the tactic of 'killing' the guardian of one's opponent in an effort to neutralize his defensive magic."[17] Yet regardless of any apotropaic allusions this scene may hold, the dramatic narration of a bloodstained sword shearing the boar off a helmet could not be a clearer illustration of defeat. In coupling the approach of Grendel's mother with this memorable image, the *Beowulf* poet links her to the destruction of something—whether boar or helmet—that ought to offer protection. While this imaginative simile does not name any particular tribe, it is evoked during Grendel's mother's imminent attack on Heorot and the Danes. This passage provides a further link between boars, Danes, and tragedy, rather than the protection which we might imagine this highly symbolic piece of armor to provide.

The elaborate, hypothetical analogy drawn between Grendel's mother's attack on Heorot and a boar sheared from a helmet in battle is mirrored by the way in which a grieving Hrothgar recalls past battles fought alongside his friend and counselor Æschere a few lines later in the next fitt. After Æschere is killed by Grendel's mother during her nighttime attack, the realization of his death the next morning means that *sorh is geniwod / Denigea leodum* (1322a–1323b, "sorrow is renewed for the Danish people"). Æschere, Hrothgar tells Beowulf, was:

> min runwita ond min rædbora,
> eaxlgestealla ðonne we on orlege
> hafelan weredon, þonne hniton feþan,
> eofferas cnysedan. (1325–28a)
>
> [my private counselor and my chief advisor, my shoulder-companion when we guarded our heads in battles, when foot-soldiers clashed together; crashed against boar-helmets]

Boar-helmets are again evoked at a moment of particular tragedy for the Danes, as Hrothgar's closest companion is slain unawares. In both of these passages, the boar shines through as an emblem not of victory but of two absent, violent battles, imagined surrounding the sorrowful context of Æschere's unexpected death.

In both Æschere's death and the Finn digression, the protective figure of the boar becomes instead a symbol of destruction. It appears that within the narrative structure of *Beowulf*, the boar is so strongly linked to the Geats that it is only seen to function protectively when borne by them. Both Æschere's death and the Finn digression are moments not just of non-Geatish tragedy, but of particularly Danish tragedy: another attack on Heorot, during which Hrothgar's closest companion is killed, and a failed attempt at peace between the Danes and the Frisians, remembered as a moment of feuding and death in Danish history. In contrast, every time a boar is linked to the Geats throughout the poem, the moment is one of their triumph, suggesting that *Beowulf* holds the boar as an emblem of particularly Geatish victory.

The poem's next boar images come at a moment of significant success for the Geats, appearing immediately before Beowulf battles and defeats Grendel's mother. First, one of the Geatish warriors shoots a sea serpent at Grendel's mere, and it is quickly dragged to shore *mid eoferspreotum* (1437b, "with boar-spears"). In addition to continuing the association of Geats and boars at moments of victory, this slaying of a sea-serpent with a boar-spear also introduces a symbolic opposition of snakes and boars—common throughout early Germanic culture—that makes the absence of boar imagery from Beowulf's later fight against the dragon so surprising. Just as the boar was associated with armor and protection, so too were serpents linked to the "bite" of attacking swords in early Germanic literature and archaeology.[18] Hatto has noted the resonance of "snake-swords compounded with venom, snake-swords which bite to kill and whose wielders feed or blood them on their enemies" against which the boar took on a symbolic role as defensive agent in early Germanic culture.[19] The Geatish killing of this sea-serpent shows the boar in victory over its symbolic opposite.

A few lines later, the long description of Beowulf arming himself as he prepares to descend into the mere also contains boars and helmets which successfully protect the Geats from attacking snakes and swords. Prominent in Beowulf's armor is *se hwita helm* (1448a, "the shining helmet"), which is *besette swinlicum, þæt hine syðþan no / brond ne beadomecas bitan ne meahton* (1453–1454, "beset with boar figures, so that never afterwards might swords or battle-blades be able to bite").[20] Glosecki rightly comments that as "Beowulf gets ready to dive into the mere, the poet hints that the helmet guards his head with something more than metal."[21] Yet whether offering apotropaic or simply symbolic protection, the visual link between the boar figure and the Geatish warrior's impending victory could not be clearer in these passages.

For the Geats, the image of the boar is evoked at moments of significant triumph. It has been argued that, "since *Beowulf* connects the boar crest with Danes and Geats alike—and since the Vendel helmets and the Torslunda die show the image being used elsewhere in Scandinavia, too—we cannot limit the belief in this guardian to any particular tribe."[22] Yet while it is clear that boar images cannot be attributed exclusively to one Germanic tribe on an archaeological or cultural basis, *Beowulf* draws a literary distinction between the way that the boar figure functions for the Geats and for the Danes. While the poem does depict the boar helmet as worn by Danes and Geats alike, it appears only at moments of victory for the Geats, and only at moments of defeat for the Danes. Within this poem, the boar is a particularly Geatish emblem of victory.

This function of the boar as a sign of Geatish victory is even more evident in its last appearance in the poem, which occurs after Beowulf's triumphant return to Hygelac's court. At the beginning of fitt XXXI, Beowulf concludes the narration of his battles in Denmark with a promise to give all the treasure he has received in reward from Hrothgar to his Geatish king and kinsman, Hygelac. Beowulf orders this hard-earned wealth to be brought in before the Geatish court, and the first—and thus most prominent—of these objects is an *eaforheafodsegn*, a boar-banner: *Het ða in beran eaforheafodsegn* (2152, "he then commanded to be brought in the boar-banner"). *Eaforheafodsegn* is a *hapax legomenon*, but the collocation *eafor* + *heafod* + *segn* continues the imagery of boars atop heads which has been so prevalent in the poem already. The presentation of this object to Hygelac not only marks a striking moment of Geatish triumph within the poem's narrative, but the physical object of the banner itself also now serves as a permanently visible symbol and a tangible reminder of the story of Beowulf's victories within the Geatish court.

The narrative impact of these boars in the poem is greater than the sum of their parts. All of the passages that mention boars occur during the first two-thirds of the poem, while Beowulf and his Geatish troops are still young warriors. Every mention of a boar object takes place prior to the passage at the end of fitt XXXI, when *eft þæt geiode ufaran dogrum / hildehlæmmum ... /... Beowulfe brade rice / on hand gehwearf; he geheold tela / fiftig wintra* (2200–2209a, "afterwards it happened, in later days, in the crash of battle ... that the broad kingdom passed to Beowulf, into his hand; he held it well for fifty winters"). No boars—on helmets, spears, banners, or otherwise—appear at any point in the final third of the poem, from the moment that the kingdom passes into Beowulf's hands onward. This is a surprising omission in and of itself, given the frequency with which boar helmets appear as an emblem of battle in the earlier portions of *Beowulf*. Yet the absence of boars from the last portion of the poem is even more striking when considered in light of the symbolic opposition of serpents and boars noted above. Beowulf's descent into Grendel's mere pits both *wyrmcynnes fela* (1425b, "many of serpent-kind") against the Geatish *eoferspreotum* (1437b, "boar-spears") and his boar-beset helmet against the serpentine bite of an enemy's blade (1453–1454). This symbolic opposition of boars and serpents on armor and weapons suggests that, when an *ongan / deorcum nihtum draca ricsian* (2210b–2211, "one began, a dragon, to rule in dark nights"), a boar helmet should be the first defensive weapon Beowulf would reach for when preparing for battle.[23]

I suggest that the absence of any boar imagery from Beowulf's last fight is just as meaningful as its presence in his earlier battles. Within *Beowulf*, the boar appears not only as an emblem of the Geats, but it also has particular resonance as a symbol of youthful heroism rather than one associated with aged kingship. The prominence of boar helmets during Beowulf's youth emphasizes the inevitability of his victories in the first two thirds of the poem, while understanding that the boar image possesses this particular narrative function explains its absence from the poem's elegiac final third, when Beowulf's death looms large. As Beowulf himself knows, his battle with the dragon must happen *swa unc wyrd geteoð* (2526b, "as fate allots for the two of us"), and totemic protection cannot save a man fated to die. The absence of boar images from the final third of the poem suggests that the boar in *Beowulf* is not only an emblem of the Geats, but also one with particular symbolic resonance for the Geats as warriors in their youth, before Beowulf becomes king.

The argument that the boars of *Beowulf* are associated specifically with the Geats as warriors in their prime, I suggest, is strengthened by the narrative positioning of the Geatish warrior Eofor, whose bloody slaying of the Swedish king Ongentheow is remembered in a lengthy flashback to the battle of Ravenswood in the final portion of the poem. Without implying that every name-element in *Beowulf* ought to be interpreted literally, I think it is reasonable to assume that the symbolic resonances of the warrior brothers Eofor and Wulf would have been closer to the surface for the poem's audience than those of characters with compounded names. The figure of Eofor both recalls and heightens the connections that the *Beowulf* poet had drawn between boars and Geatish warriors in their prime in the earlier portion of the poem, embodying in his very character, as he does, what had earlier only been emphasized by objects: physical boars are linked to the Geats only in the narrative present of the poem, while the boar character of Eofor appears only in flashbacks to the past. The Swedish-Geatish wars take place long before Beowulf becomes king, further supporting the argument that boars appear in victory only for the Geats during their age of youthful warfare. Moreover, the *Beowulf* poet uses the figure of Eofor in order to sharpen the contrast between a past age of victory for the Geats in their prime and the grim future that awaits the tribe after Beowulf's death.

The Geatish-Swedish wars and the battle of Ravenswood are recalled after Beowulf has died, during the "Messenger's Prophecy," which recounts these events in far more detail than the narrative requires at this point. The poem places a heightened emphasis on this bloody battle, in which Eofor is the embodiment of a ferocious and victorious Geatish warrior. The *Beowulf* poet uses the association between boars and the Geats as warriors which he has built up throughout the poem in order to sharpen the contrast between this heroic past age and the harsh future which is to come. Eofor's appearance in the narrative after Beowulf's death heightens the poem's linkage of boars to the Geats in an earlier age. The messenger's prophecy reminds the Geatish tribe of a time when they achieved significant victory in battle, something which is unlikely to occur again for quite some time.

The figure of the boar, then, has greater symbolic resonance in *Beowulf* than it has been granted. Yet alongside this symbolic resonance comes structural significance. In one of his many careful studies of *Beowulf*, Geoffrey Russom has argued that, "Grendel's mere provides a center for *Beowulf* that is comparable to the center of Norse mythic history."[24] This chapter has surveyed the poem not from the epic vantage point of Norse mythology, but from the smaller scale of the humble *swín*. Yet its conclusions find that even the boars of *Beowulf* lend structural coherence to the work. It is thus, I hope, a fitting tribute to one of the poem's greatest champions and scholars.

NOTES

[1] This chapter is dedicated to Rick in gratitude not only for his field-defining scholarship but also his enthusiasm and kindness as a teacher of undergraduates—the reason I entered this profession. In the words of *Maxims I: lean sceal, gif we leogan nellað, þam þe us þas lisse geteode* (l. 70); *Anglo-Saxon Poetic Records*, vol. 3 (The Exeter Book), ed. George Philip Krapp and Elliot Van Kirk Dobbie (New York: Columbia University Press, 1936). I would like to thank Frederick M. Biggs, Stephen J. Harris, and M. J. Toswell for their kind assistance with this chapter.

[2] See Stephen O. Glosecki, *Shamanism and Old English Poetry* (New York: Garland, 1989), pp. 181–210 and review by Geoffrey Russom, *Speculum* 66 (1991): 637–9; Rosemary Cramp, "*Beowulf* and Archaeology," *Medieval Archaeology* 1 (1957): 57–77; A. T. Hatto, "Snake-swords and Boar-helms in *Beowulf*," *English Studies* 38 (1957): 145–60; Heinrich Beck, *Das Ebersignum im Germanischen*, Quellen und Forschungen zur Sprachund Kulturgeschichte der Germanischen Völker, N. F. 16 (140) (Berlin: De Gruyter, 1965); George Clark, "Beowulf's Armor," *English Literary History* 32 (1965): 409–41; A. Margaret Arent, "The Heroic Pattern: Old Germanic Helmets, *Beowulf*, and *Grettis saga*,"

in *Old Norse Literature and Mythology*, ed. Edgar C. Polomé (Austin: University of Texas Press, 1969), pp. 130–99 (and plates); William A. Chaney, *The Cult of Kingship in Anglo-Saxon England: The Transition from Paganism to Christianity* (Manchester: Manchester University Press, 1970), pp. 121–27; Caroline Brady, "Weapons in *Beowulf*: An Analysis of the Nominal Compounds and an Evaluation of the Poet's Use of Them," *Anglo-Saxon England* 8 (1979): 79–141; and Roberta Frank, "The Boar on the Helmet," in *Aedificia Nova: Studies in Honor of Rosemary Cramp*, ed. Catherine E. Karkov and Helen Damico (Kalamazoo, MI: Medieval Institute Publications, 2008), pp. 76–88.

[3] Hatto, "Snake-swords and Boar-helms in *Beowulf*," p. 155.

[4] See Hatto, "Snake-swords and Boar-helms in *Beowulf*," and discussion below on the symbolic opposition of these two animals.

[5] Hatto, "Snake-swords and Boar-helms in *Beowulf*," p. 160, is one of many to argue that, "there is perhaps also direct evidence for boar-mask warriors on the fringe of the Germanic world in the first century A.D." in the form of Chapter 45 of Tacitus's *Germania*. While Hatto is careful to note that this potential evidence can be placed only "on the fringe of the Germanic world," see Frank, "The Boar on the Helmet," pp. 79–80, for an overview of the problems in connecting Tacitus to the boar helmets extant from Anglo-Saxon England.

[6] Hatto, "Snake-swords and Boar-helms in *Beowulf*," pp. 155ff; see also Cramp, "*Beowulf* and Archaeology"; Arent, "Old Germanic Helmets, *Beowulf*, and *Grettis saga*" and plates therein; *Klaeber's Beowulf: Fourth Edition*, ed. R. D. Fulk, Robert E. Bjork, and John D. Niles (Toronto: University of Toronto Press, 2008), pp. 135–37, n. 303b–6a, 303b, and referenced plates; and R. L. S. Bruce-Mitford, *The Sutton Hoo Ship Burial: A Handbook* (London: British Museum, 1968; 3rd edn. 1979).

[7] Hatto, "Snake-swords and Boar-helms in *Beowulf*," pp. 155 and 160. As Frank, "The Boar on the Helmet," notes, the use of the boar as a military symbol was not unique to the Germanic world, as it also appears on the equipment of early Celtic and Roman warriors and in later Norse skaldic poetry.

[8] All citations to *Beowulf* are by line number to *Klaeber's Beowulf: Fourth Edition*, ed. Fulk, Bjork, and Niles, and all translations are my own, unless otherwise noted.

[9] There is disagreement over how to translate the full passage, which reads, *eoforlic scionon / ofer hleorber[g]an gehroden golde, / fah ond fyrheard; ferhwearde heold / guþmod grimmon* (303b–306a), amending MS *grummon*. See *Klaeber's Beowulf: Fourth Edition*, ed. Fulk, Bjork, and Niles, pp. 135–37, n. 303b–6a, for a good overview of the problems and varying interpretations which have been proposed. I follow the reading of Bruce Mitchell and Fred C. Robinson, *Beowulf: An Edition* (Oxford: Blackwell, 1998), p. 58 n. 303b–7a, whose solution leads to the translation, "boar-figures shone over cheek-guards, ornamented with gold; shining and fire-hardened, it held guard over life." Regardless of whether or not the boar images and/or helmets of the men are what guard their lives in this

passage, the link between the Geatish warriors and boar helmets is clear.

[10] The helmets also reflect their nobility: as Cramp, "*Beowulf* and Archaeology," 60, notes: "The length of the poet's descriptions in ll. 303 ff. or 1448 ff. is a measure of the aristocratic importance of the helmet." Glosecki, *Shamanism and Old English Poetry*, p. 194, notes further that the boar figure "seems to have been closely associated with royalty." Likewise, Chaney, *The Cult of Kingship in Anglo-Saxon England*, p. 121, notes that "Certain animals are peculiarly associated with the king, and of these one of the most important was the boar."

[11] Glosecki, *Shamanism in Old English Poetry*, p. 193. Hatto, "Snake-swords and Boar-helms in *Beowulf*," p. 156: "No animal displays more desperate courage when brought to bay, as hunters of former ages well knew. On the defensive he was the most formidable beast in Europe. In Homer he ranked with the lion."

[12] This episode is illuminated by the fragmentary *Fight at Finnsburg*; see *Klaeber's Beowulf: Fourth Edition*, ed. Fulk, Bjork, and Niles, pp. 273–90, for edition, commentary, and notes, and p. 180ff for notes on the Finn Digression.

[13] As Glosecki, *Shamanism and Old English Poetry*, p. 194 notes of this passage: "The poet uses the boar figure virtually as an appositive for *æþeling* 'prince, nobleman.'"

[14] *Klaeber's Beowulf: Fourth Edition*, ed. Fulk, Bjork, and Niles, p. 273.

[15] *Klaeber's Beowulf: Fourth Edition*, ed. Fulk, Bjork, and Niles, pp. 274–75.

[16] Roberta Frank, "The Boar on the Helmet," p. 82, has noted: "A boar-helmet is mentioned in each of the three sections or fitts leading up to Beowulf's killing of Grendel's mother." She argues: "The emphasis on boar power in the first part of the poem is deliberate, as is the setting in *fyrndagum*, in old heathen times." I argue for a further distinction between the ways in which boar helmets are associated with Danes and Geats.

[17] Glosecki, *Shamanism and Old English Poetry*, p. 195.

[18] See Hatto, "Snake-swords and Boar-helms in *Beowulf*" and Hilda Ellis Davidson, *The Sword in Anglo-Saxon England: Its Archaeology and Literature* (Woodbridge: The Boydell Press, 1962), p. 104ff.

[19] Hatto, "Snake-swords and Boar-helms in *Beowulf*," p. 155.

[20] As Cramp, "*Beowulf* and Archaeology," p. 62 notes: "Here the plural form of *swinlicum*, where only one helmet is in question, seems to refer not to one figure set on the helmet's top as at Benty Grange, but to two or more little figures, perhaps set over the cheek-guards as at Sutton Hoo."

[21] Glosecki, *Shamanism and Old English Poetry*, p. 192.

[22] Glosecki, *Shamanism and Old English Poetry*, p. 194.

[23] Translation following Geoffrey Russom, "At the Center of *Beowulf*," in *Myth in Early Northwest Europe*, ed. Stephen O. Glosecki (Tempe, AZ: Arizona Center for Medieval and Renaissance Studies, 2007), pp. 225–40 at p. 226; see pp. 225–6 for discussion of the "until one began..." formula. The dragon is repeatedly referred to as both *draca* and *wyrm*.

[24] Russom, "At the Center of *Beowulf*," p. 235.

New Applications for Word-Foot Theory

Megan E. Hartman
University of Nebraska at Kearney

GEOFFREY RUSSOM'S WORD-FOOT THEORY stands out from other studies of early Germanic poetic form because where other scholars ask *what*, Russom asks *why*: word-foot theory was developed to explain what motivated poets to make the choices they did. In doing so, Russom reminds scholars that not only the poets, but also the audience, pay attention to metrical patterns. Although Anglo-Saxon interlocutors would not have scanned the poems in the same way that modern scholars do, they would still have needed to understand the metrical patterns being used to appreciate the aesthetics of the poetry. Good poetry must be straightforward enough that the audience can follow the metrical patterning, Russom argues, whereas bad poetry is overly complex and becomes obscure. While poets use some varied or unusual patterns for both practical and artistic reasons, they temper the complexity of unusual verses by making other features in the verse simpler.

This theory has opened up several new modes of inquiry. In addition to structural concerns, such as why some metrical patterns are more common than others or what makes a marginal verse, Russom has used word-foot theory to investigate such issues as the dating of poetry and the continuity between Old and Middle English alliterative verse.[1] As metrical studies continue to move forward, word-foot theory could be applied in yet further directions. In this chapter, I discuss its relevance for some kinds of stylistic and generic analysis. Where early studies of Old English meter looked largely at the corpus as a whole, some emerging studies acknowledge stylistic differences among different poems or groups of poems.[2] The application of word-foot theory advances these studies because it illuminates ways in which the syntax and genre intersects with the meter, thereby illustrating what different sorts of metrical patterns these factors might engender.

According to Russom's system of scansion, each verse, or half-line, consists of two feet, which are formed by combinations of primary stress, marked with S, secondary stress, marked as s, and unstressed elements, marked as x (I use this system of metrical notation, supplemented by references to Sievers's five types). The first of word-foot theory's most fundamental principles is that "*foot patterns* correspond to native Old English word patterns," and "the foot patterns most easily perceived are those that correspond to the most common word patterns."[3] For this reason, each foot, ideally, consists of a single word. Yet the additional function words necessary to relate a narrative must be added in somehow. According to word-foot theory, an unstressed word can either replace an unstressed syllable in a typical word pattern (as in *geong in geardum* Sx/Sx: A1 "young in the courtyards" [*Beowulf* 13a]) or stand before the foot as an extrametrical word (as in *folce tō frōfre* Sx/(x)Sx: A1 "as a consolation to the people" [*Beowulf* 14a]).[4]

These extrametrical words can either create or alleviate complexity. In verse patterns that open with an S position, additional words add complexity, though that complexity can be limited if the drop (the unstressed position) is still short and the words are clitics, which Russom considers "less word-like."[5] In verses that open with a light foot—an unstressed initial position—additional syllables and particles (which are "more word-like") decrease complexity because they mark the position as an independent foot.[6] Word-foot theory maintains that poets attempt to limit complexity as much as possible so that the audience would be able to pick out and appreciate the aesthetic value of the metrical patterns as it hears the poem recited.

Although conservative poets (conservative poems for my purposes here include *Beowulf*, *Genesis A*, *Guthlac A*, *Exodus*, and *Daniel*) seem to make limiting complexity a priority, other poets consistently compose marginal verses, frequently through long drops with extrametrical words.[7] This sort of "loose" poetry has often been considered the work of an inferior poet. While this assessment might be true in some cases, the principles that underlie word-foot theory suggest a second possible interpretation: if the main motivation for keeping verses short is to limit complexity, poets operating under an unusual set of constraints may have used longer verses while limiting the complexity in other ways. Applying this theory to *The Battle of Maldon* and the two *Maxims* poems reveals that these poems, which both diverge from traditional composition because they consistently contain long drops, each have a distinctive way of organizing the drops.[8] The differences in structure show both that these unusual features are not general sloppiness and that the poets took some care to organize the unstressed material and limit the complexity of their verse. Thus, because of differences in syntax and genre, these poets shifted their priorities and composed lines that differ stylistically from conservative poetry but would have been recognized and appreciated by an audience.

The Battle of Maldon and Maxims I & II: Poems at the Margins

Old English poems deemed irregular by modern scholars generally either contain many violations of rules that seem inviolable or have verses that differ from the four-syllable ideal either more often or to a greater degree than traditional poems such as *Beowulf* (or both).[9] Both *Maldon* and the *Maxims* poems contain some irregularities of both types, but ones of the latter type differentiate the poems more fully from traditional poems.[10] Comparing *Maldon* and the two *Maxims* poems to *Beowulf*, for example, shows where their particular irregularities lie and what makes them alike.[11] The similarity comes across most strongly when comparing the frequency of unstressed words in each poem. The table below provides the incidence of verses with one to five unstressed words in *Maldon*, *Maxims I & II* (taken together), and *Beowulf*:[12]

	1 word		2 words		3 words		4 words		5 words		Total	
	#	%	#	%	#	%	#	%	#	%	#	%
Maldon	122	18.7	190	29.4	85	13.1	33	5.1	2	.31	432	66.8
Maxims	100	27.8	90	25.0	16	4.2	0	0	1	.28	207	57.5
Beowulf	333	22.2	289	19.3	124	8.3	15	1.0	2	.13	763	50.9

As the table shows, *Maldon* contrasts sharply with *Beowulf* in terms of the willingness the poets have for using unstressed words. Although *Beowulf* has a higher incidence of verses with only a single unstressed word, *Maldon* has a higher incidence of verses with multiple unstressed words, as well as more unstressed words in total. Even *Maldon*'s relative lack of verses with exactly one unstressed word shows the degree to which the poet adds unstressed words to the poem: when deviating from what Russom considers the two-word norm, the *Maldon* poet is more likely to do so to a larger degree than to a smaller one.

The contrast between *Beowulf* and the *Maxims* poems is not as stark, especially because *Beowulf* contains a larger proportion of verses with three or more words in the drop. Significantly, though, the high incidence of verses with one or two words in the drop in the *Maxims* poems makes their incidence of verses with unstressed words higher overall. While not as willing to use a larger number of unstressed words, then, the *Maxims* poets certainly made extensive use of unstressed words in small quantities. The larger number of unstressed words in both poems affects other aspects of the drop as well. The length of the drops can similarly distinguish these poems from those of a more conservative composition. The table below shows the difference in incidence and length of the polysyllabic drops.

	2 syllables		3 syllables		4 syllables		5 syllables		6 syllables		7 syllables		Total	
	#	%	#	%	#	%	#	%	#	%	#	%	#	%
Maldon	257	39.7	88	13.6	47	7.3	26	4.0	4	.62	1	.15	423	65.4
Maxims	117	32.5	28	7.8	9	2.5	2	.56	0	0	0	0	156	43.3
Beowulf	487	32.5	150	10.0	43	2.9	13	.9	1	.07	1	.07	695	46.3

Maldon here, in a way similar to the comparison above, has a higher incidence of verses with polysyllabic drops than *Beowulf*, with a more pronounced difference in the longer verses. In particular, the verses with four- and five-syllable drops occur, while not often, at least with some frequency in *Maldon*, and less than half as often in *Beowulf*. In contrast, the drops in the *Maxims* poems are of a comparable length to *Beowulf* or shorter.[13] However, while the normal verses look similar, the hypermetrical verses in the two poems do not.[14] Both of the *Maxims* poems have an unusually high number of these hypermetrical verses, and the drops in these verses are not as consistently short as those in conservative poems.[15] The table below gives the incidence of the different drop lengths in the onsets of the two groups of poems, *Maxims* and the conservative poems:

	0		1		2		3		4		5		6		7	
Maxims	#	%	#	%	#	%	#	%	#	%	#	%	#	%	#	%
Sx onset	0	0.0	32	36.4	25	28.4	16	18.2	10	11.4	3	3.4	2	2.3	0	.00
xx onset	0	0.0	0	0.0	8	13.1	19	31.2	14	22.9	13	21.3	5	8.2	2	3.3

Conservative	#	%	#	%	#	%	#	%	#	%	#	%	#	%	#	%
Sx onset	5	5.3	50	52.6	28	29.5	11	11.6	1	1.0	0	0.0	0	0.0	0	.00
xx onset	0	0.0	0	0.0	24	16.1	48	32.2	53	35.6	21	14.1	2	1.3	1	.67

Here the difference in drop length is more similar to that between the drop length of normal verses in *Maldon* and *Beowulf*: the incidence of shorter drops remains comparable, but as the drops get longer, the numbers start to fall away more quickly in the conservative poems. For the heavy onset, the longest drop in the conservative poems is four syllables, while the *Maxims* poems have as many as six. The light onset tends to be longer in all poems, since it is a foot with no stressed position, yet the conservative poems have very few examples over five syllables long while the *Maxims* poems have more, making for drops that stand out for their length just as much as those in *Maldon*.

Thus, while by no means identical, *Maldon* and the two *Maxims* poems seem to show a general loosening of the metrical strictures exemplified by word-foot theory, varying from the norm of the conservative poems in both the length and content of the drops. It would be possible to argue that these poems therefore represent bad poetry: the poets could not maintain the same careful control over their line that a poet such as the *Beowulf* poet could, but instead needed to add function words in multiple locations. However, close attention to just how these two poets accommodate these length increases shows that at least one other explanation is possible.

Different Principles of Organization

Although word-foot theory is based on the idea that foot patterns imitate word patterns, the governing principle is even more basic: poets prefer metrical patterns that are recognizable and easy to understand. Keeping the verses short seems to be the simplest way to minimize complexity, but some poets may have had other priorities. In the face of these priorities, an adept poet could increase the complexity of the most basic feature—composing longer lines with more words—while reducing the complexity in other ways, thereby maintaining metrical patterns that the audience could follow.

Maldon's Style: Accommodating Linguistic Change

A brief passage from *Maldon* illustrates the way in which the poet expands the drops:

(1) Þā þæt Offan mǣg	ǣrest onfunde,
(x)x/Sxs (B1)	Sx/(x)Sx (A1)
þæt se eorl nolde	yrhðo geþolian,
(x)x/Ssx (C1)	Sx/(x)Sx (A1)

hē lēt him þā of handon	lēofne flēogan
(x)Sx/(xx)Sx (aA1)	SxSx (A1)
hafoc wið þæs holtes,	and tō þǣre hilde stop;
Sx/(x)Sx (A1)	(xx)xx/Sxs (B1)
be þām man mihte oncnāwan	þæt sē cniht nolde
(xxx)xx/(x)Sx (A3)	(x)x/Ssx (C1)
wācian æt þām wīge,	þā hē tō wǣpnum fēng
Sx/(xx)Sx (A1)	(xx)x/Sxs (B1)

[When the kinsman of Offa first came to know that, that the earl did not wish to put up with cowardice, he caused him then, the dear one, to fly from his hand, the hawk toward the forest, and he advanced to the battle; by that, one could know that the young man did not wish to weaken at the battle, when he took up weapons.] (*Maldon* lines 5–10)

In this passage, only one verse has the minimum four syllables. Two more have polysyllabic drops but still maintain the ideal two-word pattern, and the rest have polysyllabic drops containing multiple words. These words fall largely into one of three categories: pronouns, prepositions, and demonstratives. Of course there are others as well, such as conjunctions (e.g. *þa* in 5a or *and* in 8b) or finite verbs (e.g. *let* in 7a and *mihte* in 9a), but more than twice as many fall into one of the first three categories. The distinction is important because those are the categories of words most influenced by the incipient shift from a synthetic to an analytic language.

Old English was just beginning to move toward analytic syntax in the tenth century, which in turn made more function words necessary in normal prose.[16] In particular, normal prose contained more articles to clarify the case of a noun, more prepositions to specify the function of a noun, and more pronouns to identify the subject when it could not easily be gleaned from the verb conjugation. The *Maldon* example illustrates these exact alterations. Of the eleven common nouns in the passage, five are accompanied by an article. Furthermore, five of the nouns function as something other than a subject or direct object, and each one is accompanied by a preposition. These words all could have been omitted by an earlier or more traditional poet. Similarly, of the seven finite verbs in the passage, six have an overtly stated subject, two of which are personal pronouns. Thus, the long drops in *Maldon* do not result purely from an inability of the *Maldon* poet to compose verses with one or two words consistently, but also from syntactic usages which reflected language contemporary to the poem.

Although this contemporary syntax complicates the verses, the *Maldon* poet simplifies other features to limit the overall complexity. The following table shows that the number of verses with more complex patterns in *Maldon* as compared to *Beowulf* and *Maxims I* and *II* has decreased in favor of type A and B verses:

	A		**B**		**C**		**D**		**E**		**Remainders**	
	#	%	#	%	#	%	#	%	#	%	#	%
Beowulf	671	40.1	260	17.3	291	19.4	179	11.9	99	6.6	0	0
Maldon	337	52.1	139	21.5	98	15.2	39	6.0	33	5.1	1	.15
Maxims	199	55.3	38	10.6	47	13.1	54	15.0	15	4.2	7	1.9

Almost three-quarters of *Maldon* is made up of Sievers types A (Sx/Sx) and B (x/Sxs), as opposed to less than two-thirds in *Beowulf*, while the most complex verses—those with falling or clashing stress—all occur less often than they do in *Beowulf*, sometimes significantly so. This dependence on the simple, natural-sounding alternating stress patterns makes a regular rhythm that is easier to follow. In part, this shift to alternating stress may not have been a conscious choice by the poet: it can also be explained by another element of language change.[17] When stress began to weaken on word-final syllables, the frequency of true compounds decreased, which in turn caused the number of verses with falling stress to decrease.[18] Compounds are not necessary to form type D and E verses; a poet could instead use a word containing a disyllabic root plus an inflectional ending, or compose a verse using three stress words. The *Maldon* poet might have even found the latter structure useful because it creates space for a moderately stressed particle at the end of a line. Yet doing so would add an extra complex feature to the verse, since the two feet would have three words carrying stress instead of two. Such verses do occur in *Maldon*, especially as a type D4 (e.g. *wand wācne æsc*: S/Sxs "brandished the slender spear" [*Maldon* 43a]), but they are not the norm: the poet more regularly uses true compounds or at least trisyllabic simplexes to compose types D and E, and, perhaps consequently, does not do so as often. In this way, language change seems to have catalyzed a stylistic change in composing with type D (S/Ssx or S/Sxs) and E (Ssx/S or Sxx/S) verses, and the *Maldon* poet chose the less complex way to institute that change: mostly, the poet formed these verse types only with compounds and otherwise avoided them.

In addition to simplifying the verse types, the poet also seems to have taken care in distributing unstressed syllables across the verses. The table below shows the incidence of polysyllabic drops in each verse type as a percentage of the total number of verses with a polysyllabic drop in *Maldon*:

	2 syllables		**3 syllables**		**4 syllables**		**5 syllables**		**6 syllables**		**7 syllables**		**Total**	
	#	%	#	%	#	%	#	%	#	%	#	%	#	%
Type A	110	26.0	17	4.0	4	1.0	0	0.0	0	0.0	0	0.0	131	31.0
Type A3	3	0.7	14	3.3	31	7.3	20	4.7	3	0.7	1	0.2	72	17.0
Type B	87	20.6	34	8.0	4	1.0	3	0.7	0	0.0	0	0.0	128	30.3
Type C	52	12.3	21	5.0	8	1.9	2	0.5	1	0.2	0	0.0	84	19.7
Type D	2	0.5	2	0.5	0	0.0	0	0.0	0	0.0	0	0.0	4	1.0
Type E	3	0.7	0	0.0	0	0.0	0	0.0	0	0.0	0	0.0	3	0.7
Remainders	0	0.0	0	0.0	0	0.0	1	0.2	0	0.0	0	0.0	1	0.2
Total	**257**	**60.8**	**88**	**20.8**	**47**	**11.1**	**26**	**6.2**	**4**	**1.0**	**1**	**0.2**	**423**	**100**

Word-foot theory posits that verses can most easily receive extrametrical syllables when they open with a drop. The majority of polysyllabic verses in *Maldon* (67.14%) accord with this theory and are of type B, C, or A3. It might seem surprising that, individually, the incidence of type A and B verses with a polysyllabic drop is practically equal, and that type A verses comprise a greater proportion of the polysyllabic drops than types C (x/Ssx) and A3 (xxx/Sx). However, the vast majority of the type A verses have disyllabic drops, which are relatively simple. Given that type A verses make up over half of the poem, it is hardly surprising that this moderately expanded version would be so prominent. Longer verses of type A are rarer. For verses with trisyllabic drops, type B is most prominent, and only types that open with a drop have five or more syllables.

When compared to *Beowulf, Maldon* may not seem quite as regular: in *Beowulf,* 72.09% of the verses with a polysyllabic drop are types A3, B, or C, and only 25.61% of them are type A. The general trends are similar, but *Beowulf* consistently conforms more closely to the standards suggested by word-foot theory. Yet a more general distribution of polysyllabic drops and unstressed words is to be expected in *Maldon* given the nature of the language change. Many of the grammatical words that occur so frequently in *Maldon* are clitics and must therefore be placed beside the word they are proclitic to; as a result, clitics attached to nouns that occur later in the verse fall in verse-medial drops. Nevertheless, the poet seems to take care in where verse-medial polysyllabic drops occur. First, most are in type A verses, while the incidence of medial polysyllabic drops in types D and E

(1.65%) is roughly the same as that in *Beowulf* (2.3%).[19] This disproportionate difference suggests that the poet might have made an effort to keep the unstressed words out of the most complex positions. Second, none of the medial drops is extraordinarily long. The longest is four syllables, of which there are only four examples (all type A). All the drops with five or more syllables, including the one irregular verse, open with an unstressed position. Furthermore, among verses with an opening drop, type A3 can most easily receive numerous function words, and, accordingly, the incidence of A3 verses exceeds that of type B and C for verses with a four-syllable drop and up.[20] Certainly, ease of composition must have been a motivation here, since A3 verses are easier to compose, but using this verse type also helps the poet to work function words into the poem with the least amount of disruption possible.[21]

It would seem, then, that the poet controls the metrical complexity quite closely in *Maldon*. Although the length of the verses increases, the complexity of verse types decreases. The poet includes some complex verse types, creating a degree of variety in the poem, but such verses generally appear in their most basic instantiations. Longer verses, with multiple unstressed syllables made of several independent words, tend to open with a drop, where these extra syllables decrease rather than increase the complexity. Such limits to complexity suggests that the poet did have control over the composition but focused on different priorities; rather than concentrating on the principles that drive classical Old English verse, the poet found a way to make accessible verse while integrating the function words that characterize the contemporary diction.

The *Maxims* Style: Integrating Formulaic Diction

The two *Maxims* poems appear similar to *Maldon* because they, too, have long drops that often contain multiple unstressed words. However, a look at the types of words the *Maxims* poets use and how they organize them in the drops reveals a significant difference. While both poems have a range of unstressed words, those most frequently used in the *Maxims* poems are different from those in *Maldon*. Here, the unstressed words often fall into two different categories: finite verbs of minimal stress, usually a form of *beon* or *sculan*, and prepositions.[22] Furthermore, these words are not typically placed into the specific drops where they would be least disruptive. As the previous table on p. 80 shows, where *Maldon* contains both more type A and type B verses than *Beowulf*, the *Maxims* poems only contain more type A. In fact, since these poets also use some type D verses, the incidence of types B and C goes down, leaving fewer verses that open with an unstressed position.

Unsurprisingly, then, the additional words and syllables do not occur most frequently in types B and C verses. Even though almost all of these verses have at least one independent word in the opening drop—only one type C verse in *Maxims I* does not—there are simply not enough of these verse types in the poems to contain the majority of the unstressed words.

Instead, most of the polysyllabic drops appear in type A verses, as the table below demonstrates for *Maxims I & II*:

	2 syllables		3 syllables		4 syllables		5 syllables		6 syllables		7 syllables		Total	
	#	%	#	%	#	%	#	%	#	%	#	%	#	%
Type A	76	48.7	9	5.8	0	0.0	0	0.0	0	0.0	0	0.0	85	54.5
Type A3	1	0.6	2	1.3	3	1.9	1	0.6	0	0.0	0	0.0	7	4.5
Type B	13	8.3	13	8.3	4	2.6	1	0.6	0	0.0	0	0.0	31	19.9
Type C	21	13.5	4	2.6	2	1.3	0	0.0	0	0.0	0	0.0	27	17.3
Type D	2	1.3	0	0.0	0	0.0	0	0.0	0	0.0	0	0.0	2	1.3
Type E	2	1.3	0	0.0	0	0.0	0	0.0	0	0.0	0	0.0	2	1.3
Remainder	2	1.3	0	0.0	0	0.0	0	0.0	0	0.0	0	0.0	2	1.3
Total	**117**	**75.0**	**28**	**17.9**	**9**	**5.8**	**2**	**1.3**	**0**	**0.0**	**0**	**0.0**	**156**	**100**

Type A alone makes up over half of the verses with a polysyllabic drop in these poems, as opposed to 41.67% for all the verses that open with a drop combined. This division certainly seems unusual, since poets generally avoided complex medial drops. Yet it is also important to note that these type A verses tend to be relatively short: the drops never exceed three syllables. The longer drops, which are few in number, appear in the more standard types A3, B, and C (though none of the verses grows as long as those in *Maldon*). Thus, the *Maxims* poets do not completely disregard the general principles of conservative composition proposed by word-foot theory, but they seem, in some ways, to stray from them even more than the *Maldon* poet.

The greater deviation in the *Maxims* poems suggests a third motivation for the poets' compositional style, namely, the traditional language that tends to mark the gnomic statements governing these two poems, which focus on the nature of things and how they are ordered.[23] Such statements are often formed in one of the following ways:

(2)(a) wyrd byð swīðost.
Sx/Sx(A1)
Winter byð cealdost,
Sx/(x)Sx (A1)
lencten hrīmigost
Sx/Ssx (D*2)
(hē byð lengest ceald),
(x)x/Sxs (B1)

[Fate is strongest. Winter is coldest, springtime frostiest (it is longest cold)] (*Maxims II* 5-6)

(b) Rǣd sceal mid snyttro,
Sx/(x)Sx (A1)
ryht mid wīsum,
Sx/Sx (A1)
til sceal mid tilum
Px/xP (remainder)

[Council must come by means of wisdom, lawfulness by means of the wise, good must come by means of the good.] (*Maxims I* 22–23a)

In Example 2a, the poet uses *byð* to link together a noun with its quality, in these three cases, a superlative quality, to describe their nature. In Example 2b, the second typical verb for gnomic statements, *sceal,* pairs with a preposition to show how things are connected. In both cases, two stressed words are linked together by a finite verb, possibly with another function word. Because the statement starts with the noun in question, the stressed noun opens the verse followed by the unstressed words in the drop.

The verses above all take up exactly one verse, one half-line. Sometimes the maxim can go longer, as in Example 2c:

(c) ecg sceal wið hellme
Sx/(x)Sx (A1)
hilde gebīdan.
Sx/(x)Sx (A1)
Hafuc sceal on glōfe
Sx/(x)Sx (A1)
wilde gewunian,
Sx/(x)Sx (A1)
wulf sceal on bearowe,
Sx/(x)Sx (A1)
earm ānhaga,
S/Ssx (D2)

[The sword must experience battle against a helm. A hawk must remain wild on the glove, a wolf must be in the grove, the miserable solitary one.] (*Maxims II* 16b–19a)

In this case, each maxim consists of two verses, but offset so that it enjambs, starting in the off-verse and ending in the on-verse. Even so, the pattern looks similar to the verses in Example 2b. The poet starts with a noun, which is described by using *sceal* together with a preposition, in this case to illustrate its proper place. To that, the poet adds an extra piece of information —generally an infinitive or a noun phrase in variation—to specify how the audience ought to understand the initial noun. This pattern adds detail while keeping the statement relatively short and preserves the same opening pattern of a type A verse with multiple words in the first drop, making it similar to the shorter example.

What is significant about all of these statements is the way they consist of a small, finite number of verses, which appear in a list. This format gives them the greatest rhetorical impact. Because the maxim is confined to a small and distinct unit, it is easy to remember and stands out as a clear, unique piece of wisdom. When the poet collects these metrically distinctive snippets into a long list, the resulting form marks the composition as a wisdom poem. However, putting gnomic statements of this kind repeatedly into one or two verses requires that the poets disrupt the basic principles of verse composition. Each statement must have a finite verb. As a particle, verbs can be stressed or unstressed, but when they are unstressed, they tend to come in an opening drop. In the construction above, the verb can do neither, since the verses open with a noun and already include another stress word. Because these verbs are lexically weak—a linking verb and an auxiliary—it is not unheard of for them to be in a verse-medial drop. Still, having so many unstressed, verse-medial verbs in a single poem is unusual. When the maxim also requires a preposition, the drop becomes just a little bit longer and more complex.

Once again, though, the poets compensate for the complexity with another method to create simplicity and foster understanding: repeated formulaic diction. The repetitive nature of the formulaic construction effectively delimits both maxim and verse when several formulas from the same system form a list. All three examples above illustrate this technique. The verses from Example 2a are formed from the system NOUN + *bið* + SUPERLATIVE. Examples 2b and 2c both stem from the system NOUN + *sceal* + PREP PHRASE to describe the proper place of an object, and each instantiation in Example 2c adds an additional verse. The second verse is not as structured; it often takes the form of X + INF, though sometimes it is formed from ADJ + NOUN to create variation, and sometimes it contains an additional modifier phrase. Even with some variables, though, the pattern is clear.

The *Maxims* poets repeatedly use the same formulaic system to compose verse after verse, which made the verse patterns easy to comprehend: after the first few wise sayings, the meter is clear, despite the unusual structure of the verses. The formulaic technique is particularly evident in *Maxims II*, which is composed almost entirely through the use of the two formulae illustrated in Examples 2a and 2c: in the 132-verse poem, 93 verses are formed from one of the two systems. *Maxims I* is not quite so regular because it frequently expands on the pithy maxims with narrative explanations. Even so, the poet uses short stretches of formulaic diction, limiting the complexity of the composition at those moments. Both poems, then, offer similar patterns of diction and meter: the genre adds the complexity to the metrical pattern while simultaneously allowing for an alternate method to contain that complexity.

The poets' use of formulaic diction is also prominent because it extends to the hypermetrical verses in the poems. Although hypermetrical verses typically lack formulaic language, probably because they contain such long drops, the *Maxims* poets use formulas extensively in their hypermetrical passages. The *Maxims II* poet uses hypermetrical systems that relate to the ones used in normal verse:

(3)(a) Wind byð on lyfte swiftest,
[Sx/(x)Sxsx (HA1)]
þunar byð þrāgum hlūdast.
[Sx/Sxsx (HA1)]

[Wind is, in the air, swiftest, thunder is at times loudest.] (*Maxims II* 3b–4a).

(b) Þyrs sceal on fenne gewunian
[Sx/(x)Sxxsx (HA1)]
āna innan lande. Ides sceal dyrne cræfte,
[Sx/Sxsx (HA1)] [Sx/Sxsx (HA1)]
fǣmne hire frēond gesēcean.
[Sx/(xx)Sxsx (HA1)]

[The giant must dwell in the fen, alone in the land. A lady, a woman, must with secret craft seek her friend.] (*Maxims II* 42b–44a)

Example 3a is related to Example 2a, illustrating a superlative quality. In this case, though, the verses contain an extra adverbial modifier, making them more specific. Example 3b is related to Examples 2b and 2c, showing the proper place. In Example 2c, the two-verse system allows the poet to include either an infinitive to illustrate an action or a second noun in variation. By switching to hypermetrical meter, the poet can include both. In this way, even the longer, more complex patterns generated by hypermetrical meter fit clearly in the organizing principles.

The *Maxims I* poet does not use any adapted versions of the normal gnomic formulae but does use a specific formulaic system that could be equally familiar because it is common throughout the poetic tradition. Haruko Momma first pointed out a system for gnomes that occurs in several wisdom poems, as well as in gnomic statements in narrative poems, which she describes as "[ADJ/INTERJ + COPULA + PRONOUN] + [PARTICLE + (...) + VERB]."[24] She focuses on the instances of the formula that create a type HA verse, but a related version also exists as a type HB. Example 4 illustrates the two versions:

(4) (a) Earm biþ sē þe sceal āna lifgan
[Sx/(xxx)Sxsx (HA1)]
[Wretched is he who must live alone.] (Maxims I 172) 25

(b) Dol biþ sē þe his dryhten nāt
[Sx/(xx)xSxs (HB1)]
[Foolish is he who does not know his lord.] (*Maxims I* 35a)

Not only are these verses complex because they are hypermetrical, they are also unusual for hypermetrical verses because of three features. First, the verses have many heavy extrametrical syllables before the cadence. While hypermetrical verses generally accept more extrametrical words, the number in *Maxims I* exceeds what is usual in traditional poems: verses of this formula can have as many as five extrametrical syllables. The words that fill these positions make these drops even heavier, since the extrametrical material consists of several separate words, many of which are particles.[26] Second, the syntax is complex because there is a clause break in the middle of the verse. While clause breaks often come at the caesura in the middle of the line, they rarely occur in the middle of a verse. The combination of the clause break and the heavy material could make the verse particularly ambiguous because the particles in the long drop could receive some degree of stress, making it seem as though the verse might end before it really does. Finally, some of the verses end with a cadence in a type B verse, as *Maxims I* 35a does.[27] In general, type B is avoided for the hypermetrical cadence because it creates an added element of ambiguity in the verse: the final drop of the onset and the initial drop of the cadence would be contiguous, making the verse appear to have only five positions.[28] These three elements together could make the verses difficult for the audience to follow. However, these verses belong to a formulaic system, which resolves the difficulties. The *Maxims I* poet uses this system eight times, and it appears at least five other times in other poems.[29] Indeed, the fact that this system appears so often suggests that it may have been a gnomic standard, something to be expected in this type of poem.

Thus, the formulaic language of the *Maxims* poems acts similarly to the simplified verse patterns in *Maldon*: it lessens the complexity in a new way, thereby facilitating audience understanding of the poetics. Likewise, analysis of the shift in priorities reveals what was most important to the poets: pithy statements that put gnomic wisdom in one to two verses. While neither *Maxims* poet composes the entire poem this way, both do so to a large extent, especially the *Maxims II* poet. Because this traditional diction takes precedence over other matters of verse composition, these poems look quite different from *Beowulf*. Yet far from showing a general loosening of the lines, they differ in a specific way that reflects their genre, which allows the poet to maintain straightforward, if genre specific, metrical patterns.

Conclusions

A close analysis using word-foot theory shows that although the *Maldon*- and *Maxims* poets seem to compose similarly marginal verses, they in fact differ in their compositional style, producing very different poems with variant stylistic techniques. These techniques differ substantially from the traditional noun-heavy diction, often filled with variation, found in the more conservative poems such as *Beowulf*. The *Maldon* poet focuses instead on contemporary language, writing a poem with syntax that would echo everyday prose. This decision requires both more unstressed words in longer unstressed positions and fewer verses with secondary stress. Nevertheless, the poet is clearly aware of these changes and creates alternate organization, focusing on the type A and B verses that decrease the complexity of the line and organizing the longer drops so that the extrametrical words frequently mark a light foot. The *Maxims* poets, on the other hand, are more concerned with traditional diction, specifically the vocabulary and syntax that highlights the gnomic aspects of their sayings. The same diction that adds complexity to the metrical pattern by requiring long drops in unusual places also allows for a decrease in complexity with repeated lists of formulaic statements, which both mark the poetry as proverbial and establish clear verse patterns.

These examples are not meant to suggest that scholars should necessarily assume that all poems are well-composed and try to piece together a new style. Rather, two important qualities distinguish these poems in particular. First, the poets add complexity that affects a universal principle throughout their poem, rather than composing unusual verses erratically and with different irregularities. The latter pattern would suggest a poet who cannot sustain a form rather than a poet with an alternate style.[30] Second, each poet develops an alternative method to limit complexity. In this way, the poets do not seem to be disregarding compositional norms—indeed, the simplifying strategies they use suggest they may have been very much aware of them—but rather, they focus on the underlying principle of making the meter accessible. A stylistic analysis using word-foot theory therefore allows scholars to shift their priorities when analyzing the poems, focusing on why the poets would change their style in these ways and how we can analyze the poems given the priorities that word-foot theory has uncovered.

NOTES

[1] See Geoffrey R. Russom, "Dating Criteria for Old English Poems," in *Studies in the History of the English Language: A Millennial Perspective*, ed D. Minkova and R. Stockwell (Berlin: Mouton de Gruyter, 2002), pp. 245–65; and "The Evolution of Middle English Alliterative Meter," in *Studies in the History of the English Language II: Unfolding Conversations*, ed Anne Curzan and Kimberly Emmons (Berlin: Mouton de Gruyter, 2004), pp. 279–304.

[2] See, for example, Thomas Cable, *The English Alliterative Tradition* (Philadelphia: University of Pennsylvania Press, 1991); Jonathan Roper, "Metre in the Old English 'Metrical' Charms," in *Oral Charms in Structural and Comparative Light*, ed. Tatyana Mikhailova, Jonathan Roper, Andrey Toporkov, and Dmitri Nikolayev (Moscow: PROBEL, 2000), pp. 116–21; Thomas A. Bredehoft, *Early English Metre* (Toronto: University of Toronto Press, 2005); and Megan E. Hartman, "Poetic Attitudes and Adaptations in Late Old English Verse," *Leeds Studies in English* 43 (2012): 73–91.

[3] Geoffrey Russom, *Old English Meter and Linguistic Theory* (Cambridge: Cambridge University Press, 1987), p. 2.

[4] References to *Beowulf* come from R. D. Fulk, Robert E. Bjork, and John D. Niles, eds., *Klaeber's Beowulf and the Fight at Finnsburg*, 4th ed. (Toronto: University of Toronto Press, 2008). All other references to Old English poems refer to George P. Krapp and Elliott van Kirk Dobbie, eds, *The Anglo-Saxon Poetic Records*, 6 vols (New York: Columbia University Press, 1931–53). This edition does not include marks of vowel length in the text, but because they are useful for metrical studies, I have added them here. Translations are mine.

[5] A clitic is one of three categories of words first posited by Hans Kuhns: stress words (nouns, lexical adjective and adverbs, and non-finite verbs), which

always receive stress; clitics (prepositions, conjunctions, and determiners) which do not receive stress unless delayed; and particles (finite verbs, pronouns, non-lexical adjectives and adverbs, and conjunctions that join complete clauses), which may or may not receive stress. See Hans Kuhn, "Zur Wortstellung und -betonung im Altgermanischen," *Beiträge zur Geschichte der deutschen Sprache und Literatur* 57 (1933), rep. in *Kleine Schriften 1* (Berlin: Gruyter, 1969), pp. 4–5.

[6] See Russom, *Old English Meter,* p. 38. and Geoffrey Russom, "Purely Metrical Replacements for Kuhn's Laws," in *English Historical Metrics*, ed. C. B. McCully and J. J. Anderson (Cambridge: Cambridge University Press, 1996), p. 33.

[7] R. D. Fulk demonstrates that these poems all contain conservative features such as contraction, West Germanic parasiting, and adherence to Kaluza's law in *A History of Old English Meter* (Philadelphia: University of Pennsylvania Press, 1992). Russom reinforces Fulk's conclusion with metrical evidence in "Dating Criteria."

[8] I look at both *Maxims* poems together because they are similar in structure in many ways and analyzing the similarities shows some of the peculiar features of this type of poem.

[9] Examples of inviolable rules are that each line contains alliteration, verses consist of four positions, and verses always come in pairs.

[10] Donald Scragg in particular enumerated the features that make *Maldon* irregular: defects in alliteration, drops that deviate substantially from the norm, greater reliance on type A and B, a weak caesura, and more repetition; see Donald Scragg, ed., *The Battle of Maldon* (Manchester: Manchester University Press, 1981), pp. 28–35. Others follow Scragg's argument, focusing particularly on the abundance of function words and lack of metrical variety to argue that the poet was stylistically uncertain and the poem lacked rhetorical force; see, for example, T. A. Shippey, *Old English Verse* (London: Hutchinson, 1972), pp. 188–9; D. G. Scragg, "The Battle of Maldon: Fact or Fiction?" in *The Battle of Maldon: Fact and Fiction*, ed. Susan Cooper (London: Hambledon Press, 1993), pp. 23–4; Gerald Morgan, "*Spectamur Agendo*: The Universality of *The Battle of Maldon*," in *Text and Gloss: Studies in Insular Learning and Literature Presented to Joseph Donovan Pheifer*, ed. Helen Conrad O'Briain, Anne Marie D'Arcy, and John Scattergood (Dublin: Four Courts Press, 1999), pp. 182–206; but cf. Edward B. Irving, Jr., "The Heroic Style in 'The Battle of Maldon,'" *Studies in Philology* 58 (1961): 457–67, which argues that putting "worn formulas of poetic diction" into a new heroic context gives them new life. The metrical features of the *Maxims* poems have not been studied as extensively, but A. J. Bliss does note some irregularities in the composition, calling *Maxims I* in particular "notoriously difficult and idiosyncratic"; see *The Meter of Beowulf*, rev. ed (Oxford: Blackwell, 1967), p. 96; and Paul Cavill claims that the *Maxims* poems use "slightly different patterns of metre from most Old English verse" in *Maxims in Old English Poetry* (Cambridge: D. S. Brewer, 1999), p. 168.

[11] My data from *Beowulf* comes from five 150-line samples: lines 1–150, 301–451, 837–985, 1251–1400, and 2444–2593. I average the different passages

in order to account for the stylistic differences that might result from narrating different types of scenes.

[12] Except where otherwise specified, the data only account for the normal, as opposed to hypermetrical, verses. Because hypermetrical verses are different in structure, the same expectations for drop length and filler do not apply.

[13] By itself, *Maxims II* does have more verses than *Beowulf* with disyllabic drops (41.23%), but it does not otherwise stand out.

[14] According to word-foot theory, hypermetrical verses are verses in which the second foot (also referred to as a cadence in this context) overlaps with a normal verse; they generally take the form Sx/Sxsx or xx/Sxsx (Russom, *Old English*, pp. 59–63). Similarly to drops in normal verses, the drop in the xx onset tends to be longer than that in the Sx onset, though both of the drops in the initial hypermetrical foot seem less regulated than normal drops.

[15] Here I refer to conservative poems overall rather than simply *Beowulf* because with only twenty hypermetrical verses, *Beowulf* cannot provide useful statistical data.

[16] Fulk shows that the shift began because stress on word-final syllables was weakening, making many of the inflectional endings fall together (*A History*, p. 252). While not complete until 1250, the shift begins in the tenth century, as illustrated by shifts in the syntax such as a higher incidence of SVO word order, an increase in function words, and a greater tendency for impersonal verbs to have a stated subject; see Elizabeth Traugott, "Syntax," in *The Cambridge History of the English Language*, ed. Richard M. Hogg, vol. 1 (Cambridge: Cambridge University Press, 1992), pp. 285–6.

[17] Cable notes the consistent decline in types C, D, and E verses across the Old English period and argues that poems with a low incidence of these verses were written later; see "Metrical Style as Evidence for the Date of *Beowulf*," in *The Dating of* Beowulf, ed. Colin Chase (Toronto: Toronto University Press, 1997), pp 77–82.

[18] Compounds with true secondary stress differ from quasi-compounds with tertiary stress because they occur more often in the on-verse and they add poetic diction. Without a clear distinction between the two, the motivation to use them decreased; see Fulk, *A History*, pp 253–56.

[19] Although the most basic version of a type D verse (S/Ssx) has no place to put unstressed words, they can occur in a type D* (Sx/Ssx) or a type D4 (S/Sxs).

[20] The first drop of a type A3 verse must be particularly heavy because it takes the place of a stressed position.

[21] Russom, "Dating Criteria," pp. 251–52.

[22] For a more detailed explanation of how these verbs operate in gnomic poetry, see Marie Nelson, "'Is' and 'Ought' in the Exeter Book Maxims," *Southern Folklore Quarterly* 45 (1981): 109–122.

[23] In fact, these poems focus so exclusively and broadly on the nature of things that it can be difficult to articulate exactly what holds the poems together.

Most scholars agree that the poems are agglutinative in nature; that the topics, which often seem obvious and banal, vary widely; and that the poets connect the different ideas as much through sound patterning, word play, and syntactic repetition as through central themes; see T. A. Shippey, *Poems of Wisdom and Learning in Old English*, (Cambridge: D. S. Brewer, 1976), pp. 12–18; Elaine Tuttle Hansen, *The Solomon Complex: Reading Wisdom in Old English Poetry* (Toronto: University of Toronto Press, 1988), pp. 157–76; Carolyne Larrington, *A Store of Common Sense: Gnomic Theme and Style in Old Icelandic and Old English Wisdom Poetry* (Oxford: Clarendon Press, 1993), pp. 120–133; and Paul Cavill, *Maxims in Old English Poetry* (Cambridge: D. S. Brewer, 1999), pp. 156–83. This type of loose organization emphasizes that the poems present a variety of important kernels of wisdom, and that such a list is infinite in nature. Cavill further argues that this type of list imposes a kind of order on the world, making each individual gnome an important piece of the larger puzzle (*Maxims*, pp. 174–83).

[24] Haruko Momma, "The 'Gnomic Formula' and Some Additions to Bliss's Old English Metrical System," *Notes and Queries, n.s.* 4. (1989): 423–4. A normal verse version of this system does also exist: it maintains the opening ADJ/INTERJ + COPULA + PRONOUN for the first clause, but then has only PARTICLE + VERB, as in *Wel is þām þe mōtun* (*Christ* 1079b). However, the normal-verse version does not appear in *Maxims I*.

[25] This verse does not have a verse pair, which is another unusual feature, though not one specifically tied to the hypermetric composition.

[26] Bredehoft, *Early English Metre*, is particularly strong on issues concerning extrametrical particles; see pp. 37– 50, *passim*.

[27] Other examples are *Maxims I* 59a and 111a.

[28] Max Kaluza, "Die Schwellverse in der altenglischen Dichtung," *Englische Studien* 21 (1895): 377.

[29] Momma points out three examples in *Maxims I*: 37a, 69a, and 172b in "The 'Gnomic Formula,'" p. 424. In addition to these, five other verses should probably be considered part of the same system: 35a, 37a, 59a, 59b, and 11a. The verses in other poems are *The Wanderer* 112a and 114b, *The Seafarer* 106a and 107a, and *Daniel* 232a.

[30] As an example, Fulk points out that *The Meters of Boethius* has a number of metrical and stylistic irregularities that cannot be accounted for by language change and are probably due to the marginal skill of the poet (*A History*, pp. 251–52).

The Old English *Metrical Psalms*: Practice and Theory of Translation

Haruko Momma

New York University

Theorizing linguistic phenomena is a task so daunting that only a few bright minds have the courage to take it upon themselves. Others may only aspire to follow their dazzling example.

Introduction

The Old English *Metrical Psalms* are a remarkable set of texts with a string of superlatives attached to them. First, this is by far the longest extant body of Anglo-Saxon verse to be attributed to a single poet or at least to a single project. The metrical psalms of the Paris Psalter alone add up to 5,040 alliterative long-lines; but they are, strictly speaking, a fragment in that they begin at Psalm 51 in the manuscript.[1] Smaller fragments of metrical psalms are found in three other manuscripts: the so-called *Benedictine Office* or the Junius *Office* (129 lines), the Eadwine Psalter (169 lines), and the *Menologium* (3 lines).[2] Because some of the metrical psalms quoted in the Junius *Office* come from the first fifty psalms, these fragments, large and small, are likely to have ultimately derived from a common source that encompassed the entire psalter. Second, the text of the *Metrical Psalms* is the most versatile of all the extant Old English poems in terms of its applicability. The great majority of Old English poems occur in single manuscripts, and even the relatively few poems that are found in two or more manuscripts appear in the same or similar contexts. In contrast, the Old English *Metrical Psalms* are quoted in four manuscripts and used diversely: as a translation in a bilingual psalter (i.e., the Paris Psalter, s. xi med.); as glosses to a Latin psalter (i.e., the Eadwine Psalter, s. xii med.); as a major ingredient for a bilingual pseudo-liturgical office—or what M. J. Toswell describes as "a treatise on the content and purpose of the eight daily Offices" (i.e., the Junius *Office*, s. xi, 3rd quarter); and as a discrete quotation in a catalogue poem (i.e., the *Menologium*, s. xi^{1}–xi^{2}).[3] Third, the Old English *Metrical Psalms* hold an important position in the history of biblical translation, as they comprise the first known example of verse rendition of a large portion—and, most likely, the entire text—of the psalter in the English language or, for that matter, in any postclassical European language.[4]

Despite these remarkable characteristics, the Old English *Metrical Psalms* have been reserved for scholars who are interested either in the contents and contexts of psalms in Anglo-Saxon literature or in the peculiar nature of the poetic language of the text. Until very recently, however, even the latter group of scholars has tended to express a rather poor opinion about the *Metrical Psalms*. I am not going to recite the litany of unfavorable comments amassed by the psalter poet but, instead, quote a brief statement made by M. S. Griffith in his insightful essay of 1991, because this remark sums up the general opinion of scholars from the last century: the metrical vernacular text of the Paris Psalter is "a pedestrian and unimaginative piece of poetic translation."[5] Such an evaluation is inevitable if one focuses on what this verse composition is *not*: it is not wrought in classical Old English meter, its vocabulary is not sufficiently poetic, its diction is not rich with variation or poetic formulas, and so on.[6]

The last decade has seen, however, the rise of interest in the Old English *Metrical Psalms*, and various efforts have been made to see this verse text in a new light. To illustrate such a movement, I will here briefly mention two recent monographs, one by Thomas A. Bredehoft and the other by Emily V. Thornbury. In *Early English Metre* (2005), Bredehoft takes issue with the Old English *Metrical Psalms* as part of the "corpus of post classical tenth- and eleventh-century poetry," which as a group "works on metrical principles markedly different from those of classical verse," even though it has "clearly descended from them."[7] In addition to the *Metrical Psalms*, Bredehoft assigns to this corpus some of the Chronicle poems from the second half of the tenth century onward, some of the *Metrical Charms*, *The Judgment Day II*, *The Battle of Maldon*, *Instructions for Christians*, *An Exhortation to Christian Living*, *A Summons to Prayer*, *Durham*, and the Sutton Brooch inscription. Together, poems in this group "total over 6000 lines of verse," thus forming a body of texts large enough to warrant a metrical system of its own.[8] In *Becoming a Poet in Anglo-Saxon England* (2014), Thornbury groups the *Metrical Psalms* with a number of other late Old English poems that are "distinctively different in form from 'normal' or 'classical' verse." While her approach to postclassical Old English poetry is similar to that of Bredehoft, she underlines the importance of a cultural factor: the mode of this set of postclassical Old English poems is "connected in its subject matter with the sphere of Latin culture."[9] As a result, her list of late Anglo-Saxon verse slightly differs from that of Bredehoft: it does not include, for example, secular poems such as the *Battle of Maldon*, the *Metrical Charms*, and the Chronicle poems, while accommodating a greater range of translated verse (e.g. the *Meters of Boethius*) and religious poetry (e.g. *Kentish Hymn*, *Kentish Psalm* or *Psalm 50*, *Riddle 40*, *Seasons for Fasting*).[10]

This chapter will analyze the poetic language of the Old English *Metrical Psalms*, sometimes by comparing different versions of this verse composition with each other and sometimes by comparing it with other Old English texts with similar contents. This comparative approach will foreground the unique nature of the *Metrical Psalms* and thereby contribute to the study of the literature of transition at large. The corpus of alliterative texts from the late Anglo-Saxon and early post-Conquest periods is not only immense but also diverse, and, as implied by the slight difference between Bredehoft's and Thornbury's lists of texts mentioned above, we have yet to work out a precise classificatory system for postclassical alliterative composition. In order to categorize and classify, we must first discern and map out similarities and differences existing among the individual items. The next section will analyze the overlapping passages of metrical psalms in different manuscripts to argue, with Bredehoft, that the *Metrical Psalms* seem to have enjoyed a level of authority shared by very few other Old English poetic texts. The section after that will consider the nature of this textual authority by contrasting the strategy of translation used for the *Metrical Psalms* with those used for two other Old English renditions of psalms, that is, the *Kentish Psalm* and the prose translation of psalms in the Paris Psalter. The analysis of these three Old English texts, to be conducted in the light of Eugene Nida's theory of translation, will show that the text of *Metrical Psalms* stylistically falls between the other two. The last section will argue that the psalter poet's mixed style of translation may not be elucidated fully either by Nida's two contrastive categories of dynamic equivalence and formal correspondence or by other theories of translation that use dichotomous concepts to define their critical domain. By way of suggesting a non-binary model of translation for the *Metrical Psalms*, I will conclude with a brief discussion on the idea of acculturation as it may be applied to the psalter poet's stylistic register and the cultural implications of his work.

Variants and Textual Authority

In *Authors, Audiences, and Old English Verse*, Thomas Bredehoft considers a reason for the prominent place that the *Metrical Psalms* seem to hold in the body of English literature produced or copied in the eleventh and the twelfth centuries:

> The reuse or citation of *The Metrical Psalms* in four separate contexts would seem to suggest that this work was widely known and felt to be authoritative. From an Anglo-Saxon perspective the psalms in *The Metrical Psalms* were perhaps the most authoritative of all surviving Old English poetry, even though they do not survive in a complete manuscript of their own right.[11]

This section will support Bredehoft's claim through internal, linguistic evidence and further identify how textual authority may be gauged in Anglo-Saxon vernacular poetry.

Generally speaking, when we compare the multiple versions of a given Old English poem, we find them to be noticeably different from each other. To take the example of *Soul and Body I* and *Soul and Body II*, recorded in the Vercelli Book and the Exeter Book, respectively, the overlapping portions of these two poems vary in more than one way. Comparing lines 19 through 21 of these two poems, for instance, we find that the variants in these two versions belong to several linguistic levels:

> Lyt ðu gemundest
> to hwan þinre sawle þing siðþan wurde,
> syððan of lichoman læded wære! (*Soul and Body I*, 19b–21)
>
> Lyt þu geþohtes
> to won þinre sawle sið siþþan wurde,
> syþþan heo of lichoman læded wære! (*Soul and Body II*, 19b–21)[12]
>
> [Little did you consider/think what the condition/fate of your soul was going to be when it would be led from the body!]

In the first line of the passages cited here, the nominative singular form of the second-person personal pronoun (i.e. "thou") is spelled either with an <eth> as *ðu* or a <thorn> as *þu*. In the second line, the instrumental of *hwæt* (i.e., *hwon*) is presented either as *hwan* or *won*. In the third line, the subject of this adverbial clause is expressed in *Soul and Body II* as *heo* (referring back to the feminine noun *sawle* in the second line), whereas it is unexpressed but understood in *Soul and Body I*. But the two passages also differ from each other at the lexical level: in the first line, the verb of the main clause is *gemunan* "to consider, mind" in *Soul and Body I* and *þencan* "to think" in *Soul and Body II*. These two verbs are synonyms, although their connotations are not exactly the same. In the second line, the subject of the noun clause is *þing* in *Soul and Body I* and *sið* in *Soul and Body II*. In the translation provided above, I have rendered *þing* and *sið* as "condition" and "fate" respectively, but each of these nouns covers a much wider semantic field: the definitions of the former include "thing," "cause," "affair," and "respect," and the latter may also mean "journey," "departure," "time," and "experience."[13] Semantically, both readings make good sense, but the different choice of the subject noun in each clause gives this passage a slightly different emphasis on the soul's claim made while berating the body in the grave.[14]

It has long been noted that Anglo-Saxon scribes were, generally speaking, not as meticulous as they might have been when copying vernacular poems (as opposed especially to Latin texts).[15] Or if we were to take the perspective of the scribes, they may be said to have been more inclined to assume a creative role when they transcribed poetic texts in the vernacular. This fascinating phenomenon is theorized by Katherine O'Brien O'Keeffe in her foundational book *Visible Song*, where she applies the concept of "residual orality" to multiple versions of Old English poems and argues that Anglo-Saxon scribes did not attribute the same degree of textual authority to vernacular poems as they did to Latin writing.[16] Old English verse was textually flexible to the point of being almost unfixable. It was in the public domain, so to speak, in that those who had the art of "exchanging words" were entitled to quote, borrow, adapt, or alter poetic word-sequences stored either internally in their "breast coffers" or externally in the manuscripts (cf. *Beowulf* 871a–4b).

This general tendency does not seem to apply to scribes who copied the Old English *Metrical Psalms*. When we compare the two overlapping passages recorded in the Paris Psalter and the Junius *Office*, for example, we immediately notice that they are virtually identical: for example,

Leofað sawl min   and þe lustum hereð,
and me þine domas   dædum fultumiað.
(118.175.1–2, Paris Psalter)

Leofað sawul min   and ðe lustum hereð,
and me þine domas   dædum fultumiað.
(118.175.1–2, Junius *Office*)[17]

> [My soul will live and praise you joyfully, and your judgments will help me certainly.]

The only differences between these two corresponding passages are variant spellings (*sawl* as opposed to *sawul*) and the use of the allographs <þ> and <ð> for the accusative *þe/ðe*. In these two manuscripts, the only corresponding passages that use different lexical words (as opposed to grammar words) are:

> Beseoh on þine scealcas swæsum eagum. (89.18.1, Paris Psalter)
>
> Geseoh þine scealcas swæsum eagum. (89.18.1, Junius *Office*)
>
> [Look upon/behold your servants with benevolent eyes]

Here the verb chosen for the imperative clause is *beseon* "to look, regard" in the former and *geseon* "to see, behold" in the latter. But even this variant is, strictly speaking, morphological, because these two verbs, though one is intransitive and the other is transitive, share the same stem *seon*. In the Eadwine Psalter, there are two blocks of quotations from the Old English *Metrical Psalms* (90.16.1–95.2.1 and 142.9.1–4).[18] In both blocks, the variants are mostly linguistic, unless they concern erasures, additions, or omissions.[19]

In contrast, the overlapping portion found in the Paris Psalter and the *Menologium*, though it is only three alliterative lines long, shows a greater degree of difference:

> Þis ys se dæg þe hine drihten us
> wisfæst geworhte wera cneorissum,
> eallum eorðtudrum eadgum to blisse. (117.22.1–3, Paris Psalter)
>
> Þis is se dæg þæne drihten us
> wisfæst worhte, wera cneorissum,
> eallum eorðwarum eadigum to blisse. (*Menologium*, lines 60–2)
>
> [This is the day that the sagacious Lord has appointed as joy for us, for the generations of men, all blessed earthly descendants/earth-dwellers]

In addition to the usual range of linguistic variants, these corresponding passages contain different compound nouns: the hapax *eorðtudor* "earthly offspring" in the Paris Psalter and *eorðwaru* "earth-dwellers" in the *Menologium*. Here we seem to observe a degree of scribal freedom comparable to the one recognized in such classical Old English poems as the two

Soul and Body poems. This flexibility should probably be attributed to the scribe of the *Menologium* (or the scribe of one of its exemplars) rather than the scribe of the Paris Psalter (or the scribe of one of its exemplars), because this catenulate poem, which lists festivals according to the liturgical calendar, exhibits many traits of classical verse and occurs in the manuscript as an independent piece side by side with *Maxims II* and a version of the *Anglo-Saxon Chronicle*.[20]

The example of the *Menologium* aside, the close proximity of the overlapping passages recorded in the other three manuscripts containing the *Metrical Psalms* is in stark contrast to the divergence found in the multiple versions of other Old English poems. This difference may not be attributed solely to a greater degree of caution exercised by those who copied the *Metrical Psalms*, for even they were probably not entirely free of errors.[21] And yet these witnesses to the *Metrical Psalms* contain very few variants that involve lexical words. If scribes who copied other Old English poems were from time to time both careless and carefree as to lexical accuracy, those who transcribed the *Metrical Psalms* might have been occasionally careless but hardly carefree as to lexical accuracy.

Dynamic Equivalence and Psalm Translation

If the *Metrical Psalms* comprised one Old English poetic composition that Anglo-Saxon scribes treated with what might be called textual fidelity, how is this singular nature reflected in the text? This section will examine the peculiar nature of the *Metrical Psalms* through the lens of Eugene Nida's theory of translation in which he recommends dynamic equivalence as a preferred principle. First proposed in the 1960s, "dynamic equivalence" pertains to the quality of a translation in which the message of the original text has been so transported into the receptor language that the response of the receptor is essentially like that of the original receptors. According to this definition, the primary task of the translator is to produce a text that would solicit from the receptor audience a response comparable with the one that the source text has received from the original audience by changing the "form of the original text" as needed. Those who are concerned about textual fidelity in translation may question such an attitude towards the source text. But a translation of dynamic equivalence is intended to preserve the "message" of the source text so that the receptor text made on this principle, despite its altered form, should still be considered "faithful" to the source text. In this paradigm of translation, those who insist on preserving the form of the source text are said to subscribe to the principle of "formal correspondence," which, according to one definition, pertains to the "quality of a translation in which the features of the form of the source text have been mechanically reproduced in the receptor language."[22] As the use of the word "mechanical" here implies, the principle of formal correspondence is deemed less effective than that of dynamic equivalence. The message is not conveyed by the medium in its absolute sense but, rather, by a medium that would lead the receptor audience to a comparable place within the world constructed by the receptor or target language.

Since much of Nida's work is based on the practice of biblical translation, we may be tempted to ask: what response did the psalms receive from the original receptors? But such a question would only invite more questions: In which language? In what community? We may instead rephrase the question slightly and ask how such an audience was *imagined* by the translators and receptors of psalms in the Anglo-Saxon vernacular. Even though this question is still too large to afford a single, clear-cut answer, I will address the issue by turning to a number of Old English texts that deal with this biblical material. The *Kentish Psalm*, a free verse rendition of the *Miserere* or Psalm 50, begins with a prologue in which the anonymous poet establishes the background for the psalm:[23]

Dauid wæs haten diormod hæleð,
Israela bręga, æðelæ and rice,
cyninga cynost, Criste liofost.
Wæs he under hiofenum hearpera mærost
ðara we an folcum gefrigen hæbben. (*Kentish Psalm*, lines 1–5)

[David was the name of a brave hero,
lord of the Israelites, noble and powerful,
the most courageous of kings, dearest to Christ.
He was under the heavens the most renowned of harpers,
of whom we have heard among the peoples.]

These are just the first five lines of the poem's thirty-line prologue, but we are already transported into the world of Old English poetry. David, the presumed author and reciter of the psalm, is a courageous warrior endowed with numerous (and somewhat formulaic) superlatives: the bravest of kings, the most famous of harp-playing poets, the truest of singers, and so on. He is not dissimilar to some of the heroic characters in traditional Old English verse, such as King Hrothgar of *Beowulf*.

In her analysis of the *Kentish Psalm* in the light of the polysystems theory of translation, M. J. Toswell examines the poem's prologue as a paratext, that is, "a text introductory to and perhaps explanatory of the translation." Paratexts are of particular importance for translation studies, "because they provide some way into thinking about the purpose and approach of the translator."[24] The paratext of the *Kentish Psalm* gives us an example of how the original reception of this penitential psalm may have been re-conceived for the sake of an Anglo-Saxon vernacular audience. Yet the register of the poem raises a new question. Nida's theory of translation privileges function over form, and this hierarchy is usually maintained even when the source text is verse: because "rhythmical forms," compared to non-rhythmical or prose forms, "differ far more radically in form, and hence in aesthetic appeal," translators should remember the general rule that "certain rhythmic patterns must often be substituted for others." Nida, however, makes an exception for Bible translation: "the usual procedure is to attempt a kind of dignified prose where the original employs poetry, since, in general, Biblical content is regarded as much more important than Biblical form."[25] Given the importance of the content of the Bible, a translator of psalms may prefer prose as a medium so that he or she may be able to convey the contents of the text more readily without being encumbered by the demands of prosody.

If the common medium for translating verse from the Bible is, as Nida suggests here, dignified prose, we may find a good specimen in the vernacular section of the Paris Psalter, where the first quinquagene is all in prose. The authorship of the prose psalms is now traditionally placed in Alfred. Based on this assumption, Robert Stanton, for instance, writes that this is "by far the closest, most conservative translation Alfred did," even though "the additions and changes the king makes are often highly significant."[26] To take the opening of Psalm 50 as an example, the Old English prose rendition reads:

> Miltsa me, Drihten, æfter þinre mycelan mildheortnesse (50.1)[27]
> [Have mercy on me, Lord, according to thy great kindheartedness]

When we compare this passage with the corresponding Latin in the Roman Psalter,

> Miserere mei Deus secundum magnam misericordiam tuam

we realize that the translation here is almost word for word. The only difference concerns the re-positioning of the possessive pronoun *tuam* "thy" from the end of the noun phrase to its beginning in accordance with the syntax of Old English. This example demonstrates that the Old English prose translation of psalms generally conveys the "content" of the source text faithfully. But how does it deliver its "message"? In the Paris Psalter, the Old English prose psalms (except for Psalm 1) are preceded by prose introductions in Old English.[28] Like other introductions in the psalter, the introduction to the *Miserere* begins with an exposition on the occasion for the original recitation of the psalm:

> Dauid sang þysne fiftigoðan sealm, hreowsiende for ðam ærendum þe Nathan se witga him sæde, þæt wæs, þæt he hæfde gesyngod wið Ureus þone Cyðþiscan, þa he hine beswac for his wifes þingum, þære nama wæs Bersabe. (Int. 50, 1°)
>
> [David sang this fiftieth psalm in sorrow because of the messages that the prophet Nathan told him; that was, that he had sinned against Uriah the Hittite, when he deceived him because of the issues concerning his wife, whose name was Bathsheba.]

Seen from the perspective of the modern theory of translation, the presentation of Psalm 50 in the Paris Psalter creates a slight gap in the expectation of vernacular receptors, because it begins with an introduction, a paratext, stating that this psalm was sung by the original reciter, and then proceeds to offer the main text in Old English prose. The gap is a product of the translation, because the Latin title, which in the manuscript is placed between the Old English introduction and the bilingual main text, simply reads *VOX DAUID AD POENITENTIAM* "Voice of David in penitence."[29]

As we have seen, the poet of the *Kentish Psalm*, with his choice of form familiar to the receptor audience, takes a functionally dynamic approach to Psalm 50. After introducing David as a harp-wielding king in the prologue, he begins the psalm proper in the following fashion:

> Miltsa ðu me, meahta walden,   nu ðu wast manna geðohtas,
> help ðu, hælend min,   handgeweorces
> þines anes,   ælmehtig god,
> efter þinre ðære miclan   mildhiortnesse.   (*Kentish Psalm*, lines 31–4)
>
> [Have mercy on me, lord of might, because you know men's thoughts;
> help, my savior, the handiwork
> of your own, almighty lord,
> according to your great kindheartedness.]

Compared to the simple sentence in the Old English prose translation we have just examined, the *Kentish Psalm* uses a complex sentence, stretching over four alliterative lines, to render the same Latin text. Of these four lines, the second and third lines have no direct correspondence with the Latin, for they are a paraphrase of the first half-line: the imperative clause *miltsa ðu me* "have mercy on me" is rephrased as *help ðu ... handgeweorces / þines anes* "help ... the handiwork of your own," and the vocative noun phrase *meahta walden* "mighty ruler" has generated two variations, that is, *hælend min* "my savior" and *ælmehtig god* "almighty god." Like its prologue, the main part of the *Kentish Psalm* is filled with traditional poetic diction. The poem would likely have given its vernacular audience the impression that the psalm was recited in a way not dissimilar to the traditional vernacular poems.[30]

As a vehicle of translation, the form of the *Kentish Psalm* has a limitation of its own, however. The Anglo-Saxons were familiar with the tradition of biblical exegesis by which passages from the Old Testament were interpreted according to Christian hermeneutics. We may observe just such an operation at work in the treatment of the Old English prose psalms. In his essay "The Old English Introductions to the Prose Psalms of the Paris Psalter," Patrick P. O'Neill explains how introductions to the individual prose psalms are constructed around a "fourfold scheme" conveying (1) an historical interpretation, (2) a moral or tropological interpretation, (3) an allegorical or mystical interpretation, and (4) a second historical interpretation, which replaces the more common anagogical interpretation.[31] To take Psalm 50 as an example, the Old English introduction, as we have seen, begins with the historical interpretation, that "David sang this fiftieth psalm in sorrow." But this paratext goes on to reveal the deeper layers of meaning for the psalm:

> and heac he witgode on þam sealme be Israela folce, hu hy sceoldon hreowsian hyra hæftnyd on Babilonia; and eac be Sancte Paule þam Apostole; and be ælcum rihtwisum men he witgode, hu hy sceoldon syngian and eft hreowsian. (Int. 50, 2°–4°)
>
> [and also in the psalm he prophesied about the Israelites, how they were to bemoan their captivity in Babylonia; and also about Saint Paul the Apostle; and he prophesied about every righteous man, how they were to sin and then repent afterwards.]

The song of David that was sung after his meeting with Nathan should therefore be understood also as a prophecy about the Babylonian captivity (the second historical interpretation), Saint Paul (mystical), and any righteous man who repents his sin (tropological).[32] As a poem of lament sung by a king on an historical occasion, the register of traditional Anglo-Saxon vernacular poetry may have sufficed for producing dynamic equivalence in the receptor text. If the psalm were to be interpreted as a text containing prophetic signification, the language of classical verse might not have been the most efficient medium to convey the message. The poet of the *Kentish Psalm* seems to deal exclusively with the (first) historical interpretation of the *Miserere*, for his paratext zooms in on the figure of David. As Toswell points out, he does not even mention the prophet Nathan in the prologue.[33]

While the Old English prose psalms and the *Kentish Psalm* present two distinct models for rendering this biblical material, the *Metrical Psalms* fall somewhere between these two stylistic extremes. This verse translation differs from the Old English prose psalms in its use of alliterative meter rather than dignified prose. When we examine the psalter poet's rendition of the same passage from Psalm 50 (which is recorded in the Junius *Office*):

> Mildsa me, mihtig drihten,   swa ðu manegum dydest,
> æfter ðinre þære mycelan   mildheortnysse. (50.1.1–2, Junius *Office*)
>
> [Have mercy on me, mighty lord, as you have done for many,
> according to your great kindheartedness.]

we find that he has chosen exactly the same words that the translator of the Old English prose psalms uses to render the first three words in the source text; that is, *Miserere*, *mei*, and *deus*: *miltsa*, *me*, and *drihten*.[34] In order to turn these three Old English words into a full alliterative line, however, the psalter poet has added the adjective *mihtig* "mighty" to the a-verse and supplied the adverbial clause *swa ðu manegum dydest* "as you have done for many" to form the b-verse by itself. This passage also differs from the corresponding passage in the *Kentish Psalm*, since the psalter poet, even though he is believed to have been familiar with traditional Old English poetic diction, has refrained from free-wheeling use of variation.[35] While the poet of the *Kentish Psalm* spends as many as four alliterative long-lines on the first clause of the psalm, augmenting the passage with variations on the imperative clause and the vocative noun, the psalter poet devotes only two lines to the same passage, adding one adjective and one adverbial clause to satisfy metrical requirements without, however, altering the semantic contents of the text.[36]

Towards a Non-Binary Model of Translation

Based on the comparison of the three Old English renditions of psalms conducted in the previous section we may summarize the psalter poet's strategy of translation as follows. He uses a unique style of verse with which to convey the content of the source text more faithfully than the traditional style of Old English poetry. Modern critics may exclude the *Metrical Psalms* from the literary canon of Old English literature, because this verse composition is different from other poems. For the Anglo-Saxon receptor audience, however, the *Metrical Psalms* commanded an exceptional degree of textual authority precisely because, I believe, they were different from traditional verse. Because the psalter poet still uses alliteration and syntax specific to Old English poetry, however, his translation could deliver to the receptor audience the message that the psalms were meant to be sung in their original context.

The psalter poet's strategy, by which he adapts only some of the verse techniques, has given rise to a text that belongs neither to traditional poetry nor to dignified prose. The psalter poet's mixed style may not be fully understood in the light of Nida's principles of correspondence, because this theory of translation would place the *Metrical Psalms* somewhere in the middle of the spectrum created by dynamic equivalence and formal correspondence (or "gloss translation").[37] The difficulty surrounding the theorization of the *Metrical Psalms* does not necessarily derive from Nida's preference for function over form. Arguably the most famous challenge for his principles of correspondence comes from Lawrence Venuti, who, in his essay "Translation as Cultural Politics," contends that dynamic equivalence is nothing other than a method of translation that promotes "domestication." As a principle of translation, domestication would exercise "ethnocentric violence," because it reconstitutes a foreign text

> in accordance with values, beliefs and representations that pre-exist it in the target language, always configured in hierarchies of dominance and marginality, always determining the production, circulation, and reception of texts. Translation is the forcible replacement of the linguistic and cultural difference of the foreign text with a text that will be intelligible to the target-language reader.

While the translator "always exercises a choice concerning the degree and direction of the violence at work in his practice," he should nonetheless strive to counter this violent act of linguistic "terrorism" with linguistic foreignization. For a conscientious translator, this is an ethical choice, because it helps him place "an ethnodeviant pressure" on the cultural values of the target language and hence "register the linguistic and cultural difference of the foreign text, sending the reader abroad."[38]

According to this paradigm of foreignization and domestication, however, the psalter poet would be deemed to have committed ethnocentric violence by replacing the form of his source text with the form of his native verse to make it more intelligible for his receptors. Such a claim is, of course, preposterous, and this preposterousness derives from the difference in the cultural landscape of the psalter poet and the cultural landscape in which and for which Venuti's essay was written. Published in 1993, "Translation as Cultural Politics" is fundamentally a critique of the "Anglo-American tradition" of translation, in which the target language—that is, Modern English—is said to be intent on valorizing "transparent discourse on every foreign culture."[39] In contrast, English for the psalter poet was a local language still on its way to cultural elaboration, while Latin was the language of prestige that held a key to knowledge and salvation.

We may note that the pairing of domestication and foreignization in Venuti's theory of translation is not dissimilar to the pairing of dynamic equivalence and formal correspondence in Nida's. The only difference between the two is the question of which end of the spectrum is to be privileged: Nida recommends translation that makes formal adjustments to familiarize the source text for the receptors, whereas Venuti endorses translation that brings in foreign elements to defamiliarize the target (or receptor) language. Theory of translation has long tended to define the domain of practice with two opposite categories, be they domestication versus foreignization, formal correspondence versus dynamic equivalence, words versus meaning, and, if we were to give a wider sense to "translation," the letter versus the spirit.[40] When placed on a spectrum formed by such binary concepts, the *Metrical Psalms* are destined to be thrust into the median range and branded a translation of compromise that is neither fish nor fowl. Rather than working out a binary that would enable the psalter poet to claim his place on the privileged end of the spectrum, I suggest that we see his translation as a product of acculturation. As an anthropologically informed concept, acculturation, according to one of its earliest definitions, "comprehends those phenomena which result when groups of individuals having different cultures come into continuous first-hand contact, with subsequent changes in the original culture patterns of either or both groups."[41] The key here is that the process of acculturation may result in transmutation of both source culture and target culture. The psalter poet has replaced the form of the source text with that of alliterative verse so that his translation would have allowed the Anglo-Saxon receptors to imagine songs of David as poems not unlike theirs. But the unusual diction of his verse may have challenged the receptors' assumptions and encouraged them to seek the deeper, prophetic signification of the text outside their cultural comfort zone. The psalter poet has created a translation of acculturation—part domesticating and part foreignizing—that would have allowed the receptor audience to have access to this biblical book neither in their own cultural domain nor in the cultural domain of the source text, but, rather, in a third place that is both like and unlike the other two.[42]

NOTES

[1] Pss. 51.6–150.3. For the length of the metrical psalms of the Paris Psalter, I have relied on Daniel Donoghue's count in his *Style in Old English Poetry: The Test of the Auxiliary* (New Haven, CT: Yale University Press, 1987), p. 6.

[2] The title "Junius *Office*" was proposed by Christopher A. Jones as a replacement for the traditional title *Benedictine Office*, which is "a misleading name at best"; see Christopher A. Jones, ed. and trans. *Old English Shorter Poems. vol. 1, Religious and Didactic* (Cambridge, MA: Harvard University Press, 2012), p. 284.

[3] M. J. Toswell, *The Anglo-Saxon Psalter* (Turnhout: Brepols, 2014), p. 309. For the manuscripts containing metrical psalms, see further N. R. Ker, *Catalogue of Manuscripts Containing Anglo-Saxon* (Oxford: Clarendon, 1957), items 91, 191, 338, and 367.

[4] William J. Chamberlin, *Catalogue of English Bible Translations: A Classified Bibliography of Versions and Editions Including Books, Parts, and Old and New Testament Apocrypha and Apocryphal Books* (New York: Greenwood, 1991), p. 343. Or perhaps it is better to say that this Old English poetic composition *should* hold an important place in the history of biblical translation. For example, Chamberlin does not include the metrical psalms of the Paris Psalter, although this substantial volume mentions the Old English prose translation of Psalms 1 through 50 found in the same manuscript.

[5] M. S. Griffith, "Poetic Language and the Paris Psalter: the Decay of the Old English Tradition," *Anglo-Saxon England* 20 (1991): 167–86 at p. 167.

[6] We may note, however, that many of the half-lines in the Old English *Metrical Psalms*, including the ones that seem atypical, can be rendered to the system of Old English meter; see, for example, Geoffrey Russom, *Old English Meter and Linguistic Theory* (Cambridge: Cambridge University Press, 1987), pp. 70–71. In my *The Composition of Old English Poetry* (Cambridge: Cambridge University Press, 1997), I demonstrate that the *Metrical Psalms* follow a special kind of syntax observed in Old English poetry as a whole (see pp. 181–94). See also my "Old

English Poetic Form: Genre, Style, Prosody," in *The Cambridge History of Early Medieval English Literature*, ed. Clare Lees (Cambridge: Cambridge University Press, 2013), pp. 278–308, esp. pp. 305–8.

[7] Thomas A. Bredehoft, *Early English Metre* (Toronto: University of Toronto Press, 2005), p. 10.

[8] Bredehoft, *Early English Metre*, pp. 83, 154n14.

[9] Emily V. Thornbury, *Becoming a Poet in Anglo-Saxon England* (Cambridge: Cambridge University Press, 2014), p. 225. The two formal characteristics that Thornbury associates with this group are "end stopping of lines and reduced use of marked poetic vocabulary."

[10] Thornbury, *Becoming a Poet*, pp. 223–37.

[11] Thomas A. Bredehoft, *Authors, Audiences, and Old English Verse* (Toronto: University of Toronto Press, 2009), p. 43.

[12] All citations from Old English poetry are from the Anglo-Saxon Poetic Records unless otherwise noted. All translations are my own. See Elliott van Kirk Dobbie, ed., *The Anglo-Saxon Minor Poems* (New York: Columbia University Press, 1942); George Philip Krapp, ed., *The Paris Psalter and the Meters of Boethius* (New York: Columbia University Press, 1932); George Philip Krapp, ed., *The Vercelli Book* (New York: Columbia University Press, 1932); and George Philip Krapp, and Elliott van Kirk Dobbie, eds., *The Exeter Book* (New York: Columbia University Press, 1936)

[13] J. R. Clark Hall, *A Concise Anglo-Saxon Dictionary* 4th ed. rep. (Toronto: University of Toronto Press, 1984), s.v.

[14] For a similar analysis, see Roy Michael Liuzza, "The Texts of the Old English *Riddle 30*," *Journal of English and Germanic Philology* 87 (1988): 1–15.

[15] See Kenneth Sisam, "The Authority of Old English Poetical Manuscripts," in his *Studies in the History of Old English Literature* (Oxford: Clarendon, 1953), pp. 27–44.

[16] See, for example Katherine O'Brien O'Keeffe, *Visible Song: Transitional Literacy in Old English Verse* (Cambridge: Cambridge University Press, 1990), esp. pp. 1–46.

[17] The *Metrical Psalms* quoted in the Junius *Office* are edited under the title "Fragments of Psalms, MS. Junius 121" in Dobbie, *Anglo-Saxon Minor Poems*.

[18] For the texts of metrical psalms in the Eadwine Psalter, see Peter S. Baker, "A Little-Known Variant Text of the Old English Metrical Psalms," *Speculum* 59 (1984): 263–78 and Patrick P. O'Neill, "Another Fragment of the Metrical Psalms in the Eadwine Psalter," *Notes and Queries* 35 (1988): 434–36.

[19] See further the apparatus in Baker's edition of 90.16.1–95.2.1 ("A Little-Known Variant Text," pp. 273–8), and O'Neill, "Another Fragment," p. 435. One interesting variant that involves a lexical word occurs in the passages for Psalm 93.18, line 2, in the Paris Psalter and the Eadwine Psalter, where the adverb *eæc* "also" appears only in the latter (see Baker, "A Little-Known Variant Text," p. 281).

[20] For the text and context of the *Menologium*, see further Bredehoft, *Authors,*

Audiences, and Old English Verse, pp. 113–30, M. J. Toswell, "The Metrical Psalter and *The Menologium*: Some Observations," *Neuphilologische Mitteilungen* 94 (1993): 249–57, and Nicholas Howe, *The Old English Catalogue Poems* (Copenhagen: Rosenkilde and Bagger, 1985), pp. 74–86.

[21] See Baker, "A Little-Known Variant Text," pp. 265–66. Baker here discusses the metrical psalms copied in the Paris Psalter and the Eadwine Psalter.

[22] The definitions of these two principles are taken from the glossary in Eugene A. Nida and Charles R. Taber, *Theory and Practice of Translation* (Leiden: Brill 2003), pp. 200–01. Nida first proposed the principle of dynamic equivalence in his *Toward a Science of Translating* (Leiden: Brill, 1964). An excerpt from this book is provided in Lawrence Venuti's *Translation Studies Reader* under the title "Principles of Correspondence" (pp. 153–67). Nida's principles of correspondence have since undergone modifications, and his theory of translation has solicited a great many responses. For a useful summary of the reception of Nida's theory, see Lawrence Venuti, ed. *The Translation Studies Reader* 2nd ed. (New York: Routledge, 2004), pp. 147–48.

[23] According to the enumeration used in both the Roman Psalter and the Vulgate.

[24] M. J. Toswell, "The Old English *Kentish Psalm* and Polysystems Theory," in *Old English Literature and the Old Testament*, eds. Michael Fox and Manish Sharma (Toronto: University of Toronto Press, 2012), pp. 315–38 at p. 330.

[25] Nida, "Principles of Correspondence," p. 166.

[26] Robert Stanton, *The Culture of Translation in Anglo-Saxon England* (Cambridge: D. S. Brewer, 2002), p. 121. For the debate on Alfred's authorship for the prose psalms and other texts, see Janet M. Bately, "Lexical Evidence for the Authorship of the Prose Psalms in the Paris Psalter," *Anglo-Saxon England* 10 (1981): 69–95, and M. R. Godden, "Did King Alfred Write Anything?" *Medium Ævum* 76 (2007): 1–23.

[27] Citation from the prose psalms of the Paris Psalter are taken from Patrick P. O'Neill, ed. *King Alfred's Old English Prose Translation of the First Fifty Psalms* (Cambridge, MA: Medieval Academy of America, 2001).

[28] See further Patrick P. O'Neill, "The Old English Introductions to the Prose Psalms of the Paris Psalter: Sources, Structure, and Composition," *Studies in Philology* 78 (1981): 20–38.

[29] Bertram Colgrave, Kemp Malone, and Knud Schibsbye, *The Paris Psalter: MS Bibliothèque nationale fonds latin 8824* (Copenhagen: Rosenkilde and Bagger, 1958), f. 63r.

[30] For the additional information offered by the layout of the manuscript of the *Kentish Psalm*, together with the added Latin verses, see Sarah Larratt Keefer, "Respect for the Book: A Reconstruction of 'Form', 'Content', and 'Context' in Two Vernacular Poems," in *New Approaches to Editing Old English Verse*, eds. Keefer and Katherine O'Brien O'Keeffe (Cambridge: D. S. Brewer, 1998), pp. 21–44, at pp. 24–30.

[31] O'Neill, "Old English Introductions," pp. 26–27.

[32] See further O'Neill, *King Alfred's Old English Prose Translation*, pp. 270–71.

[33] Toswell, "Old English *Kentish Psalm*," pp. 331–32.

[34] Cf. Phillip Pulsiano, ed., *Old English Glossed Psalters, Psalms 1–50* (Toronto: University of Toronto Press, 2001), pp. 723–25.

[35] See Griffith, "Poetic Language and the Paris Psalter," pp. 182–83.

[36] See Anya Adair, "Joy as a Metaphor for Volition: Old English *Lustum, Estum,* and the Giving of Gifts," *Notes and Queries* 60 (2013): 343–49, esp. pp. 346–47, for the psalter poet's judicious choice of words to be added for this purpose.

[37] In the earliest configuration, a translation of formal correspondence is called a "gloss translation" (e.g., Nida, "Principles of Correspondence," p. 156).

[38] Lawrence Venuti, "Translation as Cultural Politics: Regimes of Domestication in English," *Textual Practice* 7 (1993): 208–23 at pp. 208–10.

[39] Venuti, "Translation as Cultural Politics," p. 215.

[40] For the last two contrastive pairs, see Jerome, "Letter to Pammachius," p. 24, and Saint Paul's Second Epistle to the Corinthians 3:6.

[41] Robert Redfield, Ralph Linton, and Melville J. Herskovits, "Memorandum for the Study of Acculturation," *American Anthropologist* 38 (1936): 149–52 at p. 149.

[42] The "third place" created by the *Metrical Psalms* and possibly also by other early medieval English texts very much remains a *terra incognita*, although it may have a parallel existence with Homi Bhabha's "third space" in, for example, *The Location of Culture* (London: Routledge, 1994), pp. 19–39. See also M. J. Toswell, "How Pedantry Meets Intertextuality: Editing the Old English Metrical Psalter," in *New Approaches to Editing Old English Verse*, eds. Keefer and O'Brien O'Keeffe, pp. 79–93. I would like to thank Patrick O'Neill, Hironori Suzuki, Wanchen Tai, and Benedick Turner.

Polyptoton in Old English Texts

M. J. Toswell
University of Western Ontario

IN THE ROYAL PSALTER, in many ways one of the most intriguing manuscripts of the late tenth century in Anglo-Saxon England, there occurs a bilingual proverb: *Selre byð oft feðre þænne oferfeðre*, translated by Arngart as "Better often loaded than overloaded."[1] In his book on maxims, Paul Cavill simply provides this proverb, noting that it also appears in the *Durham Proverbs* and that it is a translation from the Latin *Meliora plura quam grauia honera fiunt*. His conclusion in the section is that the "fairly large number of proverbs in Old English that derive from non-native sources, both learned and popular, makes evident the fact that proverbs were a means by which lore and learning were transmitted."[2] Earlier in the chapter Cavill discusses the rhetorical patterning of proverbs, noting that each proverb has some pattern in concept, sound, or structure, and that generally proverbs in Old English follow a paradigmatic form, although they rarely take advantage of the metaphorical possibilities of the genre. Thomas Bredehoft, finding the same proverb in the manuscript in the context of a confessional prayer that he recognizes as poetic, argues that here, as often elsewhere in Old English, the proverb too is poetic—in this case a one-line poem, but still a poem.[3] My own interest in the proverb is that the rhetorical patterning that interested the Old English translator of this text was polyptoton, the playing off of words with the same root in different ways, as the rhetorical technique providing part of the somewhat sing-song emphasis that many proverbs offer. In this case the root *feðer* juxtaposes against its prefixed form *oferfeðer,* "laden" against "overladen." Polyptoton provides the charm of the proverb, while its structure comes from the opening *Selre byð*, "It is better." The locution does not appear difficult or unusual in Old English, but straightforward and sensible, and its rhetorical patterning seems quite natural in the vernacular. That is, the proverb's use of polyptoton both makes good sense and makes the saying a memorable one: it offers the kind of wisdom that might impel someone to make two trips with less of an armload than one with a teetering stack of books, or to write a good three hundred words of an article rather than a bad thousand in a sitting. Since it is the nature of proverbs to be memorable (and frequently repeated), the rhetorical patterning seems only appropriate. The use of polyptoton as the focus, however, is well worth pursuing as a rhetorical technique in its own right; that is, the extent to which polyptoton functions as a pattern of repetition in Old English offers us another lens on the stylistic preferences of Anglo-Saxon thinkers and writers.

As a rhetorical technique, polyptoton can be difficult to assess. Students who discuss the "wording of the words" in a text tend to come to grief, and in many cases polyptoton can be rather a failing than a grace. Its basic form, in which a word repeats through at least one permutation of case, is rather simple. However, polyptoton can be striking and memorable, a rhetorical feature that adds real impact: "to dream the impossible dream," or the politicians' favorite, "I want to work for the workers," come to mind. In Old English, polyptoton in poetry intersects with many other patterns of repetition, including poetic compounding, apposition, variation, kennings, envelope patterns, and perhaps even formulas. It can therefore be difficult to determine whether polyptoton in Old English poetic texts results from the volition of the writer rather than being simply an accidental result of the patterning effects of the language. I will argue here that polyptoton functions as a deliberate rhetorical strategy in Old English poetry, both in *Beowulf* and in a variety of other texts, including the *Paris Psalter*. Often it forms part of the appositional structure of a typical dense and sophisticated Old English verse paragraph, but it can also occur on its own for a different emphatic effect. The metrical psalter, a late text which many dismiss as bad poetry and others reject as purely translation, employs polyptoton more than a hundred times in its 5039 lines, at a very rough count. This is not a high number, but it includes only the most obvious cases, in an effort to begin thinking about the effects of the technique. Polyptoton in Old English poetry functions as a regular, if infrequent, rhetorical feature, and one with some occasional grace and genuine emphasis.

If polyptoton is intentional in Old English as a rhetorical technique, to what extent is it a result of Latin rhetoric, and to what extent does it reflect vernacular enjoyment of repetition?[4] To answer these questions, it seems best to begin with prose texts that are generally recognized as heavily involved with Latin. The most obvious of these is perhaps Byrhtferth's *Handbook* or *Enchiridion*, a volume that switches back and forth from Latin to Old English, sometimes from paragraph to paragraph.[5]

Byrhtferth's effort to explain much of medieval science, notably astronomy, often means that he gives a long version in Latin, and then a slightly different version in Old English. In their edition, Lapidge and Baker patiently offer a translation into modern English for each, but some stylistic features may be occluded. Thus, in the opening section concerning the four seasons and the four elements, which today would be called the four humors, three different Old English terms are all translated as "childhood": *cildhad, cildiugoð,* and *cildyld.*[6] These occur within a sequence of three sentences, and all can indeed translate as "childhood," but it does seem that Byrhtferth wanted to vary his usage. Some would call the results variation, quite rightly; I wonder if he is heading towards polyptoton. In the next section of the manuscript, Byrhtferth discusses the year and its various calculations; he turns to explain the Latin to English clerics (with a longsuffering statement about how it would be too tedious [*langsum*] to explain the whole thing), but *we heom secgað soð to soðe* (Baker and Lapidge translate, "we tell them truly a truth").[7] *Soð to soðe* "truth as a truth" may not be the most exciting rhetorical technique, but it offers some emphasis to require attention for the explication of the six kinds of year in the computus. Moreover, Byrhtferth is writing highly technical prose, so any efforts he makes at a rhetorical flourish are worth attention. A few folios later the monk discusses concurrents: *Þære sunnan geares dagas æfter þære sunnan ryne synt to asmeagenne and synt eac to asmuganne mid scrutniendre scrutnunge* ("The days of the solar year, according to the sun's course, must be examined, and must also be studied with scrutinizing scrutiny").[8] Here Baker and Lapidge translate Byrhtferth's *asmeagenne...asmuganne*, a nascent polyptoton, as "examined...studied," but acknowledge his *scrutniendre scrutnunge* as "scrutinizing scrutiny." The repetitions, however, point to the important issues, offering clear paths for the clerks Byrhtferth was addressing (quite frequently with vocatives to keep them engaged). Byrhtferth wanted his reader to notice the repetition, perhaps not rejoicing in its excellence, but appreciating its force with a wry smile—and remembering the point.

Through the first two sections of his analysis Byrhtferth continues explicating and clarifying, using polyptotons involving readers and reading, and learners and learning, none of them signalled in the Latin interleaved texts which he then explains for clerks in English. In the third section of the *handboc* he quotes from Bede, paraphrasing from the *De schematibus et tropis* to present seventeen rhetorical figures and their use. Section fourteen reads as follows:

> Polyptoton ys þæt feowerteoðe hiw, and hyt ys þus to undergitanne: nam polon multum dicitur, toton þæt ys casuale. Þis hiw ys polyptoton: 'Quoniam ex ipso, et per ipsum, et in ipso sunt omnia, ipsi gloria in secula seculorum', and on þam sealme ys polyptoton, | þus cweðende: 'Niue dealbabuntur' and 'mons coagulatus' and 'mons pinguis' and 'mons in quo beneplacitum est De<o>.'
>
> [*Polyptoton* is the fourteenth figure, and it should be understood thus: *polon* means many, and *toton* means 'of case endings'. This figure is *polyptoton*. *Quoniam ex ipso, et per ipsum, et in ipso sunt omnia, ipsi gloria in secula seculorum* [For of him and through him and in him are all things, to whom be glory for ever]; and there is *polyptoton* in the psalm, which speaks thus: *Niue dealbabuntur* [they are made white with snow], and *mons coagulatus* [curdled mountain], and *mons pinguis* [fat mountain], and *mons in quo beneplacitum est Deo* [mountain in which it is pleasing to God].[9]

Byrhtferth interleaves Latin and Old English in this passage so completely that it can be a bit uncertain which language he is in. Baker and Lapidge point out that he takes his etymology from Remigius's commentary on Bede, and makes an error, presumably, in writing *polon* instead of *polis*.[10] The conclusion that the term implies "many cases" in the grammatical sense follows on from Bede, whose *De schematibus et tropis* is the principal source for this, as for most of the other entries in this section.[11] In other words, although Byrhtferth explicitly etymologizes the term to suggest many cases, he uses examples such as the fourfold repetition of *mons*, "mountain," which simply indicate different idiomatic usages and shades of meaning. A mountain here can be figurative, rhetorical, descriptive, and somehow curdled, for which a figurative meaning must be intended. The first example, the sequence *ex ipso...per ipsum...in ipso* offers a clearer example of the case permutations, as does *secula seculorum*, one of the classic polyptotons of the Bible, and a biblical epithet to boot. Byrhtferth and his ancestor in stylistic analysis, Bede, clearly take a liberal approach to the identification of polyptoton: case permutations in a sequence with prepositions are good, repetition of the word in two cases is also good, and even repetition of a word in various shades of meaning will do. Polyptoton is a broad house for these Anglo-Saxon thinkers. Byrhtferth's use of the term, as demonstrated from the beginning of his *handboc* and from his analysis here, suggests that this Latinate structure could work in the vernacular, and work hard. He defines the term, and uses it throughout his writing.

Byrhtferth might well have been, as Baker and Lapidge posit, the most learned Anglo-Saxon of his day, but he is rarely cited for his stylistic excellence or his rhetorical innovations. A second example from prose might be useful, in this case a text which demonstrates a different kind of Latin/Old English bilingualism. Latin translations or adaptations are the texts in which we would most expect to find polyptoton carried over from the Latin source, since it was a common rhetorical feature in Latin prose and poetry. The prose version of the first fifty psalms, associated with the circle of King Alfred, offers a good sample text of this kind. Quite commonly, where the Latin psalter has straight repetition, the adaptor uses polyptoton to get the same effect. For example:

> 23:10 Hwæt is se *gewuldroda* kyning? Hit is se *wuldorfæsta*, se þe God fore wyrcð swylc wundru.
>
> [Who is this glorious king? It is the one firm in glory, he who accomplishes such wonders before God.][12]
>
> Quis est iste rex glorie? Dominus virtutum, ipse est rex glorie.
>
> [Who is this King of Glory? The Lord of hosts, he is the King of Glory.][13]

Here, at the end of the famous 23rd psalm, the Latin repeats *rex glorie*, but the adaptor has *se gewuldroda kyning* followed by *se wuldorfæsta*. The sense changes, emphasizing not simply the repetition of God's glory and virtue, but almost implying the divine and glorious actions of the earthly and glorious king, accomplished and glorified with divine wonders in the face of God. The line also has four alliterating words with *wyrcð* and *wundru* in the clause added by the adaptor. Its central rhetorical feature, however, is the polyptoton, the play on *wuldor* "glory" which refocuses the purpose of the line with its playful use as both *gewuldroda*, the past participle taken as an adjective modifying *cyning*, and the compound adjective *wuldorfæsta*, "the one firm in glory." The polyptoton here advances from the straightforward repetition of the Latin to shift the focus of the line and offer it a link to the actions of King David (and perhaps King Alfred).

A simpler example appears in psalm 11, when the psalmist works a line through the complex but common psalmic construction of the evildoers who speak evil. After a sequence in verse 2 with *idla spræca hi sprecað* ("they speak vain speeches") and several other iterations of the verb *sprecan* and one of its synonym *cweðan*, the psalmist describes the way in which the Lord spurns these speakers:

3.(4) Ac Drihten towyrpð ealle þa facnesfullan weoloras and þa ofer-spræcan and þa yfelspræcan tungan.[14]

[But the Lord throws away all the evil lips and the tongues of the boasters and the evil-speakers.]

Disperdat dominus uniuersa labia dolosa & linguam maliloquam.

[May the Lord destroy all deceitful lips and the tongue that speaketh proud things.]

The vernacular version focuses on speech, the thing produced by the lips and tongue that are to be banished, and does so with two compounds: *oferspræcan* and *yfelspræcan*, expanding the sense and range of the original from the evil lips to those who speak too much, promising too much, and thence straightforwardly to the ones who speak evil.

Similarly, and to prove that this kind of use of polyptoton is the adaptor's own work and not something brought over from the Latin, the vernacular prologue to psalm 24 has as its second clause in the introduction the following:

and eac he witegode on þam sealme be þæs folces gehwyrfnesse of heora *hæftnyde,* þa hi on Babilonia *gehæfte* wæron.[15]

[and also he prophesied in the psalm about the return of that nation from their captivity, when they were held captive in Babylon.]

The editor of the prose psalms, Patrick O'Neill, cites pseudo-Bede as a source for this clause, but adds that the adaptor is here mistaken, as the return should be from exile, not from captivity. Perhaps here, too, the adaptor was looking for the rhetorical effect of being seized captive as being doubly emphasized, and not worrying about precision of language. The rhetoric was more important than the fact of the exile, which is, after all, often framed as a kind of captivity in the desert. Here, then, the polyptoton on *hæftnyde* and *gehæfte* offers one of the many ways in which the prose adaptor wishes to address the psalms. Whether the adaptor could prepare new material adapted into the vernacular, in the extensive prose introductions, which are drawn from a number of Latin sources, or worked closely from the Latin psalter, polyptoton for rhetorical effect was an available technique. The prose psalter text has a number of other rhetorical effects, favoring alliteration and other kinds of repetition and variation as well; it may repay further study. For now, however, polyptoton, it seems, was not just an occasional accident, but appears to have been a rhetorical technique known in learned circles in Anglo-Saxon England, explicated by Bede and Byrhtferth, and used by Byrhtferth and the translator of the prose psalter. The next question is whether it was in use in Old English poetry, in ways other than coincidence or bad practice.

We know that Anglo-Saxon poets loved to play. They worked in a highly sophisticated mode of textual production, weaving together a highly traditional vocabulary and a metrical structure that was profoundly difficult and full of constraints. They made use of formulas and conventions, reworking motifs and artfully interweaving epithets and appositive constructions so as to create dense thickets of meaning in their verse paragraphs. In his famous study of the stylistic effects in *Beowulf*, Fred Robinson argued that we achieve a "constant alertness to the semantic layering of words" as a result of the way the poet plays off "ubiquitous variations" of one term against another, and of one meaning of a given word in a particular passage contrasted to another meaning in a different passage.[16] He argues that the constant variation, what he calls the apposed word meanings, is almost a metaphor for the way in which the most sophisticated Old English poetry apposed a new Christian context against or with an older heroic world. In Robinson's construction, apposition forges the distinctive style and the central theme of Old English poetry. However, his central argument concerns the way in which a particular word appears and repeats in different syntactic and lexical contexts—while apposition is a perfectly accurate term to describe this technique, so would be polyptoton in many situations.

For example, in the opening lines of *Beowulf*, the poet has *feasceaft* (7), *gescæphwile* (26), and *frumsceafte* (45).[17] Not much later in the poem appear *frumsceaft* (91), *gesceop* (97), and *scyppend* (106). In the prologue and first fitt of the poem, forms of the verb *scieppan* and its associated nouns *scyppend*, and *sceaft* occur six times, making "shaping" and "creation" the signal word-complex of the poem's opening (some would include *scop* (78) in this complex as well). Two occurrences are straight repetition of *frumsceaft*, opposing the clearly parallel compound *feasceaft* that introduces the polyptoton. Two more refer to a possible divine figure: the genitive noun *scyppend* and the noun which looks like it is formed from the preterite singular and generally used in Old English to refer to the poet, *scop*. The last two are perhaps the most and least striking: the preterite singular form *gesceop* which reflects the term for the poet twenty lines earlier, but is central to the actual "Creation Poem" in *Beowulf*, and the unusual compound *gescæphwile*, the finite verb combined with the noun *hwil* to suggest a "shaped period of time," referring to the appropriate moment at which Scyld Scefing dies. That is, having shaped his own life to the best result for his nascent nation, Scyld chooses his time of departure. This complex is not precisely apposition, but it is precisely polyptoton, the use of different forms of the same root to indicate linkages in theme, idea, and style. Even the reuse of the adjective *won* in *wonsælig* (105) and *wonsceaft* (120), a vocabulary parallel linking together Grendel's "miserably happy" man with the dark misery of the way that things will turn out for the inhabitants of Heorot, is polyptoton.

A sequence with the verb *gewinnan* "to fight, contend" and the related noun *gewinn* "strife, struggle, fight" offers more evidence of polyptoton in this section of the poem. *Gewin* occurs in lines 133 and 191, the third person past tense singular *wan* at lines 144 and 151, and the past plural *wunnon* at line 113. These five occurrences—which take place during the section of the poem when Grendel's depredations on Heorot are devastating and the Danes are not fighting back, but running away and even trying to make bargains with the gods—seem significant. The verb occurs only three more times in the poem, meaning that fully half of its occurrences are found in this sequence; the noun as a simplex has five more occurrences, and two more as a second element in a compound. The polyptoton here underscores the fact that fighting, ironically, matters most when it does not actually take place.

To take a third example from the opening of a work by a similarly sophisticated poet, consider Cynewulf's *Juliana*, lines 1–4:

> Hwæt, we ðæt hyrdon hæleð eahtian,
> deman dædhwate, þætte in dagum gelamp
> Maximianes, se geond middangeard,
> arleas cyning, eahtnysse ahof...[18]

> [Listen, we heard about this, the hero, the one bold in deeds, persecuted and judged; that in the times of Maximian, the king without honour, who engaged in persecution throughout the world...]

The link between *eahtian* and *eahtnysse*, the verb "to persecute" and the abstract noun "persecution," is clearly a polyptoton which interleaves with a quite complicated opening section of the poem to introduce both the heroine, Juliana, and her persecutor, Maximian. Judith Weise analyzes this opening as a complex site of great ambiguity, in which the reader is obliged to decode the meaning.[19] This seems perhaps too complicated, as it does seem possible that the interlinking of the polyptoton would advise the Anglo-Saxon audience that the persecution of Maximian would be associated with the object of the verb *eahtian*, that is, the *hæleþ,* the hero, the one whose deeds are indeed to be judged as bright and shining in this poem.

Stylistic analysis of Old English poetry generally begins with *Beowulf*, the touchstone text for sophisticated poetic and metrical techniques. Polyptoton, however, overlaps in *Beowulf* with a variety of other kinds of stylistic play, and as a result its function tends to be occluded. Moreover, in a poem that already has a panoply of rhetorical techniques at work, the details of the working of one of them can seem less important. Polyptoton might well be a more significant feature of the rhetorical landscape of other Old English poems; in particular, those that offer less in the way of stylistic graces. Damian Fleming, though he does not characterize the locution as polyptoton save in passing, investigates the superlative genitive construction in a group of Old English poems, noting that the "construction seems to have made a smooth transition from Latin into Old English."[20] Such phrases imitative of the Latin as *cyninga cyning* "king of kings" or *on worulda world* "world of worlds" or "to the ends of the earth" (translating *secula seculorum*): these phrases led, as Fleming points out, to a proliferation of the genre in Old English since these constructions are by their nature alliterative, fill a half-line quite easily, look formulaic, and can even provide epithets. They are particularly common in the metrical psalter to express the concept of eternity; Fleming also finds more subtle poetic usages in *Elene* and *Christ I*. Fleming plausibly perceives the usage of the superlative genitive construction in *Elene* as a reflection of Cynewulf's interest in Hebrew poetic usage, but it may also reflect a genuinely native interest in the word-play offered by repetition of the root nouns of the construction. Jackson J. Campbell, in an earlier generation, considered elements of Latin rhetoric—including polyptoton—in the Old English adaptation of Lanctantius's *Carmen de ave phoenice* to argue that in *The Phoenix*, the "native style and bookish learning are here marvelously fused."[21] For Campbell, polyptoton is one of many elements at work in the transfer of Latin rhetorical techniques into what he perceives as formulaic usage, for extremely flexible Old English prosody. Janie Steen, whose recent book focuses on the question of Latin rhetoric and its influence on Old English verse usage, sees the issue quite differently.[22] Steen argues that the poet of *The Phoenix* is a bold and original adaptor, departing from the native poetic tradition with the use of many similes, including epic similes, and finding a new kind of poetic idiom.[23]

Polyptoton is a part of that idiom, as Steen points out. She argues that the author of *The Phoenix* is a good or excellent Old English poet mixing vernacular devices with Latinate patterns, as also evident in Cynewulf, two riddles, and *Judgment Day II*. *Judgment Day II*, an example of a late text and a close translation, makes great use of polyptoton, what Steen terms its "biblical ring."[24] She suggests that the use of Latin word-order and syntactic patterns such as polyptoton in this text mark a shift to rhythmical patterning in prose texts of the late Anglo-Saxon period. This may be part of the explanation for polyptoton in late texts. However, the salient issue is not the fact that these texts are late, but that they perforce necessitate a slightly different kind of meter: less complex in its patterns, but with the flexibility to permit other kinds of rhetorical systems. Where for *Beowulf* or in the poetry of Cynewulf, polyptoton can remain unnoticed because of the coruscating brilliance of other kinds of patterning, in poems such as *Judgment Day II* and the metrical psalter, polyptoton is more noticeable because it serves a more structural and less ornamental purpose.

To determine the extent to which polyptoton begins to partake of the structure of the verse, my last set of examples will come from the Old English metrical psalter, the longest surviving poem from the period.[25] I want to suggest that in this text polyptoton functions almost as a prosodic feature, since the meter of the text is perforce less sophisticated and complex than in such poems as *Beowulf* and the work of Cynewulf. It might even be that the poet of the metrical psalter compensated for the lack of metrical variety and the looseness of the verse by adding other rhetorical features.[26] Given that the Hebrew and Assyriac originals lying behind the Latin psalter texts the Old English poet worked from made great use of polyptoton, it remains more difficult to argue that polyptoton in this Old English text does not derive solely from the sacred source text. However, the *Paris Psalter* poet achieved some notable, or at least noteworthy, stylistic effects—effects that in general are not signalled by the Latin source. Thus, the metrical psalter has its version of what might have been called the *Beowulfian* polyptoton accruing about the notion of "shaping," involving the verb *scieppan* and associated nouns such as *scop* and *gesceaft*: at psalm 73.16, line 2 reads, *þæra gesceafta þe þu gesceope ðe*, and later in the text 103.23 ends in line 4, *þinra gesceafta, scyppend mære*. The creations God shaped for himself are later referred to as "of your creations, glorious Creator." The close connection between the two forms, alliterating with each other in both examples, suggests that the poet was well aware of the polyptoton. Often, of course, this paronymy derives from the Latin, including locutions such as "god of gods" and "lord of lords." The metrical psalter has its share of *drihtna drihten* and of *worulda woruld* occurrences, and plays on *god* and *good* are ubiquitous in the metrical psalter. The psalter poet also plays on *man* and *mann*, paronomasia noted by Roberta Frank.[27] Returning to polyptoton proper, there are frequent plays on *halig...hal...hæl*, and on *wyrcan...weorc* and other such variations. For example, psalm 61.8 begins: *Hycge him halig folc hælu to drihtne; doð eowre heortan hige hale and clæne*, "The holy people consider him as salvation from the lord; may the spirits of your hearts make themselves healthy and pure." The awkwardness of the translation here reflects the way in which the poet works out the polyptoton not fully required by the Latin. Being healthy, saved, and part of the holy folk admitted to heaven is an important collection of results, the more so if the wordplay can include alliteration and polyptoton. Sometimes what is polyptoton here will strike others as simply translation. For example, in psalm 110, verse 4, occurs *mærweorcum*, four lines later at the beginning of verse 5 appears *handgeweorc*, and at the end of verse 7 appears *wyrcean*. The combination of "glorious works," "handiwork," and the verb "to work," all of them translating to some extent from the Latin, could be so far apart from each other that they do not constitute polyptoton. But the way that the psalter poet works at creating whatever slight amount of linkage is available suggests that polyptoton was an acceptable, even approved, rhetorical technique in Old English poetry.

Polyptoton and alliteration intermingle, as for example in this group of examples:

113.21 Weorð þu ure gemyndig, mihtig dryhten,
and þine bletsunge bring ofer us;
þu gebletsudest bearn Israheles,
Aarones hus eac gebletsadest;
þu gebletsadest bliðe mode
ealle þa þe on ðe egsan hæfdan,
mycle and mæte ofer middangeard.

[Powerful lord, be mindful and bring your blessing over us; you sanctified the sons of Israel; you also sanctified the house of Aaron; you sanctified with a happy spirit all those who have fear of you (who worship you), the great and the small, throughout the world.]

Dominus memor fuit . nostri & benedixit nobis : benedixit domui israhel : benedixit domui aaron : benedixit omnibus timentibus se dominus pusillis cum maioribus.[28]

The opening line of this long verse (a combination of two from the Roman Psalter) alliterates on *m*, as does the last line. Unsurprisingly the alliteration is on *b* three times and on vowels twice in the middle of the psalm-verse. And *gebletsadest* repeats three times, but with the noun form *bletsung* the first time the locution occurs. In other words, given the constraints of the verse form, the poet succeeds in linking sound and meaning here.

In several passages the psalter poet works with *heah* and compound nouns beginning with *heah*. Many of these are unique to the metrical psalter, and while they are certainly created with alliteration in mind, it seems likely that the poet saw these constructions as also providing some continuity to the verse. Thus, starting at verse 6 in psalm 88 and continuing through the psalm are *heah gemetincg*, *heah mægen*, *heahstne*, *heahehtendra,* and even continuing into psalm 89 with *heah eadmedu*; similarly, at verse 17 in psalm 101 is *hean*, then *heahgnornunge*, *heahsæl*, and *heahgeweorc*; and at verse 108 in psalm 118 are *heahsælum* and *heahbliss*. Similar compounds exist with *wæter*, and with *þearf*, in this case as a second element. The psalter poet used the material available to offer adequate verse, and occasionally to step slightly farther. In psalm 135, for example, occurs a series using *miht* "might, strength, power":

135.8 Sette on miht dæges mære sunnan,
.9 On miht nihte monan and steorran.
.10 He Ægyptas sloh and eall heora frumbearn,
.11 And he Israhelas ealle oðlædde of Ægyptum ealle gesunde,
.12 On mihtigre mære handa
and on eallmihte earmes swylce.
.13 He readne sæ recene todælde,
.14 Lædde Israhelas ealle þurh midne.

[He established the glorious sun in power in the day; in power in the night, the moon and stars. He killed the Egyptians and all their first-born sons, and he led the Israelites all out of Egypt, all in good health through the powerful glory of his hands and also the absolute power of his arm. He powerfully divided the Red Sea, he led the Israelites completely through the middle.]

This is an intriguing passage in the psalms, a combination of praise of God with history of the departure of the Israelites from Egypt, a topic that comes up frequently in this text. In this particular psalm, the effect is that of a litany with a repeated refrain in the Latin. The Old English holds to the very short declarative statements, offering its version in one or two lines. But there is also a linkage from line to line, so that *on miht* is repeated in the first two verses, and also the first two lines. The glorious sun is set powerfully in the day, and the night has, with equal power, the moon and the stars. In the next lines, *ealle*, another very popular element in compounds and for alliteration in the metrical psalter, appears, but in verse 12 the poet returns to *miht* with both *mihtigre* and *eallmihte* (a *hapax legomenon*), so that glorious hands and also arms are powerful and strong. Finally, not relevant to the *miht* complex, verse 13 ends with *todælde* and the first word of 14 is *lædde*. While there is no polyptoton at work here, the reversal of the consonants, and the near-rhyme, both seem like intended features. The metrical psalter poet commonly has verbs at the end of lines, so putting *lædde* at the beginning is intriguing and perhaps intentional. Even in passages where the exigencies of the form and of the translation required brevity and accuracy, the psalter poet tried to balance and parallel his terms in ways that might offer a slight extra poignancy or meaning to the verse.

Students of Old English poetic style range broadly in their approaches. Their work is complicated by issues of phonology, including the poetic *koiné* of conventionalized spelling and perhaps vocabulary, and meter. Parallel usages of vocabulary, even when quite different thematic and narrative matters pertain, also occur, as does the use of oral formulae, or poetic usages based on oral or transitional narrative poetic traditions. They focus on vocabulary, considering kennings, other kinds of nominal and adjectival compounds, apposition, rank, variation, and questions of alliteration and its effect on the poetic vocabulary.[29] Repetitive patterns and their effects in various locutions are in many ways their central focus, since those who study Old English poetry tend to enjoy close reading. Readings of the extant poetry, as a result, very commonly engage in detailed analysis of words and ideas in specific passages and of word complexes throughout a work.

Much work on style in recent years has moved strongly in the direction of suggesting a highly sophisticated poetic *milieu*. That is to say, the paradigm that suggested that the Anglo-Saxon poet might compose orally and freely, but revise somewhat for a written version or perhaps sing to a scholar who would "tweak" the text when writing it in a manuscript, has fairly completely fallen out of favor (though it does still receive gracious gestures). For instance, Andy Orchard's spectacular analyses of Cynewulf's poetry, of the Exeter Book riddles, and even of Wulfstan's prose, have demonstrated highly ornate poetic structures of repetition, wordplay, rhetorical excess, and aureate diction.[30] Elizabeth Tyler has argued that collocations offer new ways of accessing the intentions and approaches of Old English poets, as she demonstrates with respect to words for treasure.[31] Tom Hall's work on consonance in Old English poetry suggests that not only the initial consonants alliterated when the poet was reaching for an impressive poetic effect, but that initial and medial consonants and consonant clusters could match. His examples are deeply impressive (though unfortunately his comprehensive analysis elucidated only two lines from the *Paris Psalter*, and one from the *Kentish Psalm 50*).[32] The many articles of Mark Griffith fall in this tradition as well, demonstrating, as so many of them do, the ways in which individual poets manipulate and structure the metrical and stylistic approaches available to them.[33]

For me, this modern consideration of style in Old English poetry dates from a remarkable article, published in *Studies in Philology* in 1978 and entitled "Artful Avoidance of the Useful Phrase in *Beowulf*, *The Battle of Maldon*, and *Fates of the Apostles*." Its author begins with consideration of ready-made phrases in *Beowulf*, comparing them to similar phrases in Homer, especially *The Iliad,* and in Serb and Croat poetry. The persistent use of such a ready-made phrase, called economy, is something that appears in some Old English poems, such as *Cædmon's Hymn*, *Meters of Boethius*, *Dream of the Rood*, and *Seasons for Fasting*. However, as the author elegantly demonstrates, this notion of economy—with its focus on the repetition of ready-made phrases, here whole-line formulas which offer easily-repeated alliterative patterns—does not appear in poems such as *Beowulf*, *Battle of Maldon*, and *Fates of the Apostles* (the latter generally attributed to Cynewulf). In fact, these poems avoid formulas, avoid verbal repetition, and engage in what the author terms "a painstaking search for variety in diction."[34] Where a ready-made verse was available, some poets chose to develop something different, clearly placing "a high value on varied expression."[35] In short, the author of this article, Geoffrey Russom, identifies three poets—one from the late Old English tradition and the other two from an earlier period, and all writing very different kinds of poetry—who agree in reaching for varied kinds of expression, eschewing the easy and readily-available cliché that was the whole-line formula. Those who do use the ready-made expression are similarly very different poets ranging across the chronological period of Old English poetry.

In this chapter, I have attempted to investigate some aspects of the use of polyptoton, a rhetorical technique that functions both in Old English prose and poetry, but which seems to be more appreciated by particular writers. The translator of the metrical psalter is a poet for whom polyptoton seems a comfortable and easy rhetorical technique. It can derive from the Roman psalter, the source text for the poet's adaptation. It can also be an addition or a reworking of an element derived from the Latin. It can be a way of bringing together a whole group of verses, or a quiet repetition in one verse. Polyptoton, that lovely rhetorical technique that trips so lovingly across the tongues of stylistics experts and no other individuals, deserves to be brought into the repertoire of prosodic techniques recognized as functioning in Old English poetry.

NOTES

[1] The Royal Psalter is British Library, MS Royal 2. B. v and the proverb is one of four bilingual proverbs or maxims added on f. 6r. See N. R. Ker, *Catalogue of Manuscripts Containing Anglo-Saxon* (Oxford: Clarendon Press, 1957), §249. For the translation see Olof Arngart, ed., "The Durham Proverbs," *Speculum* 56 (1981): 288–300 at p. 299.

[2] Paul Cavill, *Maxims in Old English Poetry*. (Woodbridge: D. S. Brewer, 1999), p. 73–74, quotation from p. 74.

[3] Thomas A. Bredehoft, "*Confessio et Oratio*: An Unrecognized Eleventh-Century Poetic Prayer," elsewhere in this volume, p. 131.

[4] The classic pieces in this field used to be Jackson J. Campbell, "Knowledge of Rhetorical Figures in Anglo-Saxon England," *Journal of English and Germanic Philology* 66 (1967): 1–20, and his "Adaptation of Classical Rhetoric in Old English Literature," in *Medieval Eloquence: Studies in the Theory and Practice of Medieval Rhetoric*, ed. J. J. Murphy (Berkeley, CA: University of California Press, 1978), pp. 173–97; see now Gabriele Knappe, *Traditionen der klassischen Rhetorik im angelsächsischen England* (Heidelberg: Carl Winter, 1996), and the article which summarizes the book's concerns, "Classical Rhetoric in Anglo-Saxon England," *Anglo-Saxon England* 27 (1998): 5–29. In the article, Knappe points out (p. 20) that a detailed analysis of rhetorical strategies in Anglo-Latin and Old English is a *desideratum* in the field, and briefly discusses some rhetorical techniques in Old English texts (pp. 20–25). She also addresses the question of teaching rhetoric, for which see also D. A. Bullough, "The Educational Tradition in England from Alfred to Ælfric: Teaching *utriusque linguae,*" in his collection of papers *Carolingian Renewal: Sources and Heritage* (Manchester: Manchester University Press, 1991), pp. 297–334. For an investigation of what Latin rhetorical texts were available in Anglo-Saxon England, see Vivien Law, *The Insular Latin Grammarians* (Woodbridge: Boydell Press, 1982), and for my purposes here especially chapter 6 on "The Exegetical Grammarians," pp. 81–97, where Law discusses some rhetoric and especially etymological speculations as they were made available for teaching

in Anglo-Saxon England. Knappe's book ranges more broadly over the field of classical rhetoric, arriving at Bede's *De schematibus et tropis* (which she cites extensively, including for polyptoton) at the mid-point. Knappe also mentions Byrhtferth's rhetoric, and includes some examples of polyptoton in her analysis of OE poetry, for which she cites Claire Wade McPherson, "The Influence of Latin Rhetoric on Old English Poetry" (Ph.D. dissertation, Washington University, 1980), which I have not seen.

[5] See *Byrhtferth's Enchiridion*, eds. Peter S. Baker and Michael Lapidge, Early English Text Society s.s. 15. (Oxford: Oxford University Press, 1995). The editors suggest in the introduction, pp. xxxi–xxxii, that Byrhtferth was interested in Latin verse, and might well have written some distichs and even the "Metrical Calendar of Ramsey." The editors later describe him as "a scholar of quite exceptionally wide learning; indeed, it would probably not be misleading to describe him as the most learned Englishman of his day" (p. lxxiv).

[6] *Byrhtferth's Enchiridion*, pp. 12–13 (Old English with facing modern English translation).

[7] *Byrhtferth's Enchiridion*, pp. 20–21.

[8] *Byrhtferth's Enchiridion*, pp. 30–31.

[9] *Byrhtferth's Enchiridion*, pp. 168–169.

[10] *Byrhtferth's Enchiridion*, pp. 330–1 in the Commentary.

[11] See Bede, *Libri II: De arte metrica et De schematibus et tropis: The Art of Poetry and Rhetoric*, ed. and trans. Calvin Kendall (Saarbrücken: AQ-Verlag, 1991).

[12] See Patrick P. O'Neill, *King Alfred's Old English Prose Translation of the First Fifty Psalms* (Cambridge, MA: The Medieval Academy of America, 2001), p. 125. It should perhaps be mentioned that in verse 8 occurs *þes wuldorfæsta kyning* "this glorious king" and in verse 9 appears the verb *gewuldrod hæfd* "that God had glorified." The Latin psalter makes great use of repetition and rhetorical techniques; the Old English prose version follows suit in its own way. O'Neill's excellent glossary helps significantly with analysis of this text.

[13] O'Neill does not provide the Latin from the Paris Psalter manuscript, because it was not the text from which the vernacular was developed. The version given here is transcribed from the facsimile edition, *The Paris Psalter*, ed. Bertram Colgrave (Copenhagen: Rosenkilde and Bagger, 1958), f. 24v with punctuation added from the standard edition of the Roman psalter: *Le psautier romain*, ed. Robert Weber. Collectanea Biblica Latina 10 (Rome: Abbaye St-Jérôme, 1953). For the manuscript see now the digital images on the website of the Bibliothèque Nationale: http://gallica.bnf.fr/ark:/12148/btv1b8451636f.r=8824.langEN.swf. The translation of the Latin is from *The Douai-Rheims Bible, Challoner revision*, available now at http://www.drbo.org.

[14] O'Neill, *King Alfred's Old English*, p. 111; Latin transcribed from Colgrave, *The Paris Psalter*, f. 10v.

[15] O'Neill, *King Alfred's Old English*, p. 126. O'Neill's commentary on this psalm is p. 211.

[16] Fred C. Robinson, Beowulf *and the Appositive Style* (Knoxville: University of Tennessee Press, 1985), p. 51.

[17] Quotations and references from *Beowulf* are to *Klaeber's* Beowulf, 4th ed, eds. R. D. Fulk, Robert E. Bjork, and John D. Niles. (Toronto: University of Toronto Press, 2008). The glossary, building as it does on an already spectacular glossary from the predecessor edition, is a truly marvellous piece of work, and very helpful for this analysis.

[18] See *Cynewulf's "Juliana"* ed. Rosemary Woolf (Exeter: University of Exeter Press, 1977), p. 21, with slightly regularized orthography.

[19] Judith A. Weise, "Ambiguity in Old English Poetry," *Neophilologus* 63 (1979): 588–91.

[20] Damian Fleming, "*Rex regum et cyninga cyning*: 'Speaking Hebrew' in Cynewulf's *Elene*," in *Old English Literature and the Old Testament*, eds. Michael Fox and Manish Sharma (Toronto: University of Toronto Press, 2012), pp. 229–252 at p. 233.

[21] Jackson J. Campbell, "Learned Rhetoric in Old English Poetry," *Modern Philology* 63 (1966): 189–201 at p. 196.

[22] Janie Steen, *Verse and Virtuosity: The Adaptation of Latin Rhetoric in Old English Poetry*. (Toronto: University of Toronto Press, 2008).

[23] Steen, *Verse and Virtuosity*, chapter 3 "The Figure of the Phoenix," pp. 35–70.

[24] Steen, *Verse and Virtuosity*, p. 81.

[25] Quotations from the metrical psalter are from *The Paris Psalter and the Meters of Boethius*. Ed. G. P. Krapp. Anglo-Saxon Poetic Records 5 (New York: Columbia University Press, 1932), and from my notes.

[26] The issue of classical as against "late" or even "debased" poetry, metrically speaking, is alive, although the debate is one of intermittent sputters. Jun Terasawa, *Old English Metre: An Introduction* (Toronto: University of Toronto Press, 2011), offers some comments and exercises to think about these issues on pages 108–115, ending with a helpful set of suggestions for further reading. Thomas A. Bredehoft tackles the issue head-on in chapter 3 on late Old English verse in his *Early English Metre* (Toronto: University of Toronto Press, 2005), arguing for a changed approach in these poems to issues of stress, resolution, anacrusis, and—presumably—distribution of verse types. Alliteration becomes his focus as the principal structural feature of this verse. For more technical, and perhaps more helpful, analyses of the changes in metrical structure over the period of Anglo-Saxon verse see Geoffrey Russom, "Dating Criteria for Old English Poems," in *Studies in the History of the English Language: A Millennial Perspective*, eds. Donka Minkova and Robert Stockwell (Berlin: Mouton de Gruyter, 2002), pp. 245–265, and "Evolution of the a-verse in English Alliterative Meter," in *Studies in the History of the English Language III: Managing Chaos: Strategies for Identifying Change in English*, eds. Christopher M. Cain and Geoffrey Russom (Berlin: Mouton de Gruyter, 2007), pp. 63–87. The latter article starts with late Old English linguistic changes having metrical effects, canvases Old Norse, and points to

ways forward into Middle English, and the former article notes that "*Maldon* and the *Paris Psalter* provide fascinating insight into metrical death but little insight into earlier periods of Old English metrical history" (p. 249).

[27] See Roberta Frank, "Some Uses of Paronomasia in Old English Scriptural Verse," *Speculum* 47 (1972): 207–226, this discussion at p. 221. It should be noted that although Frank's title heralds an analysis of scriptural verse, that is to say verse based on a Latin biblical text, her analysis includes a number of examples from Old English prose, notably from Ælfric. Her main point, that both in Latin and Old English writers were aware of etymological connections, whether obvious or not, seems correct given the range of examples from Old English that she provides.

[28] The Latin text for the metrical psalter is transcribed from the facing text of the Roman Psalter in the manuscript, Paris, Bibliothèque Nationale MS lat. 8824. Although this is not the text of the Latin psalter which was the source for the metrical psalter, it remains slightly closer than the standard edition of the text.

[29] There are many excellent studies of Old English verse practice; for the traditional approach see T. A. Shippey, *Old English Verse* (London: Hutchinson University Library, 1972), pp. 80–113, and Barbara C. Raw, *The Art and Background of Old English Poetry* (London: Edward Arnold, 1978), pp. 65–81 and 97–122. An elegant and judicious assessment is Daniel G. Calder, "The Study of Style in Old English Poetry: A Historical Introduction," in Daniel G. Calder, ed. *Old English Poetry: Essays on Style* (Berkeley: University of California Press, 1979), pp. 1–65. Calder concludes that "[a]n enquiring and open-ended methodology for Old English stylistics begins to emerge" (p. 56). I hope the open-ended methodology lauded by Calder continues to emerge.

[30] Unfortunately, most of Orchard's work in this vein comes in conference papers; e.g., most recently, on *Judith*, at "Transforming Scripture: Biblical Translations and Adaptations in Old and Middle English," May 29–31, 2014. St. Anne's College, Oxford. Some of his arguments, and some of his lists of various poetic features, are to be found in "Both Style and Substance: The Case for Cynewulf" in *Anglo-Saxon Styles*, ed. Catherine E. Karkov and George Hardin Brown. (Albany: State University of New York Press, 2003), pp. 271–305. The article includes a list of formulas in texts and shared among the Cynewulfian group, and a long list of near-misses for formulas, which may be more instructive. See also the chapter "Style and Structure" in *A Critical Companion to* Beowulf (Cambridge: D. W. Brewer, 2003), pp. 57–97 and "Appendix II: Repeated Formulas in *Beowulf*," pp. 274–314. Most useful for my purposes here is the list of noun- and adjective-compounds based on five Old English words for "war" and "battle," a total of 103 compounds, on pages 70–2. Orchard's point is the interwoven connectedness of the poetic vocabulary; mine would be in addition that the individual poet used this kind of repetition, especially polyptoton, for particular patterns of meaning.

[31] Elizabeth Tyler, *Old English Poetics: The Aesthetics of the Familiar in Anglo-Saxon England* (York: York Medieval Press, 2006), pp. 38–100.

[32] Tom Hall, "Consonance in Old English Poetry," International Society of

Anglo-Saxonists Conference. August 2011. Madison, Wisconsin.

[33] Most recently see Mark Griffith, "Old English Poetic Diction not in Old English Verse or Prose—and the Curious Case of Aldhelm's Five Athletes," *Anglo-Saxon England* 43 (2014): 99–131, but for a consideration of prosodic elements in poetic context see also "The Register of Divine Speech in *Genesis A*," *Anglo-Saxon England* 41 (2012): 63–78, and "Convention and Originality in the Old English 'beasts of battle' Typescene," *Anglo-Saxon England* 22 (1993): 179–99.

[34] Geoffrey R. Russom, "Artful Avoidance of the Useful Phrase in *Beowulf*, *The Battle of Maldon*, and *Fates of the Apostles*," *Studies in Philology* 75 (1978): 371–90 at p. 381.

[35] Russom, "Artful Avoidance," p. 387.

Confessio et Oratio: An Unrecognized Old English Confessional Poem

Thomas A. Bredehoft

The Poem

In the summer of 2005, while spending a few days working with manuscripts at the British Library, I was fortunate enough to be granted access to the Royal Psalter, a large and beautiful tenth-century English manuscript.[1] I was consulting this book for a couple of small poetic scraps it was known to contain: the *Latin-English Proverbs* printed by Dobbie in *The Anglo-Saxon Minor Poems* and the Royal scholion, which Mechthild Gretsch's work on the Royal Psalter had brought to my attention.[2] But, as one does, I also took the opportunity to look at the rest of the book as well, and I was, I have to admit, entirely surprised to turn to the very end of the book and find an unrecognized Old English poem, beneath the heading "CONFESSIO ET ORATIO."[3] Undoubtedly, this discovery was made the more easily because I had already been looking in this very book at other poetic texts that have been conventionally understood as prose: the two additional bilingual proverbs found alongside Dobbie's *Latin-English Proverbs* on folio 6v:

> Meliora plura qua*m* grauia honera fiunt;
> Selre byð oft feðre   þænne oferfeðre;
>
> [Better often loaded than overloaded]

> Omnis inuocans cupit audiri;
> Clipiendra gehwylc   wolde þ*æt* him man oncwæde;
>
> [Each one who calls out wishes that someone would answer him.][4]

These two proverbs, recorded here and in the *Durham Proverbs* collection, strike my eye as perfect examples of what I have called "late Old English verse," with alliteration in each Old English line and metrical forms that would have been acceptable even in classical Old English poetry, excepting only the placement of alliteration on the last stressed position of the final line.[5] In short, I was primed to recognize a passage of late Old English verse when I ran across it, though the prayer's relatively few modern readers and editors had only ever understood or printed the passage as prose.[6]

I tell this story simply to call attention to the special problem that the nature of Old English poetry's textualization presents to its readers: Old English poetry is conventionally written in long lines across the page, as is Old English prose. Neither modern nor medieval readers can rely upon a visible difference between verse and prose to help them recognize the genre of a particular passage. And while a number of passages of Old English are universally understood to be verse, the principle by which one can reliably distinguish between the two genres seems to have long eluded modern Old English scholars. The very nature of metrical study, which must be inductive in its methods, compounds this central interpretative problem.

That is, metrical study proceeds by taking a body of data (we might also call it verse, or even poetry), and analyzing that data in order to discover the metrical rules that it was composed to fit. The rules that different metricists discover in their analyses might well be matters for debate and disagreement, but in the absence of an Old English metrical treatise, the inductive method is really the only method available for the metrical study of Old English texts. Importantly, however, this inductive method depends crucially upon the identification of a body of data *before* the metrical analysis can begin.

For a very long time, metricists interested in Old English simply took *Beowulf* as the relevant body of data, though it has long been obvious that poems like *The Metrical Psalms*, the later *Chronicle* poems, and many other items do not match *Beowulf*'s meter at all closely. Using *Beowulf* as the database for metrical analysis, of course, has been very effective, and it is certain that we have learned a great deal from the extended study of Beowulfian meter.[7] But none of that work is at all useful for helping to determine whether some other passage of Old English is metrical or not. The data is there—there is a large body of Old English prose and verse—but before the inductive process of metrical study can begin, we must have a way to distinguish between the two.

We need not remain wholly at sea, however. While I wish I had recognized it fifteen or twenty years ago, as it would have saved me a great deal of difficult thinking, I've come to understand that the central difference between prose and verse is that, as Gerard Manley Hopkins long ago put it, verse can be defined as being characterized as "speech wholly or partially repeating the same figure of sound."[8] This definition, of course, remains frustratingly vague, as the degree of repetition involved is still undefined, and we all must recognize that some texts might shift back and forth between verse and prose. But the central difference is that verse passages must have a repeating, measured (or metered) structure, Hopkins's "figure of sound." To put it in other terms, verse—including Old English verse—must have structures that we can visualize (and print) as lines.

This conclusion, perhaps, should have been obvious all along. Classical Old English verse was recognized and lineated in printed editions, and this happened long before metrical analysis began to show any promising or detailed understanding of its metrical structure. In that sense, the history of the lineation of Old English verse should have taught us (or reminded us) that recognizing Old English verse (and lineating it) must precede metrical analysis, and that sometimes the metrical understanding might lag behind the recognition by a century or more. Regardless, however, this logic straightforwardly identifies the lineated structures W. W. Skeat used to print the bulk of Ælfric's *Lives of Saints* collection as the very defining feature of verse.[9] Although we have been slow to recognize and name these works as verse, as poems in fact, the very circumstance that they can be so successfully lineated should always have made that identification inescapable. If we have failed so far to understand Ælfric's meter, that only means we haven't yet found our Sievers: the essential identity of Ælfric's alliterative works as verse is already as clear and as persuasive as the lineations of *Beowulf* or the Junius poems were before Sieversian metrical analysis. To put it in other terms, Kemble's or Thorkelin's failure to understand *Beowulf*'s meter no more proved that *Beowulf* wasn't a poem than our failure to understand Ælfric's meter can prove that the *Lives* are not poems. We must learn to have the courage of our lineations.

In the end, it was this repeating structure, the way the passage at the end of the Royal Psalter was structured in a way that can be represented through lineation, that allowed me to recognize it as verse when I sat before it in 2005. I print it here as a poetically lineated text in order to clarify those poetic structures that I recognized as I read it.

CONFESSIO ET ORATIO

Eala þu ælmihtiga god,   unasecgendlicere mildheortnesse.[10]
eala þu god, unametenra   arfæstnysse.
eala þu god scyppend. *ond* geedstaþeliand   ealles manncynnes.
þu þe afeormast   fram fulum synnu*m*
þæra heortan þe þe andettað.   *ond* ða þe hi sylfe wregað
ætforan gesihðe   þinre mildheortnysse.
þa þu alyst fra*m* bende   ælcere unrihtwisnysse
þine mihte ic bidde   mid ealre geomerunge
þ*æt* þu ðurh menigfealdnysse   þinre mildheortnyssa me forgife
þ*æt* ic hluttre andetnysse   ætforan þe don mote
be eallu*m* minu*m* sy\n/nu*m*   þe min ingehyd me nu wregð.
ond ic soðe dædbote   ætforan þe don mote
be eallum þa*m* synnu*m*   þe ic gesyngode
on yfelu*m* geþohtu*m*.   *ond* on þwyru*m* smeageon\g/um.
on yfelre geþafunge.   *ond* on unrihtwisu*m* geþeahte.
on unclænre lustfullunge.   *ond* on fracodre gewilnunge.
on ydelu*m* wordu*m*   *ond* on yfelu*m* dædu*m*.

Ic syngode on gesihðe.   *ond* swiðe on hlyste.
eac on swæcce[11]   on stence *ond* on hrepunge.
þu, leofa drihten,   ealle lima me gesceope.
to menniscu*m* bricu*m*   gemæte. *ond* gelimplice.
ac ic earming hi awende   to deoflicum weorcum.
ond mid synnum hi befylde.   *ond* þe forseah, drihten.

.I.[12] Ic on ofermettu*m*   oft swiðe agylte.
ond þurh upahefednysse   me toforan oþru*m* tealde.
ond þine beboda, driht*en*,   dyde me unwurðe.
ond ic nolde wegan   þine wynsume geoc
ne ðine leohtan byrþene   on minu*m* bæce ferian.
ond ic unwærlice syngode   oft þurh modignysse;

.II. Ic on gyfernysse.   *ond* on oferfylle
ond on druncennysse.   wið þe, drihten, agylt
oft *ond* gelome   on untiman.

CONFESSION AND PRAYER

Lo, thou, Almighty God of unspeakable mercy,
Lo, thou, God of immeasurable grace,
Lo, thou, God, creator and restorer of all mankind,
Thou who dost cleanse from foul sins
The hearts of those who confess to thee, and those who accuse themselves
Within the sight of thy mercy:
You then release them from the bonds of all kinds of unrighteousness.
With all sorrowing, I pray for strength from you,
That you through the abundance of your mercy grant me
That I might perform true confession before you
Concerning all my sins that my conscience now accuses me of,
And that I might do true penance before you
Regarding all of the sins that I have committed
In evil thoughts, and in perverse thinking,
In the consenting to evil and in improper thought,
In unclean desire and in wicked longing,
In idle words and in evil deeds.

I sinned in sight, and strongly in hearing,
Likewise in taste, in smell, and in touching.
You, dear Lord, shaped all my limbs
For human uses, measured and proper,
But, wretched, I twisted them to devilish works
And befouled them with sins and forsook you, Lord.

I I often greatly failed in pride
And through arrogance counted myself before others,
And made myself unworthy of your commands, Lord,
And I would not bear your joyful yoke,
Nor your light burden carry on my back,
And I sinned, heedless, often through pride.

II I often in gluttony and in over-eating
And in drunkenness, against you, Lord, sinned,
Often and repeatedly and at improper times.

.III. Ic eac earming   ofer ælcum gemete
on fulum forligre   *ond* on fracodre galnysse
\me sylfne/ befylde   ge on sawle ge on lichaman.

.IIII. Ic on gitsunge   mid gitsigendum mode
swiðe oft agylte.   *ond* beswac oðre
æt heora æhtu*m*   þurh þa unrihtwisan gitsunge.
ond ic unriht oft spræc   arleaslice.
ond riht forsuwode   þurh þone sylfan leahter:~

.V. Ic þurh weamodnysse   worhte fela yfela
ond þurh manslihtas   me scyldigne dyde
wið þe, min hælend,   þa þa ic þin handgeweorc
unwyrcan dorste.   *ond* deaðe betæcan.
nu synd mine handa   þurh þone hefian gylt
mid manna blodum   þe ic þurh gebeot oft
ond þurh hatheor\t/nysse   her on life ageat
yfele befylede.   *ond* fæste gebundene
swaru*m* gyltum   þurh þa sylfan weamodnysse;

.VI. Ic on unrotnysse   oft eac agylte
ond swiðor ceorude   þonne min sawul behofode
þa ðe ic æhta forleas.   oððe leofne freond
oððe me hwæt mislamp   on þises lifes ryne.
ond ic þa ongean þe, drihten,   dyrstiglice ceorode
þurh þa unrotnysse   þe is deaðes wyrcend;

VII. I[c] syngode gelome   þurh asolcennysse
þa þa me god ne lyste don   ne gan to godes hus
ne nan ellen niman   to ænigum godan weorce.
ac ic leofode min lif   lange on asolcennysse
butan godum weorcu*m*   *ond* godu*m* biggenge;

.VIII. Ic on \i/delu*m* wuldre   eac swylce agylte
on gylplic\e/re spræce.   *ond* gylpes cepte
ond wolde beon gehered   þeah ðe ic herigendlic nære.
ond on wlence ic ferde   þurh þ*æt* idele wuldor

III I often wretchedly, beyond every measure,
In foul adultery and in filthy lust
Befouled myself, both in soul and in body.

IIII I in covetousness and with a greedy mind
Very often was guilty, and I tricked others
Out of their possessions through that unrighteous greed.
And I often spoke wrong honorlessly
And forsook right, through this same sin.

V Through anger I often wrought many evils
And through murders I made myself guilty
Towards you, my Healer, when your handiwork
I dared to undo, and to share out death.
Now are my hands—through encumbering guilt,
With the blood of men, that I often through boasting
And through anger here in this life spilled—
Evilly befouled, and I am firmly bound
By oppressive guilt through this same anger.

VI In despair, too, I've often been guilty
And complained more greatly than suited my soul,
When I have lost possessions or a dear friend
Or when some mishap came by in the course of this life
And then against you, Lord, I boldly complained
Through the despair that is the maker of death.

VII Often I have sinned through slothfulness
When I wished not to do good, nor go to God's house
Nor to take up any goodwill towards any good work:
But I lived my life long in sloth
Lacking good works and good application.

VIII In vainglory, too, I was often guilty,
In prideful speech, and I held to boasting,
And I wished to be praised, though I was unpraiseworthy
And I walked in pride through that vainglory;

ond manna lyffetunge   ic lufode to swiðe.
ond on menigfealdre glen\c/ge   ic glencged minne lichaman
ond mid sweartum synnum   mine sawle awlætte
ond wolde beon wiðutan swa þeah   wurðlice geþuht;

On eallu*m* þisum heafodleahtrum   ic healice agylte.
ond oðru*m* læssum gyltum   ic gelome syngode.
ond ic eaðe ne mæg   mines gyltes atellan.

Ic bidde swa þeah, driht*en*,   *þæt* hi beon þe geandette
mid soðre behreowsunge.   *ond* þu mine sawle g*e*hæle
fram eallu*m* synnum.   þu ðe eart sawla alysend.

Ðu sealdest us, hælend,   healicne truwan
þurh ezechiel cweþende   þinne soðan witegan
'gif se arleasa deð   soðæ dædbote
be eallum his synnum   þe he ær geworhte.
ond ealle mine   beboda g*e*hylt
ond deð rihtwisnysse.   *ond* demð rihtlice
he leofað his life.   *ond* he nane swylt.
ond ic ne gemune   ealra his mandæda.
ac he leofað on his rih\t/wisnysse   þe he sylf geworhte;'

Eac þu sylf, driht*en*,   sædest on þinu*m* godspelle.
þæt mare bliss   bið on heofenum
be anum synfullan men   gif he gecyrð to þe.
þonne be nigon ond hundnigantigan   þe nanre dædbote ne behofiað;

Underfoh me, nu, drihten,   for þinre mildheortnysse.
ond aþweah me   þurh þæs halgan gastes gife
fram eallum minum synnum   *ond* sele me staþolfæste heortan
þæt ic ælc yfel onscunige.   *ond* ælce unrihtwisnysse.
ond ic þine bebodu lufige.   *ond* þe, leofa driht*en*;

Ne læt þu me æfre bugan   to þam ærran leahtru*m*
þe ic receleas gefremode   fullice foroft
ac geedstaðela on me   þu arfæstosta hælend
swa hwæt swa ic amyrde   þurh manfulle dæda.

And the flattery of men, I loved too greatly
And with many bright things, my body I adorned
And with dark sins defiled my soul
And wished outwardly still to be held to be worthy.

In all these capital sins I was highly corrupt,
And through other, lesser faults, I frequently sinned
And I may not with ease count up my failings.

I pray you, therefore, Lord, that they be confessed
With true repentance, and that you should heal my soul
From all sins, you who are the redeemer of souls.

You granted us, Lord, a lofty pledge,
Saying through Ezekiel, your true prophet,
'If the wicked man does true penance
Regarding all his sins that he previously wrought,
And holds all of my commands
And works in righteousness and passes judgment righteously
He shall live his life and he shall not die,
And I shall not consider any of his crimes,
But he shall live in the righteousness that he himself has wrought.'

Also you, yourself, God, said in your gospel
That greater happiness shall be in the heavens,
Over one sinful man, if he turns to you,
Than for nine and ninety that should need no penance.

Receive me, now, Lord, for your mercy
And cleanse me through the holy spirit's gift
From all my sins, and grant me a steadfast heart
That I might shun each evil, and each unrighteousness,
And that I may love your decrees and you, dear Lord.

Let me never sink down to the earlier sins
That I reckless wrought, foully and often;
But rather establish in me, most grace-full Savior,
Just what I destroyed through my wrongful deeds.

Gescylde me, drihten,   wið þone swicolan deofol
þæt he me earmne   eft ne beswice
for þan þe min tyddernys   ne mæg him wiðstandan
butan þu, leofa hælend,   onlihte mine heortan
ond mid þinre mihtigan handa   me geheald wið hine;

Ðu miht eall *þæt* þu wylt   swa swa ælmihtig god.
ond þu naht ne swincst   þeah þu gescylde us
heald me for þig leofa   to lofe þinum naman
þæt ic on godum weorcum   wunian mote
oð mines lifes ende   mid soðu*m* geleafan;

Ic bidde þe nu, hælend,   *þæt* þu gehæle mine sawle
þæt ic dælnimend beo   on þam forman æriste
swa *þæt* min sawul   of synnu*m* nu arise
þæt heo þe orsorhre   on þam oþrum æriste
lichamlice arise   to þa*m* ecan life.

Syle me nu, scyppend,   gesælig geþanc.
ond þa halgan mihte   þe men þurh geþeoð
geleafan *ond* hiht   *ond* halige lufe
modes snoternysse.   *ond* mihtig geþyld.
gemetegunge. *ond* anrædnysse   rihtwisnysse. *ond* mildheortnysse.
clænnysse. *ond* cystignysse.   sibbe *ond* arfæstnysse.
soðfæstnysse *ond* welwillendnysse   wuldres drihten.
ond syle me forgifennysse   ealra min\r/a synna
ond þæ\t/ ece lif   æfter þisum lænan \life/;

Hælend crist gehyr þas word   þu ðe leofast *ond* rixast
mid þa*m* ælmihtigan fæder   *ond* þam halgan gaste
butan anginne   *ond* ende. A M E N:~

Man mot hine gebiddan   swa swa he mæg *ond* can
mid ælcum gereorde.   *ond* on ælcere stowe.
Nu is her on englisc   andetnyss *ond* gebed.
Ac se þe þis singan wylle,   ne secge he na mare
on þære andetnysse   þonne \he/ wyrcende wæs,
for þan ðe ure hælend nele   *þæt* man on hine sylfne leoge.
ne eac ealle menn   on ane wisan ne syngiað:~

Shield me, Lord, from the treacherous devil
That he may never betray me, wretch as I am,
Because my frailty may not stand against him
Unless you, dear Lord, should enlighten my heart
And with your mighty hands hold me from him.

You might do all that you wish, as Almighty God,
And you toil not at all though you shield us:
Hold me, for love of you, to the praise of your name
That I may dwell in good works
Until the end of my life with true belief.

I bid you now, Savior, that you might heal my soul,
That I may be participant in the first rising,
So that my soul will now rise up from sins
So that it the more unconcernedly in that other arising
Shall bodily rise to the eternal life.

Give me now, Creator, prosperous thought
And the holy might that men prosper through:
Belief and hope and holy love,
Wisdom of mind and mighty patience,
Moderation and resoluteness, righteousness and mercifulness
Purity and bounty, peace and virtue,
Truthfulness and goodwill, Lord of glory,
And grant me forgiveness of all my sins
And eternal life after this transitory life.

Savior Christ, hear this word, you who shall live and rule
With the Almighty Father and the holy spirit,
Without beginning and end, Amen.

A man must pray for himself, as he may and as he can,
With every voice and in every place.
Now here in English is a confession and prayer,
But he who wishes to sing this, he shall say no more
In the confession than he has committed,
For the Savior wishes not that a man tell lies on himself,
Nor do all men likewise sin in one way.

Commentary: Meter, Structure, Sources, Parallels

It is important to note, when considering this lineation, that the numbered subsections in particular (numbered in the Royal manuscript; identified by rubricated initials usually placed in the margin in Tiberius), can each be seen to feature a whole number of long lines. That is, these half-lines are indeed paired up into long lines in a fashion that appears to be entirely purposeful. That these half-lines and lines are structural elements of the text is confirmed by this repeated and consistent pairing, which would be neither functional nor consistent in prose.

Further, fewer than ten of the 130 lines reconstructed here fail to feature alliteration, and many of those may in fact be allowable exceptions: if *h*-words alliterate with vowels, as sometimes seems to be the case in Ælfrican poems, then alliteration can be seen in lines 5 *heortan/andettað*, 78 *ealle/gehylt*, and 122 *ælmihtigan/halgan*. Somewhat exceptional alliteration on prepositions or pronouns might be hypothesized in lines 71, 88, and 129. Off-rhyme or assonance presumably serves as the link in line 30. Even if none of these is allowed, alliteration in more than ninety percent of observed lines is at least roughly as consistent as can be seen in Ælfric.

Just as tellingly, the instructional passage at the end of the text appears to indicate that the whole prayer is poetic:

> Ac se þe þis singan wylle,   ne secge he na mare
> on þære andetnysse   þonne \he/ wyrcende wæs[13]
>
> [But he who wishes to sing this, he shall say no
> more in the confession than he has committed.]

The very sense of these instructions must be that individual confessors who wish to use this prayer must "sing" only the numbered sections that actully correspond to the sins they intend to confess. Indeed, the whole of the poem may be founded upon an imaginative or figurative paronomastic link between *singan* (to sing) and *syngian* (to sin) that ultimately makes use of and invokes the prayer's poetic form. Given our ability to lineate the prayer, its alliterative effects, and the explicit presence of the verb *singan* there can be little doubt about the poetic nature of the passage.

Finally, the verses and lines thus revealed appear to be perfectly consonant with the description of late Old English verse that I attempted in *Early English Metre*.[14] In that sense, the meter of the passage fits into the norms established by poems such as the *Metrical Psalms* and the alliterative, poetic works of Ælfric as typifying late Old English verse. Specifically, the range of verse types corresponds more closely to Ælfrician forms than to the comparatively classical *Metrical Psalms*; it seems likely that the date of composition for this poem lies in the early eleventh century, not long before it was recorded in the Royal Psalter.

Structurally, the poem falls into four sections. First is a general opening section (lines 1–23) closely translating the opening to Alcuin's "Deus inaestimabilis misericordiae."[15] Then follows a confessional section focused on the eight deadly sins or *heafodleahtras* (lines 24–71); the third section is a series of prayers, ending in "Amen" (lines 72–123). The final section (lines 124–30), which has often been taken as a stand-alone item or else as a preface to the next item in Tiberius A. iii, is a set of instructions indicating to the reader that, in confession, one should recite only those parts of the preceding poetic material that correspond to the sins one has wrought.

Previous editors and commentators have clearly indicated the prayer's debt to Alcuin, and there is no need, I think, to repeat that work here.[16] But the debt to Ælfric is also significant, and some account of it seems desirable. Besides numerous single verses and several full-line parallels between Ælfrician works and *Confessio et Oratio* (*CO*), three passages involve even more substantial parallels. The following three consecutive verses from *CO* are notably Ælfrician in their expression:

> mid soðre behreowsunge. *ond* þu mine sawle gehæle
> fram eallu*m* synnum.[17]
>
> [With true repentance, and that you should heal
> my soul from all sins.]

The phrase *soðre behreowsunge* is typical of Ælfric, appearing (by my count) six times in the *Catholic Homiles*, sixteen times in his poetic works, and in only two other passages in Old English: the Ash Wednesday homily in CCCC 190 and the prayer to the cross in Cotton Galba A. xiv.[18] Other texts generally link *soð* to *hreowsunge* or *hreow*. Note also how closely all three verses parallel the following passage from Ælfric's *Life of St Maur*:

> and mid soðre behreowsunga   heora sawle aþwogon
> fram eallum synnum.[19]
>
> [...and with true repentence washed their souls of all sins.]

The *CO* passage substitutes *gehæle* for Ælfric's verb, giving the line cross-alliteration, which seems to be at least an attempt at poetic improvement.

Further, the opening of the final verse paragraph at the end of *CO* is also very similar to an Ælfrician passage. The *CO* lines read:

> Man mot hine gebiddan   swa swa he mæg *ond* can
> mid ælcum gereorde.   ond on ælcere stowe.[20]

> [A man must pray for himself, as he may and as he can,
> with every voice and in every place.]

Ælfric's passage from *The Prayer of Moses* has a somewhat different effect, although using very similar language:

> Se man mot hine gebiddan   swa swa he mæg and cann
> Forðan þe se ælmihtiga god cann   ælc gereorde tocnawan.
> and on ælcere stowe   man mot mærsian his drihten.[21]

> [A man must pray for himself, as he may and as he can,
> because the Almighty God can know every voice, and in every
> place man might glorify his Lord.]

The third parallel passage is even more revealing. Here, in lines 74–82, the *CO* poet references a passage from Ezekiel:

> Ðu sealdest us, hælend,   healicne truwan
> þurh ezechiel cweþende   þine soðan witegan
> "gif se arleasa deð   soðæ dædbote
> be eallum his synnum   þe he ær geworhte.
> ond ealle mine   beboda gehylt
> ond deð rihtwisnysse.   ond demð rihtwislice
> he leofað his life.   ond he nane swylt.
> ond ic ne gemune   ealra his mandæda.
> ac he leofað on his rih\t/wisnysse   þe he sylf geworhte;"[22]

> [You granted us, Lord, a lofty pledge, saying through Ezekiel,
> your true prophet, "If the wicked man does true penance
> regarding all his sins that he previously wrought, and holds
> all of my commands and works in righteousness and passes
> judgment righteously, he shall live his life and he shall not die,
> and I shall not consider any of his crimes, but he shall live in the
> righteousness that he himself has wrought."]

Remarkably, this passage appears to be a versified version of what can be seen in the prose portion of Ælfric's Ash Wednesday homily, printed by Skeat as follows:

> Eft cwæð se ælmihtiga god. Gif se arleasa and se synfulla wyrcð dædbote ealra his synna. and hylt mine beboda. and rihtwysnysse begæð. he lifað and ne swylt na yfelu*m* deaðe. and ic ne gemune nanre his synna þe he gefremode."[23]
>
> [Then spoke the Almighty God: "If the wicked and the sinful does penance for all of his sins and holds my commands and engages in righteousness, he shall live and die no evil death, and I shall not consider any of the sins that he committed."]

Note that Ælfric does not identify Ezekiel as the source for the passage, suggesting either that the *CO* poet was working from an annotated manuscript, or simply recognized the source of the passage on his (or her) own.

These three passages together suggest that the *CO* poet had a notable familiarity with the *Lives of Saints* collection; it is at least possible that the choice of late Old English verse was perhaps inspired by Ælfric's example. The versification of the Ash Wednesday passage must either be attributed to the *CO* author, or it might suggest the hypothesis that Ælfric himself revised the Ash Wednesday material into a fully poetic rendering that no longer survives. It seems unlikely that the *CO* author is Ælfric himself: in his own lists of *heafodhleahtras*, Ælfric apparently prefers the term *modignysse* to *ofermette* for pride.[24]

What I have done here, of course, has been merely to begin the work of understanding this poem and its place within the Old English poetic corpus. Much good work, I think, remains to be done. But crucially, such work must begin with an understanding of what Old English metrical study can accomplish. In particular, it requires that we recognize that we must identify poems such as this one *before* we can even begin to worry about what sort of metrical rules their poets had in mind. I strongly suspect that other examples of late Old English verse remain to be identified: in this sense, it may be the case that the study of Old English meter now has more to contribute to our understanding of Old English literary culture than ever before.

NOTES

[1] The Royal Psalter is London, British Library, MS Royal 2. B. v. Part of the research for this chapter was completed with the aid of a research grant from the West Virginia University Faculty Senate in 2012.

[2] *The Anglo-Saxon Minor Poems*. Ed. E. V. K. Dobbie, *The Anglo-Saxon Poetic Records* 6 (New York: Columbia University Press, 1942); Mechthild Gretsch, *The Intellectual Foundations of the English Benedictine Reform* (Cambridge: Cambridge University Press, 1999).

[3] I print the poem under this title below, and I abbreviate the title as *CO*. This poem is recorded in what N. R. Ker, *A Catalogue of Manuscripts Containing Anglo-Saxon* (Oxford: Clarendon, 1957), p. 320 identifies as "a fine upright hand of the kind written at Christ Church" in the first quarter of the eleventh century, on fols. 197r–198r. The text also appears, with some mostly minor differences, in London, British Library, Cotton Tiberius A. iii, fols. 44r–45v, written near the middle of the eleventh century.

[4] Consider the following (late Old English) scansions:

Selre byð oft feðre	þænne oferfeðre
xxx/SSx	xx/SxSx
Clipiendra gehwylc	wolde *þæt* him man oncwæde
SSx/(x)S	Sx/(xxxx)Sx.

Note that if classical scansions were attempted, *ofer-* would undergo resolution, and both halves of the first proverb here would be Type C, and the whole line would feature cross alliteration. The second proverb would easily scan as Type E followed by Type A, though still with unusual alliteration on the last stress of the line.

[5] The *Durham Proverbs* have been printed recently in Richard Marsden, *The Cambridge Old English Reader* (Cambridge: Cambrige University Press, 2004), pp. 302–9, though all are there treated as prose; these two are Marsden's numbers 37 and 39. A striking number of the items in the collection, however, can be scanned as late Old English verse.

[6] Most of the passage has previously been printed (as prose) in H. Logeman, "Anglo-Saxonica Minora," *Anglia* 11 (1889): 97–120, and Phillip Pulsiano and Joseph McGowan, "Four Unedited Prayers in London, British Library MS Cotton Tiberius A.iii," *Mediaeval Studies* 56 (1994): 189–216. Note, however, that neither Logeman nor Pulsiano and McGowan print the final paragraph as part of this prayer. In their useful and precise footnote 4, Pulsiano and McGowan trace the history of the treatment of this paragraph as a "brief introduction" to the following prayer in Tiberius A. iii. The page layout in Tiberius A. iii is ambiguous on the issue, however, and the ensuing Tiberius prayer is preserved without the instructions paragraph in Oxford, Bodleian Library, MS Laud Misc. 482. In short, only in Tiberius A. iii. is the instructional paragraph placed ambiguously in between *Confessio et Oratio* and the following prose prayer; in Royal 2. B. v, it accompanies *Confessio et Oratio* unambiguously, just as the prose prayer appears in Laud Misc. 482 without it. There is no reason not to conclude that the instructions paragraph properly stands as part of *Confessio et Oratio*.

[7] Perhaps this is the place to note that, when I was first trying seriously to learn about Old English meter, it was Rick Russom's *Old English Meter and Linguistic Theory* (Cambridge: Cambridge University Press, 1987) that I found most useful. Despite its reliance on the database provided by *Beowulf* alone, that book did more to clarify for me the logic of Old English meter, and to demonstrate how a useful theory of meter must have an explanatory power, than any other book.

[8] Hopkins is cited in Roman Jakobson, "Linguistics and Poetics," in *Language and Literature*, eds. Krystyna Pomorska and Stephen Rudy (Cambridge, MA: Harvard University Press, 1987), pp. 62–94. The Hopkins material is found at p. 72.

[9] Ælfric of Eynsham. *Lives of Saints*. Ed. W. W. Skeat. Early English Text Society o.s. 76, 82, 94, and 114 (London: Oxford University Press, 1881–1900).

[10] The punctuation used for the Old English text is from the manuscript, with the addition of quotation marks around ll. 77–93. I use light modern English punctuation in the translation. There are occasional variances as a result.

[11] Although Pulsiano and McGowan report *spæcce* here, the correct reading seems to be *swæcce*, although the letter in question is ambiguously formed. Tiberius has *spræce*.

[12] The Roman numeral here is in the middle of the line of text, but II through VI are in the right-hand margin of the text, VII and VIII in the left-hand margin of their respective lines.

[13] *CO*, ll. 127–28.

[14] Thomas A. Bredehoft, *Early English Metre* (Toronto: University of Toronto Press, 2005).

[15] A recent edition of this Alcuinian prayer can be found in Jonathan Black, "Psalm Uses in Carolingian Prayerbooks: Alcuin's *Confessio Peccatorum Pura* and the Seven Penitential Psalms (Use 1)," *Mediaeval Studies* 65 (2003): 1–56.

[16] See both Logeman and Pulsiano and McGowan. There is no reason, I think, to associate any of the Old English material with Alcuin himself, but it is notable that *CO* begins by translating a passage from this important Anglo-Carolingian Latinist.

[17] *CO*, ll. 72–73a.

[18] I have not checked all these references against the printed texts, but rather cite them directly from the DOE online corpus: see *-soð-* / *-soþ-* followed by *-behreow-* / *-hreow-*.

[19] Ælfric, *Lives of Saints* VI (Maur), ll. 340–41a.

[20] *CO*, ll. 124–25.

[21] Ælfric, *Lives of Saints* XIII (Prayer of Moses), ll. 64–66.

[22] *CO*, ll. 75–82.

[23] Ælfric, *Lives of Saints* XII (Ash Wednesday), ll. 153–57.

[24] See Ælfric, *Lives of Saints* XVI (Memory of the Saints), l. 307; Ælfric, *Homilies of Ælfric: A Supplementary Collection*, ed. John C. Pope, Early English Text Society o.s. 259–60 (London: Oxford University Press, 1967–1968), IV (*Dominica III in Quadragesima*), l. 251; and in a prose passage in Ælfric, *Homilies of Ælfric* XIX (*De Doctrina Apostolica*), l. 127.

Alliterative Meter after 1450: *The Vision of William Banastre*

Eric Weiskott
Boston College

NEW INDEX OF MIDDLE English Verse (*NIMEV*) 1967.8 is a verse prophecy extant in two fifteenth- and sixteenth-century manuscripts.[1] The *Vision of William Banastre*, as I title it, has received no critical attention and has never been edited. The poem combines the tradition of vatic, anti-Saxon prophecy inherited from Geoffrey of Monmouth's *Historia regum Brittaniae* (ca. 1138) with oblique references to early fourteenth- and mid-fifteenth-century politics. The work offers at least one first-rate literary effect, an extended simile comparing a hopeless siege to sailing upwind with no rudder (ll. 7–9). The organization of prophetic language into an interview with God, conducted by Sir William Banastre, has its own pleasures. The *Vision* furnishes important evidence of the circulation of alliterative verse and the development of alliterative meter in the sparsely documented period after 1450. The meter of the *Vision* also testifies to the continuity of the alliterative tradition across the Old English/Middle English divide, a hypothesis which the honorand of this volume has supported from the perspective of his word-foot theory of alliterative meter. In what follows I introduce the manuscript texts of the *Vision*, present a critical edition of the poem with textual notes, and contextualize the metrical form of the poem in terms of the durable poetic tradition to which it belongs.

The *Vision* occurs in Oxford, Bodleian Library, MS Hatton 56 (late fifteenth c.), fols. 37br–8v (henceforth **H**), and Oxford, Bodleian Library, MS Rawlinson C.813 (early and mid-sixteenth c.), fols. 142v–44v (henceforth **R**).[2] **H** is a large collection of prophecies in Latin and English. Its contents include a vision ascribed to Thomas Becket (Latin), "the proficie of Sybyll & Merlyn" (English), "prophetia s. Edwardi confessoris" (Latin), a vision ascribed to Hildegard of Bingen (Latin), and a prophecy attributed to Bede (English). Probable references in the *Vision* to events of the 1460s and early 1470s, if accepted, would set a more precise terminus post quem for the production of **H**, previously dated to ca. 1450 on historical and paleographical grounds. **R** is composed of two originally distinct compilations. The first compilation (fols. 1–98, early sixteenth c.) contains lyrics, verse prophecies, and other items in English; it is well-studied and has been edited in full as the "Welles Anthology."[3] The *Vision* appears in the second compilation (fols. 103–67, mid-sixteenth c.), which contains a number of prose and verse prophecies in English and is relatively neglected. To judge from the binding, the two compilations were bound together in the seventeenth century, presumably with the intention of producing a compendium of English prophecies.

In **H**, the text of the *Vision* is written in a single column in an unbeautiful secretary hand with Anglicana elements. In **R**, the text of the poem is laid out as prose and written in secretary hand, with a change of ink and handwriting after verse 85a. Prose format for verse remained an (increasingly uncommon) option in fifteenth- and sixteenth-century English book production, and it was historically associated with the alliterative meter.[4] The *Vision* carries the same title in both manuscripts: the title appears in English in **H** as "Part of þe visioun of Sire William Banastre knyght" and in Latin in **R** as "Pars visionis domini Willielmi Banistre milytis." This title is conceivably attributable to the poet. There is no indication, however, that the received text belongs to a longer sequence on the same theme. The **R** text of the poem is not noted at *NIMEV* 1967.8.

The spelling of the extant texts strongly suggests that the *Vision* circulated in northern copies. Characteristic forms include *als* "as," *atover* "all over," *ga* "go" (infinitive), *hase* "has," *kepis* "keep" (pl. indicative), *mykel* "much," *the tane* "the one (of the two)," *þeym* "them," *til* "to" (prep.), *trei* "three," and *wate* "wet." **R** includes northern dialectal features not found in **H**, for example, *bludy* for 12a *blody*. The provenance of **H** and **R** is unknown, however, and northern spellings alternate with southern or standard forms such as *as* "as," *gedir* "gather," *hath* "has," *thre* "three," and *to* "to" (prep.). The spellings *wȝan* "when" (*wgan* in **H**) and *wirke* "make, work" are rare overall in the anchor texts of *A Linguistic Atlas of Late Mediaeval English* (*LALME*).

The provenance of the poem itself is difficult to determine. Certain items of vocabulary and details of phonology are characteristic of northern dialects, for example, *bus* "must" (impersonal auxiliary) <OE *bihofian*, *gar* "make" (auxiliary) <ON *gera*, *mon* "shall" <ON *munu*, and *trei* "three" alliterates *tr-*. However, alliterative poetry had always been composed in a literary standard or *koiné* that combined features of multiple spoken dialects. The rare verb *spritte* "leap" <ON *spretta*, found elsewhere in Middle

English only in *Sir Gawain and the Green Knight* (l. 2316), is probably an alliterative poetic word that never had appeared, or no longer appeared, in everyday speech in any region. Moreover, the alliterative tradition was increasingly colored northern in literary culture over the course of the fifteenth century. For example, all eight of the unrhymed alliterative poems datable after 1450 have connections to Scotland, whether thematic or geographical.[5] There was thus both motive and opportunity for a southern poet to adorn an alliterative poem with words like *gar* and *mon*. Anti-Saxon rhetoric became fashionable in fifteenth-century prophecy and is no sure indicator of Scottish provenance. The best evidence for northern provenance might be thematic: possible references to Bamburgh and Lesbury, Northumberland (l. 83a), if accepted, would support a Percy family connection.[6]

Like other late medieval English prophecies, the poem is laced with coded allusions to contemporary politics. For example, mention of a king "Wandrand in wild kith [...]/ Amonges þe wild lyons" "wandering in a wild region ... among the wild lions" (ll. 31–32a) who will be "fond as a fawcoun [...]/[...] fleand" "found flying like a falcon" (ll. 33–34a) almost certainly refers to Scotland, from the lions in its royal arms, and Richard, duke of York, from the falcon featured on his heraldic badge. Two allusions may be particularly valuable for dating the poem. First, God foretells an important battle that will take place "by þe Mawdeleyn day" "on Magdalene Day (July 22)" (l. 58). This recalls the Battle of Falkirk, fought on July 22, 1298, in which the English under Edward I defeated the Scots under William Wallace. The prediction may refer more proximally to the Battle of Edgecote Moor, July 26, 1469, the first military expression of the rebellion of Richard Neville, earl of Warwick, against Edward IV. Authors of political prophecies were wont to recycle references in this way. Second, God speaks of "a day of satlyng [...]/ A metyng of a mariage" "a day of reconciliation ... An illusion of a marriage" (ll. 88–89a) between the opposing camps in the poem, warning, "Shall neuer your trews last | half ouer fyve wynter" "Your truce will not last much more than five years" (l. 92). The Treaty of Edinburgh—Northampton (1328) ended the First War of Scottish Independence, providing for the marriage of the daughter of Edward III of England to the son of Robert I of Scotland; the truce was to last only five years before the Second War of Scottish Independence broke out. More proximally, in December 1470, Henry VI's son was married to Richard Neville's daughter in order to cement Neville's reversal of loyalty. A tentative *terminus post quem* for the composition of the poem can therefore be fixed at summer 1469 or winter 1470/1471. Before this time, references to "þe Mawdeleyn day" and "A metyng of a mariage" would have had no definite connection with the dynastic conflict in which Richard ("a fawcoun") was embroiled. In any case, the poem cannot have been composed before 1450, when Richard first engaged in a power struggle with Henry VI, and more likely not before 1455, when Richard and the Yorkists first took up arms against Henry and the Lancastrians.

The *Vision* belongs to a long tradition of English political prophecy that begins with the "Prophetie Merlini" in Geoffrey's Latin *Historia* and runs well into the seventeenth century in Latin and the British vernaculars.[7] From the fourteenth century to the sixteenth, political prophecy, Scottish subjects, and alliterative meter increasingly overlap in perception and practice. Textual evidence suggests that the poet made use of at least two earlier verse prophecies, the *Prophecy of the Six Kings* in couplets (late fourteenth to early fifteenth c. across several revisions) and the alliterative *First Scottish Prophecy* (ca. 1450). The so-called "first revised version" of the *Prophecy of the Six Kings* in couplets (early fifteenth c.) appears in **H**.[8] It is difficult to say whether the *Vision* poet knew the original couplet version (last quarter of the fourteenth c.) or the first revised version, since the latter has not been printed. (I have seen both manuscript texts of the so-called "second revised version" of the *Prophecy of the Six Kings* in couplets and can report that this version includes neither of the lines found in the *Vision*.) Use of the *First Scottish Prophecy*, which makes reference to the Jack Cade rebellion of 1450, sets a mid-fifteenth-century *terminus post quem* for the poem, buttressing the late fifteenth-century dating offered above on historical grounds. Direct borrowing from the *First Scottish Prophecy* would fit with the relative popularity of that poem, which survives in roughly twenty manuscript copies and multiple textual states. Finally, the poet's use of punning personification (86b *Bote Hill*) and psychomachia (50a *wrecched Pride* and 51a *lele Loue*) may reflect the influence of *Piers Plowman*, whose closing passus (B 20) portrays the forces of evil, captained by Antichrist and Pride, arrayed against the forces of good.[9] *Lele loue* appears among Anima's many names (B.15.34a; cf. 11.162a, 17.220a, and 17.228a). The kaleidoscopic genre identity of *Piers Plowman*, in turn, includes political prophecy. Indeed, on fol. 140v and immediately before the *Vision* on fols. 142r–v in **R** there occur two heretofore unrecognized freestanding excerpts, each combining the same two prophetic passages from *Piers Plowman*. These excerpts take their place among other, similar uses of *Piers Plowman* as political prophecy in sixteenth-century print and manuscript culture.[10] Other echoes of extant Middle English prophecies in the *Vision* are harder to disentangle from the shared repertoire of symbols, formulae, and allusions from which the prophecies were constructed.

William Banastre (d. 1323), to whom the *Vision* is ascribed, was M.P. for Lancashire; he was reputed as an author of prophecies by the middle of the fourteenth century. Banastre is mentioned in this capacity by Sir Thomas Grey in his Anglo-Norman *Scalacronica* (1362); twice by the author of the *First Scottish Prophecy*; by the author of the popular fifteenth-century political prophecy "The King who will Find the Holy Cross," a copy of which appears in **H**; in another prose prophecy in English found in London, British Library, MS Sloane 2578 (mid-1550s), fols. 35r–37r; by John Leland in his *Collectanea* (ca. 1557) in an epitome of *Scalacronica*; and in the title of the *Whole Prophesie of Scotland, England, & some-part of France, and Denmark, Prophesied bee meruellous Merling, Beid, Bertlingtoun, Thomas Rymour, Waldhaue, Eltraine, Banester, and Sibbilla, all according in one* (first published 1603), which also contains remodeled versions of the *First Scottish Prophecy*, including the allusions to Banastre.[11] Given the conventional use of a canon of prophets to authorize vernacular prophecies, there is no reason to suppose that the *Vision* itself was known to any of these later writers.

The two extant texts of the *Vision* are relatively similar. Variation in this textual tradition was fluid but largely restricted to substitution, rewording, and rearrangement within individual lines of verse, for example, 30b *tynt* beside **R** *killyd*. As a topical vernacular poetic text, the *Vision* was characteristically exposed to textual *mouvance* in transmission. As it happened, however, scribes remade the text within a relatively narrow scope. The text in **H** is the more complete at 116 full alliterative long lines. The text in **R** lacks lines 27 (eyeskip from 27a *William* to 28a *William*), 32 (eyeskip from 32a *wild* back to 31a *wild*), 43–5 (compounded by eyeskip from 44b *yemes* to 46b *yemes*?), and 105 (eyeskip from 104a *And* to 106a *And*, compounded by dittography of l. 106). The text in **R** also lacks most of lines 56–7 and 94–5: in these cases, a scribe has reworked the received text as prose, with sentence structure superseding line structure. Twice, the first hand of **R** copied portions of lines out of order and then cancelled them, jumping from verses 10b to 12b (fol. 142v) and from verses 26a to 28a (fol. 143r). These two instances of eyeskip forward two lines of verse imply that **R**'s exemplar was, like **H**, in verse format.

HR share several evident textual errors: two twice-repeated lines (after l. 105, repeating l. 106; and after l. 111, repeating l. 110), insertion of a grammatically superfluous particle (*he shall* for presumptive *He* at l. 115, consequent on misprision of 115a *mon* "shall" <ON *munu* as "man"), and four other presumptive errors (at 22a *Therwhiles*, 83a *Lesbury*, 83b, and 98b *knowe*). Taken together, these shared errors suggest that **HR** descend from an archetype at some remove from the original. The twice-repeated lines, in which eyeskip occurred at line boundaries, also suggest that the **HR** archetype was laid out as verse, as in **H**, not as prose, as in **R**.

As the earlier of the two extant manuscript witnesses, **H** serves as the copy-text and governs the accidentals of the edited text and title. In the following critical edition, scribal punctuation is omitted, and the caesura between a-verse and b-verse is represented by a tabbed space. Paleographically uncertain or reconstructed readings are enclosed in parentheses. Punctuation is used to clarify ambiguous syntax and to indicate questions, the bounds of speeches, and the ends of larger rhetorical units, but no attempt has been made to make modern sentences of the text. Italics indicate expansion of scribal abbreviations, except that the ampersand is silently expanded to *and*. Capitalization is editorial and follows modern usage, including capitals at the beginning of each line of verse. *Y* for *þ* in abbreviations of particles such as "that" and "the" is printed *þ*. Line-initial *ff* is rendered *F*. Difficult words and phrases are accompanied by glosses, with etymologies where this has been thought useful. In the apparatus, **HR** readings are given in the form of **H**.

The Vision of William Banastre

Part of þ*e* visiou*n* of *Sir*e Will*ia*m Banastre knyght

“Lord, sey me for þe mayden love   that thou þi modir calles
What shall worthe of our kyng   lord, yf it be þi wyll?”
“I shall [þe tel], Will*ia*m   and haue sone done:
Ther shall a kyng prik westward   pr*o*pirly w*ith* pr*i*de
And gedir hym an herd   fast al out of towne   [army <OE ***hired***
And set hym in a seege[12]   til a full sory walle
But þ*at* shall be as nedelese   þ*at* þey seile þedir
Als he þ*at* buskes to a bote   þ*at* broken were þe rother
And þe wynd of þe west   were went hym agayne.
Therwiles shal Albanie bernes   buske out þerag[a]yn
And bende bakward behynde   into Bretayn*e*
And make a blody hervest   in a handwhile
And wirke bataill bi southe   whiles he þ*ere* dwellis
And whan he hers þ*at* word   þan werkis his hert
And shall warry þe sithe   þat eu*er* he was born of modir   [curse <OE ***wirgan***
Þ*at* he ne were depe þ*at* day   dolven vndir erthe
Owther sonken þer   among þe salt stremes.
So shall he greved be he shall grete   w*ith* bothe his eyen   [cry <OE ***gretan***
And he shall remeve his sege   as neu*er* kyng shold
And folow on frekely   to fynd þem in his anger   [scent (hunting)
And he þ*at* he trestis most   [s]hall tray hym sone.[13]
The[r]whiles[14] shal Albanie bernes be away   by þe west bank*es*
And ageyne to þe kith   w*ith*outen care maked
And þus shal worthe of yo*ur* lede[s]   leue þou þe sothe

Part of þe visioun of Sire William Banastre knyght] Pars visionis domini Willielmi Banistre milytis **R** [1] sey] tell **R** þe] thi **R** [2] worthe] beworth **R** [3] þe tel] **R**; tel þe **H** [4] prik] ried **R** [5] an herd] a heard **R** fast al] fall **R** towne] a town **R** [6] in a seege] seg **R** til] to **R** walle] waell **R** [7] þey seile þedir] he shall doe ther [8] were] is **R** rother] rouker **R** [9] were] om. **R** [10] Therwiles] þe wheyll **R** bernes] banneres **R** þeragayn] þe agayne **R**; þer aghyn **H** [11] bende] bynd **R** into] to **R** [13] whiles] whiell **R** [14] þan] þat **R** werkis] workith **R** [15] And] he **R** warry] way **R** sithe] tim **R** modir] his mother **R** [16] ne were] weare **R** þat day] om. **R** dolven] burried **R** erthe] þe earthe **R** [17] Owther] or eles **R** þer] om. **R** [18] he[2]] þat he **R** [20] And] om. **R** frekely] fercly **R** [21] trestis most] trostid most on **R** shall] **R**; sone shall **H** tray] betray **R** sone] sonneste **R** [22] Therwhiles] the whiell **R**; the whiles **H** bernes be] banneres **R** by] to **R** bankes] backe **R** [23] ageyne to þe] agaynste him to **R** maked] make **R** [24] þus shal worthe] this work **R** your] our **R** ledes] lede **H**; lorde **R** leue þou þe] beleve me for **R**

And alle haue I destenyed this   for þe dede of yo*ur* syn*nis*."
"Lord," [said William,][15] "þan were it good   *þat* kyng wer[e] vndir erthe."
"Now maddist þow, Will*iam*   whan þow s[o] me[ll]est."
"Lord," said Will*ia*m, "was neu*er* kyng in care cast   so mykel in a tide
Ne neu*er* holden so high on loft   and so low light."
"Will*ia*m, he shall be tened and takyn   and tynt in his owne
Wandrand in wild kith   where no man hym kennes
Among*es* þe wild lyons   [þ]*at* he hymself ken.
Than aft*er* he shall be fond as a fawcou*n*   feir at þe last
Wele faire fleand into his owne   full bold and full prest   [swift <OF
This I warn þe, Will*ia*m   on world it shall fare
And tell [me] þi[s] good men[16]   *þat* Holy Kirke kepis
And yf þei hold it for fabill   founden in towne   [concocted
It shall be by p*ro*phecy   p*re*ued at þe last.
Thre bugle(s), [William, I þe tell,   blow shall] in Bretayn
By þe last [blaste] haue bl(ow)en   þan shall blis fall
The first *þat* blowe(s) he bydes   in þe northwest;
It shall be wele blakker   þan bylle of a crawe[17]
W*ith* a treity of howles   knyt in þe myddes
And a corbid best   þe corner [þat] yemes.[18]   [crippled <OF *corber*
Trei trenta[ul]es[19]   this athel shall wirke   [trentals (thirty-part masses for the dead)

I shall send hym a kay   a curle[u] *þat* yemes[20]
And bid hym walkand be   in all his wirk*es*
Fro tide of mydnyght   vnto þe mydmorn.

25 And] for **R** haue I] þat I have **R** for þe dede] by caus(e) **R** 26 said William] **R**; om. **H** þat kyng] þat kynge þat kyng **R** were²] **R**; were lorde **H** erthe] the earth **R** 27 Now maddist þow William whan þow so mellest] H (so mellest] semes eldest H); om. **R** 28 cast] om. **R** mykel in a tide] mecke **R** 29 Ne] om. **R** holden] so holden **R** 30 William] Wyllam **R** tened and takyn] takyn tenid **R** tynt] killyd **R** 31 wild kith] the wylde fyld **R** kennes] knowith **R** 32 Amonges þe wild lyons þat he hymself ken] H (þat] for to þat H); om. **R** 33 feir at þe] far att **R** 34 Wele faire] fare **R** into] in **R** full¹] fall **R** and] om. **R** 35 on] in the **R** fare] be faell **R** 36 me þis] **R**; þise **H** good] to 37 And] or **R** fabill] a fable **R** founden in] fownd in a **R** 38 be by] be **R** prophecy] profycied **R** 39 William I þe tell blow shall] R (William] Wyllam R); shall blow I tell þe William **H** 40 last blaste] **R**; last **H** haue] om. **R** þan shall blis fall] blis shall faelle **R** 41 he] om. **R** 42 bylle] the bill **R** 43-5 om. **R** 44 þat] om. **H** 45 trentaules] trent andres **H** 46 hym] to hym **R** curleu] curill **R**; curle **H** þat yemes] with seames **R** 47 walkand be] be wakned **R** wirkes] other workis **R** 48 tide] þe tied **R** mydmorn] mydmorrowe **R**

On þe morn he shall do   þ*at* fey vpou*n* feld   [livestock <OE *feoh*
But wrecched Pride hath won þe day   and þ*at* hym likes
And þ*ere* shall lele Loue   be laught all out of lyue.
Þan at a brigge ende   mon þe bale fall
Þ*at* myracles in Holy Kirke   know shall sone aft*er*."   [reveal
"Ye whan [þat day shall] fa[l]le, lord,   for þi modir loue þ*ou* me te(ll)."
"Nou maddest þ*ou*, Will*ia*m   whan þou so mellest.
Waite a wate som*er*   and a wyndy hervest
A wakand wynt*er*   w*ith* many wery knyght*es*
And aft*er* by þe Mawdeleyn day   þan shall blode ren."[21]
"Now is mekyll wondir   lord, of thise word*es*."
"Yit it is more wondir, Will*ia*m   to tell þe þe sothe
To se a femal[22] fel   þe floure of Breteyn
And make a bro[del] to be kyng   þe kith for to kepe.   [scoundrel
This tyme shall be w*ith* care   and c[o]myng of knyght*es*
Be wele wa[l]kand aboute   and wandrynge of sorowe[23]
Bold bachelers shall be   and neithir set be othir.
The tane shall seke southward   w*ith* sore hert geven*e*
The othir ho*m*ward to her kith   w*ith* mekyll care maked
But þer shall brest a bugle   and blow in þe southwest
And whan þat bugil shall brest   so mekill blis comes
And he shall raise a ban*er*   þ*at* neu*er* none ere liftid
W*ith* þe lepard on loft   a labell atover   [band on a coat of arms (heraldry); all over
And shall bryng þe helme hangand   on þe left half[24]
The Spenc*er* shall sp[r]itte bifore   (þ)*e* ma[rshalle] shall aft*er* folowe   [leap <ON *spretta*

49 fey] fare **R**   vpoun] vpon a **R**   50 hath won þe] fordoth þat **R**   51 Loue] leue **R**   laught] laste **R**   lyue] om. **R**   52 Þan at a] om. **R**   brigge] brygges **R**   mon] muste **R**   53 Kirke] churche **R**   know] knowyth **R**   54 Ye] om. **R**   þat day shall] **R**; shall þat day **H**   falle] be faell **R**; faile **H**   lord] om. **R**   loue] lore **R**   þou] þat **R**   55 þou William] wan **R**   mellest] medleste **R**   56 Waite a wate somer and a wyndy hervest] watt a **R**   57 A wakand wynter with many wery knyghtes] knyght **R**   58 þe] om. **R**   þan shall blode] blod shall **R**   59 is] itt is **R**   60 þe²] for **R**   62 brodel] broble **H**; child **R**   kyng] a kynge **R**   63 This tyme] þe tim said **R**   comyng] ceming **H**; lovyng **R**   64 Be] with **R**   walkand] **R**; wakand **H**   65 shall be] þer shalbe þat **R**   66 tane] on **R**   seke southward] vntro **R**   sore] suare **R**   67 her kith] them right **R**   maked] mad kynge **R**   68 brest] brast out **R**   bugle] bugley **R**   69 shall brest] is blowen **R**   so mekill] som kynd of **R**   comes] doth com **R**   70 ere liftid] such was lysed **R**   71 þe] a **R**   atover] ther over **R**   73 spritte] prit **R**; spitte **H**   marshalle] **R**; ma **H**   after] after and **R**

The Mortymer for all his (m)ede wend shall out of lyue[25]
And þen flees þe broll (w*ith*) care and w*ith* sorowe [wretch
Þan is þe Bretons blode full proude and pilles þeym aft*er*
Sodenly þei shull be sought at home in þeir owne
That in a fox den þeir fare shall be founden*e*
And eu*er* as þei ar take tyne þ[ei] shall þeir hed*es*
Shal neither ga for þeym gold ne silu*er* [ransom
And þus mon worthe þe lede leve þ*ou* þe sothe.
Your kyng shall ryn to þe eldest burgh þat eu*er* was biggid
That is by [L]esbury and Bannbury on [...] is a toun[26]
And þare sike on his sides shal ly w*ith* [mekyll] care makid
And þan at þe first shall b[u]st [out] of [h]ar[ne]s [armor <OF
Bale Hill shall be bifore but þan is Bote Hill come[27] [remedy <OE *bot*
And þan bitwene yo*ur* ledes shall a laike fall [encounter <ON *leikr*
And set a day of satlyng al so myght it betyde [reconciliation
A metyng of [a] mariage and it myght mend þeir hert [illusion
But w[ȝ]an al ys touched and tumbled to þe ende
Þan shall it be but a glosyng for gold and for silu*er*
Shall neu*er* yo*ur* trews last half ou*er* fyve wynter
Ar blody sides be makid and speres be spend. [wielded
The lyou*n* has losed al þ*at* he laught hase
And geven þe lepard þe rees for hym bus raike ou*er* [he must go <ON *reika*
XXI wynt*er* w*ith* lawté and w*ith* loue
Aft*er* he shall Scotland kepe for skelpyng of sorowe [scourging

[74] mede] made **R** wend] on **R** lyue] lynne **R** [75] flees] followeth **R** broll] child **R** [76] Þan] that **R** Bretons blode] Brettayn of blude **R** pilles] puttes **R** þeym] him **R** [77] sought] senne **R** [78] a] þe **R** fare] feare **R** [79] take] takine **R** tyne] losse **R** þei[2]] **R**; þat **H** [80] Shal] the shall not be savid **R** ga for þeym] om. **R** gold ne] for golde nor **R** [81] þus mon] on this maner **R** þe[1]] of youre leve] belev **R** þe[2]] for **R** [82] biggid] made **R** [83] transposed with 84 **R** [83] Lesbury] Landesbury **H**; Lanseburg **R** [84] sides] sydde **R** ly with] by worth **R** mekyll] **R**; om. **H** care makid] woo **R** [85] bust out of harnes] **R**; best of a barons **H** [86] come] comen **R** [87] a] om. **R** [88] satlyng] setting **R** al so] yf **R** it] om. **R** [89] a] **R**; om. **H** and] yf **R** myght] om. **R** þeir hert] therwyth **R** [90] wȝan] wgan **H**; when **R** touched and tumbled] tombled and touched **R** [91] Þan shall it] it shal **R** [92] Shall neuer] om. **R** trews] truse shall not ouer] on **R** wynter] wyke **R** [93] be spend] espended **R** [94] losed al þat he laught hase] om. **R** [95] And geven þe lepard þe rees for hym bus raike] om. **R** [96] XXI wynter] on and twenty **R** lawté] lewter **R** [97] for] from **R**

Sithen he shall turn þe name of Albanye know[e][28] [generation <OE *cneo*
And of Scotland*e* w*ith* skyll*e* þ*at* skelped*de* was eu*er* [scorned
And call it Breteyn ageyn; it was a pece out geven
Partid in a mariage for movyng of sorowe. [removal
This worshipfull kyng in his myght by craft of hy*m*self
He shall manrede make to þe mekull kyng of heven [homage <OE *manræden*
And all holy of hym hold þat he has
And Holy Kirke he shall gar rise þ*at* low doun is fall
And make ilk lodesman for to loue oþ*ir*
W*ith* hert so free as it were his brothir
Þan [shall he] southward seke [þe beneson of heauen]
And whet his toskes boldly on Paris [g]a[t]es[29]
Þat no best dare hym abide ne bird on tre light
And m*er*veyles worke as he in gate walkes
For threten kyng*es* shal doute his dome vpon benke [throne <ON *bekkr*
And holly of hym hold þ*at* þei in londe haves;
Þe crois and þe holy kith shall he rule aft*er*;
[He] poysened m[o]n be as he a[t] bord sitt*es*
And w*ith* [þe] thre kyng*es* of Coleyn[30] [be] cast in þe middis." [Cologne

[98] Sithen] syth **R** Albanye] Albyoun **R** knowe] knowen **H**; kwo(n)en **R** [100] call] cause **R** out] om. **R** [101] movyng] mourning **R** [102] worshipfull] om. **R** myght] ryght **R** of] of of **R** [103] manrede make] morne in his mocke **R** mekull] myld **R** [104] of] on **R** [105] om. **R** after 105 and ilk loueliche man loue shall othir **HR** (ilk] eke a **R** loueliche] lowe leage **R** loue] loue þei **R**) [106] ilk] ike a **R** for to] to **R** [107] it] he **R** [108] shall he] he shall **H**; shall þe **R** þe beneson of heauen] **R**; with besynes **H** [109] on] vpon **R** gates] **R**; walles **H** [111] merveyles] meruelouse **R** gate] gret **R** after 111 þat no best dare hym abide ne bird on tre sit **HR** (bird] stir nor **R**) [112] doute] beat **R** dome] denne **R** benke] a banke **R** [113] of] on **R** þei in] in þe **R** [114] kith] kirk **R** rule] om. **R** [115] He] he shall **HR** mon] man HR as] at **R** at] **R**; at þe **H** [116] And] om. **R** þe] **R**; om. **H** be] **R**; om. **H**

Having suggested a post-1450 date for the *Vision* on historical and textual grounds, I turn now to consider its metrical form. The *Vision* is in the variety of alliterative meter characteristic of the last phase of the alliterative tradition, before its disappearance from the active repertoire of verse forms around 1550. Recent developments in the study of alliterative meter can serve to contextualize the poetic form of the *Vision*; the meter of the *Vision*, in turn, can clarify and consolidate progress in Middle English alliterative metrics. In what follows, I summarize the consensus view of Middle English alliterative meter, compare it to the meter of the *Vision*, and point to one avenue for future research. I conclude by addressing the position of alliterative verse in late medieval literary culture more broadly.

Recent studies have gone some way toward solving the riddle of Middle English alliterative meter, while at the same time uncovering evidence of continuity between Old English meter, Early Middle English alliterative meter, and Middle English alliterative meter.[31] The new metrical scholarship refocuses questions of literary history, poetics, and the cultural meaning of meter. In particular, the alliterative tradition appears to have been both more durable and more dynamic than proponents of a so-called Alliterative Revival supposed. These recent studies have focused on the late fourteenth and early fifteenth centuries, the period to which most of the extant Middle English alliterative poems can be referred. Alliterative meter after 1450 remains less well understood. Yet if the conclusions of this recent scholarship hold, late alliterative poems like the *Vision* belong to the same centuries-long trajectory of formal development that links *Beowulf* (?eighth/tenth c.) to Lawman's *Brut* (ca. 1200) and the *Brut* to *Sir Gawain and the Green Knight* (late fourteenth c.).

Geoffrey Russom has been a pioneer on the question of continuity in the alliterative tradition. His important essay, "The Evolution of Middle English Alliterative Meter," coordinates his word-foot theory of Old English meter with Thomas Cable's rules for the Middle English b-verse in order to plot a developmental trajectory for alliterative meter. This essay appeared four years before Nicolay Yakovlev's Oxford dissertation, which makes the same demonstration from different theoretical principles, and five years before a review essay in which Cable stated that "[t]here had to have been some kind of evolutionary process" connecting Old English verse to Middle English alliterative verse.[32] Russom further developed the thesis of continuity in two essays on the Middle English a-verse.[33] The ramifications of this new research paradigm extend backward from the fourteenth and fifteenth centuries as well as forward from the ninth and tenth. The work of Cable, Russom, Yakovlev, and others indicates the importance of pursuing the development of alliterative meter and the alliterative tradition across the traditional linguistic/political period boundary of the Norman Conquest. Indeed, this work has begun to suggest the incoherence of the received period terms "Old English" and "Middle English" as such. The meter of the *Vision* focuses attention on the last phase of the alliterative tradition, but Old English language and meter remain relevant as reference points in the deep history of form and phonology. As I will show, Old English etymologies and metrical contours exert historical pressure on the scansion of the *Vision*.

As is to be expected in a rapidly expanding research area, specialists disagree about many details of the emergent metrical model as well as the broader ramifications for literary history. Two proposals, however, enjoy critical consensus. Both concern the b-verse or second half of the Middle English alliterative long line, which is more tightly constrained than the a-verse or first half. First, the b-verse must have exactly two lifts or metrically stressed syllables and exactly one long dip or sequence of two or more metrically unstressed syllables. The long dip may occur before or between the two lifts but not after them. When presenting their independent discoveries in the late 1980s and early 1990s, Cable and Hoyt Duggan agreed on these basic requirements but disagreed about the end of the line: Cable argued that a short dip was obligatory there, while Duggan argued that it was optional.[34] For Cable, then, the acceptable b-verse patterns are (x) Sx...xSx and x...xS(x)Sx, while for Duggan they are (x)Sx...xS(x) and x...xS(x)S(x), where S represents a lift and x represents an unstressed syllable in a dip. Cable and Duggan's disagreement about meter also involved a disagreement about metrical phonology, in particular the availability of historically justified final *-e* in alliterative meter. Though it concerns a seemingly minor detail, the question of the final short dip and historical *-e* turns out to have far-reaching implications for understanding of the Middle English alliterative meter, its relationship to pre-1300 incarnations of alliterative meter, and the position of the Middle English alliterative corpus in literary history. While differing over the scansion of historical *-e*, Cable and Duggan nonetheless agreed that a long history of metrical practice lay behind the fourteenth-century corpus.

The second point of consensus concerns phonology. As shown in greatest detail by Yakovlev, in fourteenth-century alliterative meter medial and final short dips (as in x...xSxSx) normally consist of schwa or word-final /i/.[35] Some qualification is needed in this case, since clear exceptions to Yakovlev's so-called non-schwa principle do occur in the extant corpus. Yakovlev found virtually no exceptions in the final short dip (<0.1% of verses in a large sample corpus) but a minority of convincing exceptions in the medial short dip. Many of the exceptions involve separate words in the medial short dip, for example, *Gawain* 2433b *I schal se hit ofte* (xxSxSx). The non-schwa principle thus appears to be an example of an incomplete systematization of meter, at least in the medial short dip. Fourteenth-century poets normally filled medial and final short dips with schwa and word-final /i/, but in the history of verse form the non-schwa principle came to constitute a criterion of metricality in the final short dip but less so (or not at all) in the medial short dip.

In order to scan Middle English alliterative verse, one needs a way to map words onto lifts and dips. Metrists generally attribute the stress assignment of alliterative poetry to grammatical category membership. A broad distinction obtains between function words (articles, prepositions, pronouns, etc.), which typically do not receive metrical stress, and content words (nouns, adjectives, lexical adverbs, etc.), which typically do. On this point Cable and Duggan concur.[36] Here, too, there are significant literary-historical implications to be drawn out. The prosodic hierarchy used in Middle English alliterative poetry would have seemed very artificial by the late fourteenth century in comparison to the phrasal and rhythmically conditioned stress assignment used in syllabic meters, as in the opening line of Chaucer's *Canterbury Tales* (metrically stressed function words underlined): *Whán that Áprille wíth his shóures sóote*. Here the function words *Whan* and *with* receive metrical stress due to their position beside prosodically lighter words and the expectation of an alternating (iambic) rhythm; such effects of metrical promotion do not occur in the same way in alliterative verse. Despite the growing artificiality of the prosodic hierarchy, Old English poetry and Early Middle English alliterative poetry relied on the same broad distinction between function words and content words. Thus the prosodic hierarchy of fourteenth-century alliterative poetry appears to have been inherited from earlier iterations of alliterative meter.[37]

Another consideration affecting scansion is metrical phonology, that is, which historically justified forms of a word count in meter. Here, Cable and Duggan differed most profoundly. Cable posited a variety of historically motivated final *-e*'s and inflectional endings in fourteenth- and early fifteenth-century alliterative meter despite the loss of these *-e*'s from spoken Middle English a century or so earlier. Metrically significant phantom syllables include the vocalic endings of Old English, Old French, and

Old Norse nouns with *-e* (as in *erth(e)* "earth" <OE *eorðe*; *ile* "island" <OF *isle*; and *kirk(e)* "church" <ON *kirkja*) and Old English feminine nouns that acquired an analogical *-e* in the Early Middle English period (as in *bliss(e)* "bliss" <OE *bliss* (f)), as well as the inflectional *-e*'s of infinitive verbs, weak and/or plural adjectives, and certain petrified datives in stereotyped phrases. Yakovlev, with reference to *Sir Gawain and the Green Knight*, and Ad Putter, Judith Jefferson, and Myra Stokes, with reference to a large sample corpus drawn from many poems, have argued in favor of Cable's view of the availability of historical *-e* in alliterative meter.[38] Duggan, by contrast, posited a contemporary phonology for alliterative poetry, in line with the findings of historical linguists. However, Duggan then found it necessary to admit grammatically determined exceptions to the metrical system. Thus, where Cable would scan a b-verse like *Gawain* 1517b *dulful stoundez* SxxSx, counting the (unwritten) inflectional *-e* in the plural strong adjective *dulful*, Duggan would scan it SxSx but accept it as metrical on the grounds that equivalent grammatical constructions had hardened into a formula prior to the loss of linguistic *-e*. I follow Cable in scanning historically justified *-e*'s where possible, since I would expect Duggan's grammatically determined exceptions to engender other, non-formulaic exceptions to the metrical system. That is, if the numerous b-verses like *Gawain* 1517b scan SxSx, then there should also occur some b-verses like **often stoundez* (SxSx), with no possibility of historical *-e* to make the long dip. The same argument holds for the end of the line. If b-verses like *Gawain* 4b *þe trewest on erthe* (*erthe* <OE *eorðe*) scan xSxxS, one would expect to find some b-verses like **þe trewest þat was* (xSxxS). Yet b-verses like **often stoundez* and **þe trewest þat was* are vanishingly rare in the fourteenth-century corpus.

An important implication of the availability of historical *-e* is that metrical phonology and linguistic phonology are not necessarily isomorphic at any given moment in the evolution of metrical traditions. I follow Cable in assuming that meter is a system of mental structures with a historically mediated relationship to linguistic form. The counterintuitive assumptions "that alliterative rules fixed in the twelfth or thirteenth century remained fixed—and active—a century or two after pervasive loss of grammatical function for final <*-e*> in northerly dialects" and "that alliterative poets, including some who also wrote in iambic foot-counted meters, maintained a special conservative set of usages for just those occasions when they were composing alliterative poetry," both rejected by Duggan in his most recent essay on *-e*, are strongly supported by the metrical distribution of words with *-e* in alliterative verse.[39] The arguments about *-e* put forward by Cable, Yakovlev, and Putter, Jefferson, and Stokes suggest the extent to which it is insufficient to rely on the reconstructions of historical linguists to determine the metrical-phonological entities manipulated by alliterative poets—a particularly important consideration for the editor of an alliterative verse text. Lags between linguistic developments and metrical developments also characterize Old English and Old Norse meters, as Russom has demonstrated.[40] For these reasons, I rely on considerations of etymology and the history of meter, rather than presumed dialect, in proposing scansions.

Another level of representation that must be carefully distinguished from meter is orthography. Words, not spellings, are the proper objects of metrical analysis. The presence or absence of written *-e* does not dictate the presence or absence of metrical *-e*. This is clear in the case of *Gawain* 1517b *dulful*, for instance, where the word happens to have been spelled without *-e* by the scribe but scans with a metrically detectable phantom syllable. Conversely, in *Gawain* 30a *laye* "lay, poem" <OF *lai*, the written *-e* is not etymologically justified and no *-e* is counted in meter. Nor do such mismatches between written and metrical *-e* betoken scribal misunderstanding of meter or require emendation, since *dulful* and *dulfulle* are both intelligible renderings of *MED* Online, "dōlful," and *laye* and *lay* are both intelligible renderings of *MED* Online, "lai (n.(2))." Middle English spelling was variable and was not primarily intended to represent the etymologically significant aspects of a word form. Editorial insertion or deletion of *-e* in cases like 1517b *dulful* and 30a *laye* may be defensible on pedagogical grounds, but it would amount to a kind of metrically aware punctuation, not substantive correction. I have not engaged in such punctuation in this study. My scansions should be understood to represent words or lemmata, not scribal spellings.

The meter of the *Vision*, and by implication other post-1450 alliterative poems, differs in one important respect from the consensus model of fourteenth-century alliterative meter. While the requirement of exactly one long dip in the b-verse is still fully in effect, the requirement of a final short dip has been partially eroded. So for example one finds 1b *that thou þi modir calles* (xxxSxSx), 8b *þat broken were þe rother* (xSxxxSx), and 16b *dolven vndir erthe* (SxxxSx; *erthe* <OE *eorðe*) beside 6b *til a full sory walle* (xxxSxS; *walle* <OE *weall*), 34b *full bold and full prest* (xSxxS; *prest* <OF), and 104b *hold þat he has* (SxxxS; infinitive *hold*). The acceptable b-verse patterns in the *Vision*, then, are (x)Sx...xS(x) and x...xS(x)S(x). However,

patterns with a final short dip continue to predominate: 107 of 116 b-verses (92%) have a final short dip, counting historical *-e* where possible. Treatment of the final dip in the *Vision* testifies to a transitional moment in verse history. Finally, the non-schwa principle applies: schwa occupies 106 of the 107 final short dips. The exception is 85b *harnes* "armor" <OF *harnois*. There is only one exception to the non-schwa principle in the medial dip: 100b *it was a pece out geven* (xxxSxSx; *pece* <OF *pais*). Like the exceptions in the fourteenth-century corpus, *Vision* 100b shows a separate word in the medial dip. Perhaps Yakovlev's non-schwa principle is best understood as a constraint on multisyllabic words, without prejudice to monosyllables, though it is not clear why this should be so.[41]

The evidence of the meter of the *Vision* suggests that historical *-e* continued to be available to alliterative poets at this late date. Several times, *-e* fills the metrically necessary long dip, for example, 14b *þan werkis his hert* (xSxxSx; *hert* <OE *heorte*), 18b *with bothe his eyen* (xSxxSx; *bothe* <OE *ba þa*), 21b *shall tray hym sone* (xSxxSx; infinitive *tray*; *sone* <OE *sona*), 47b *in all his wirkes* (xSxxSx; pl. *all*), and 109b *on Paris gates* (xSxxSx; genitive sg. *Paris*). There occur no b-verses in the *Vision* with the pattern xSxSx where *-e* is not at issue, which strongly implies that *-e* counts in verses like 14b. Historical *-e* also fills the final short dip, as in 14b *hert* and 21b *sone*. Counting *-e*, including petrified datives in 5b *out of towne*, 37b *in towne*, 51b *all out of lyue*, and 74b *out of lyue*, there are only nine b-verses in the *Vision* without a final short dip; discounting *-e* apart from *-es* in plural nouns, there are 59. This lopsided distribution strongly implies that *-e* must still be counted where possible at line end. If *-e* did not count, one would not expect such a high proportion of patterns without a final short dip (50 of 59 or 85%) to end in a word with historical *-e*. The significance of historical *-e* in a late fifteenth-century alliterative poem further underscores the constitutive difference between the history of language and the history of meter. Linguistically conservative scansions like *tray* (Sx) were only thinkable in the late fifteenth century in the context of an enduring metrical tradition.

Possible evidence of the loss of *-e* is limited to four instances: 9b *were went hym agayne* (x(x)SxxSx; subjunctive sg. *were* <OE *wære*; *agayne* <OE *ongeanes*), 15b *þat euer he was born of modir* (xxxxxS(x)xSx; *born* <OE *boren*), 89b *and it myght mend þeir hert* (xxxS(x)xSx; infinitive *mend*; *hert* <OE *heorte*), and 107b *as it were his brothir* (xxS(x)xSx; subjunctive sg. *were*). However, discounting *-e* in 15b *born*, 89b *mend*, and 107b *were* leads to non-schwa vowels in medial short dips (15b *of*, 89b *þeir*, and 107b *his*).

These three verses thus pose a difficult scansional choice between a violation of the non-schwa principle and innovative metrical phonology on the one hand and an asystematic pattern with two long dips on the other. Verse 107b has a third option: it may show metrical promotion of *as* rather than *were*, for the metrically acceptable pattern SxxxxSx. Scansional choices like these reveal the pressure points through which metrical systems are deformed and reformed over time. The particular choices posed by 15b, 89b, and 107b also illustrate the inextricability of meter and metrical phonology in the experience of scansion (and, inferentially, composition).

Three b-verses in the *Vision* pose more specialized difficulties of scansion. Two verses may exhibit asystematic patterns with two long dips: 25b *for þe dede of your synnis* (xxSxxxSx; *dede* <OE *dæd* (f) with analogical *-e*; or omit prosaic *þe*, xSxxxSx) and 103b *to þe mekull king of heven* (xxSxxxSx with metrical demotion of *king*; or three lifts, xxSxSxSx). Like 103b, 73b *þe marshalle shall after folowe* may be scanned with three lifts, with stress on syntactically inverted adverbial *after*. Patterns with two long dips or three lifts are relicts in the history of form, the result of an incomplete systematization of the requirements of exactly two lifts and one long dip. (**R** has the metrical but clearly inferior *by cause of yor sinnes* at 25b; at 103b, **R** has *to þe myld king of heauen*, metrically equivalent to the **H** reading.) Verse 80b *gold ne siluer* has the pattern SxSx, with no long dip, unless *gold* counts an inorganic *-e* or *ne* replaces a form of "neither" (but 110b *ne* evidently makes a short dip). **R** has a thoroughly reworded line here. The b-verse pattern SxSx, Sievers Type A in Old English meter, may be another relict in the history of form. Systematic in Old English, it occurs sporadically in alliterative poetry as late as the *Conflict of Wit and Will* (early/mid fourteenth c.) and possibly *Sir Gawain and the Green Knight* (13b *Felix Brutus*).[42]

In the new work on alliterative meter since 1985, the extent to which the a-verse is governed by metrical rules remains thoroughly controverted. Cable argued for asymmetry between a-verse and b-verse patterns: the a-verse must have a metrical pattern disallowed in the b-verse.[43] Cable's hypothesis covers the vast majority of a-verses, but clear exceptions occur in around 5% of verses, even taking into account Yakovlev's non-schwa principle, for example, *Gawain* 3a *Þe tulk þat þe trammes* (xSxxSx, schwa in final dip). A-verse/b-verse asymmetry appears to be another example of an incomplete systematization of meter, and one with a long historical trajectory: Early Middle English alliterative meter exhibits ca. 35% asymmetry between a-verse and b-verse patterns, a figure midway between Old English meter (ca. 5% asymmetry) and Middle English alliterative meter (ca. 95% asymmetry). The problem of asymmetry is also embedded in the more infamous problem of a-verses with three (alliterating) content words, for example, *Gawain* 2a *Þe borȝ brittened ond brent.* Cable and Duggan both scan a-verses like *Gawain* 2a with three lifts, one on each content word, whereas Noriko Inoue and Putter, Jefferson, and Stokes maintain that all a-verses have exactly two lifts, positing contextual demotion of one of the three content words in verses like *Gawain* 2a.[44] More recently, Inoue and Stokes have argued for tight constraints on the length of dips in both the a-verse and the b-verse of Middle English alliterative poetry, assuming a variety of *ad hoc* elisions and metrical doublet forms in order to eliminate apparent exceptions.[45] Finally, Yakovlev argues that final long dips are prohibited in the Middle English a-verse as in the b-verse, positing compound stress in the final word of a-verses like *Gawain* 4a *Watz tried for his tricherie* (xSxxxSxSx not xSxxxSxxx).[46] In support of this scansion, Yakovlev observes that a-verses with apparent final long dips in *Sir Gawain and the Green Knight* overwhelmingly (207 of 210 instances or 99%) have only two content words, and that the vast majority of these a-verses end in a word capable of carrying secondary stress on its final or penultimate syllable (*tricherie* in *Gawain* 4a).

Yakovlev's brilliant observation tells against the existence of final long dips in the Middle English a-verse, since final long dips, if they were a legitimate metrical feature, ought to have occurred approximately as often in a-verses with three content words like *Gawain* 2a as in a-verses with two content words like *Gawain* 4a. It also buttresses the case for three-lift a-verses, for two reasons. First, if a-verses like *Gawain* 2a were metrically equivalent to a-verses with two content words, they ought to end with words like *tricherie* approximately as often. Second, over 200 a-verses like *Gawain* 4a must now be assigned a third metrical stress in order to avoid the unmetrical final long dip. A prohibition against final long dips in the Middle English a-verse would also have precedents in the history of meter: final long dips do not occur in Old English meter or in Early Middle English alliterative meter.[47] Yakovlev's insight invites further investigation into apparent final long dips in the a-verse of Middle English alliterative poems other than *Gawain*.

The meter of the *Vision* tends to confirm Yakovlev's findings. Of fourteen a-verses with an apparent final long dip, thirteen (93%) have only one or two content words (accent marks on content words; apparent final long dips underlined): 7a *But þat shall be as nédelese* (*nede-* <OE *nyd* (f)

with analogical *-e*), 25a *And alle haue I déstenyed this*, 32a *Amonges þe wild lýons* (*lyons* <OF *liun*), 38a *It shall be by próphecy* (*prophecy* <OF *profecie*), 45a *Tréi tréntaules* (*trentaules* <OF *trentel*), 47a *And bíd hym wálkand be*, 80a *Shal neither gá for þeym*, 83a *That is by Lésbury and Bánnbury*, 89a *A métyng of a máriage* (*mariage* <OF), 91a *Þan shall it be but a glósyng* (*glosyng* <OF *gloser* + OE *-ung* (f)), 101a *Pártid in a máriage*, 106a *And máke ilk lódesman*, and 116a *And with þe thre kýnges of Cóleyn* (*Coleyn* <OF *Coloine*).[48] The exception is 88a *And sét a dáy of sátlyng* (*satlyng* <OE *sehtlian* "bring to an agreement" + *-ung* (f)). This regularity supports Yakovlev's conclusions and suggests that the prohibition against final long dips survived in alliterative meter into the fifteenth century. Verses like 38a should be scanned with compound stress on the last word (*próphecý*), while verses like 80a should be scanned with promotion of the last function word (*gá for þéym*). In the case of 88a, perhaps the analogical *-e* of Old English *-ung* was no longer metrically significant for this poet; or perhaps the verse has four lifts. The prohibition against final long dips conforms to a universal principle of closure, whereby the endings of metrical units (in this case, the a-verse) are more tightly constrained than the beginnings. As Russom has observed, the principle of closure also accounts for the structure of the Middle English alliterative long line, in which the repertoire of acceptable a-verse patterns is relatively large and the repertoire of acceptable b-verse patterns is relatively small.[49]

It is now possible to draw together the strands of this chapter—the meter of the *Vision*, alliterative verse prophecy, the history of form, and literary history—in a broader discussion of the place of alliterative poetry in literary culture. To pose the question in an acute form: what did the alliterative meter mean to the poets who used it, the scribes who transmitted it, and the audiences who received it after 1450? Elsewhere, I have introduced the concept of "verse history" as a method for approaching such questions.[50] Verse history is literary history focalized through the history of poetic form. Coordination of formalism and historicism in the study of medieval English poetry can counterbalance ahistorical understandings of literary form as well as unformalized understandings of literary history. Russom has aptly criticized Eduard Sievers's *Fünftypensystem*, the most influential theory of Old English meter, for its lack of historical dynamism.[51] It is a great virtue of Russom's word-foot theory that it predicts and accommodates metrical evolution. As emphasized above, progress in Middle English alliterative metrics has also come in part from the adoption of a deeper historical perspective. Contextualization of the meter of the *Vision* involves not only the synchronic expression of form but also the historical developments that underlie and shape the expression of form. Verse history seeks to synthesize several kinds of evidence about metrical traditions, of which metaliterary remarks such as Chaucer's Parson's allusion to "'rum, ram, ruf' by lettre" (*Canterbury Tales* X 43) are only the most obvious.[52]

The two surviving manuscript contexts for the *Vision* direct attention in the first instance to the poem's status as a prophecy. Indeed, the *Vision* was likely received as prophecy first ("þe visioun of Sire William Banastre knyght") and alliterative poetry second. The two formal categories, metrical and generic, became increasingly intertwined over the course of the fifteenth century and into the sixteenth, as preceding references to the *First Scottish Prophecy*, *Piers Plowman*, and the *Prophecies of St. Thomas of Canterbury* make clear. No fewer than six of the eight unrhymed alliterative poems datable after 1450 are political prophecies. Four of them survive in two late manuscripts (London, British Library MSS Cotton Vespasian E. viii and Sloane 1802) and in the printed *Whole Prophesie of Scotland, &c.* (1603), issued to celebrate the accession of a Scottish king (James VI) to the English throne (as James I), a key prediction of medieval English political prophecies. Two others, the *Vision* and the *Ireland Prophecy*, appear in large post-1450 manuscript anthologies of prophecies and political writings. The genre of these alliterative poems accounts in large part for their transmission and preservation.

In the sixteenth century, writers associated alliterative meter with prophecy explicitly. In the preface to his 1550 print edition of *Piers Plowman*, Robert Crowley takes pains to dispute the authenticity and interpretation of two passages that might be construed as political prophecies ("And that which foloweth and geueth it the face of a prophecye is lyke to be a thinge added of some other man than the fyrste autour" and "Loke not vpon this boke therfore, to talke of wonders paste or to come," STC 19906, ii^v^). Crowley is here discussing those same two prophetic passages excerpted twice in **R**. Significantly, Crowley titled his edition *The Vision of Pierce Plowman*, and later commentators would read the poem in this form as well as continuing to read manuscript copies. In a passing mention of *Piers Plowman* in his *Arte of English Poesie* (1589), George Puttenham dubs Langland "a very true Prophet" of the Reformation before describing the form of *Piers Plowman* as "but loose meetre" (STC 20519.5, 50). These notices join the evidence of the eight extant post-1450 alliterative poems in suggesting the extent to which alliterative meter and political prophecy overlapped in perception and practice after 1450.

From the retrospect of the sixteenth century, then, the *Vision* marks an early stage in the marginalization and radicalization of the alliterative tradition after 1450. The view from the fourteenth and earlier centuries is rather different. Since the publication of Thorlac Turville-Petre's *The Alliterative Revival* (1977), scholars have been most interested in understanding fourteenth- and fifteenth-century alliterative verse as a contemporary cultural phenomenon. Analysis of a metrically constituted corpus in its most immediate generic, historical, political, and codicological contexts can reveal the reciprocal pressures exerted by verse traditions and literary communities. Within the past fifteen years, John Scattergood, Christine Chism, and Alex Mueller have each contributed monographs that profitably take this route, exploring points of contact between the extant fourteenth- and fifteenth-century alliterative corpus and contemporary politics, political geography, historiography, and literary genre (especially romance).[53] This research succeeds in counterbalancing older views of the Alliterative Revival as an isolated, atavistic protest movement by reinscribing alliterative poetry in the multilingual literary culture of late medieval England. In these terms, post-1450 alliterative poetry is most legible as a late contribution to "a penumbra shading off on every side into other forms of writing," to borrow Derek Pearsall's formulation.[54] In the case of the *Vision*, "other forms of writing" could include not only (non-alliterative) political prophecy but also dream vision, allegory, biblical exegesis, *Brut* chronicle, and the historiography of the Wars of Scottish Independence and the Wars of the Roses. This list represents several promising avenues of inquiry not taken in this chapter because they lead beyond the bounds of a single poetic tradition.

For all its historical and cultural capacity, a limitation of this research agenda has been its narrowly synchronic perspective. Ideally, one wants to know not only how alliterative poetry responded to and bled into "other forms of writing" in the late fourteenth- and early fifteenth-century literary scene, but also how the observable configuration of literary traditions ca. 1400 arose and disintegrated. At its best, post-1977 historicism accentuates rather than solves the problem of form, which is a historical problem. Viewed under the rubric of verse history, progress in Middle English alliterative metrics offers a powerful new way of conceptualizing the life and death of poetic traditions. If the thesis of continuity holds, the so-called Alliterative Revival was a non-event in literary history—in contrast to both Turville-Petre's arguments and the nationalistic views against which he was reacting. By "non-event" I mean prosodic business as usual, a moment in verse history neither foundational nor fatal. In 1470 the *Vision* poet simply selected an available meter whose prior development extended at least 785 years, counting forward from the approximate date of *Cædmon's Hymn*, the earliest datable Old English poem. Like other poets who utilized the alliterative meter, the *Vision* poet offers no explicit comment on metrical form or poetic style.[55] To judge from surviving evidence, there never was an *ars metrica* for the alliterative meter. In the context of a well-established verse tradition, theorization of poetic practice was unnecessary.

If the view of the *Vision* as a quiet contribution to a durable poetic tradition is less immediately satisfying than the late-medieval historicist view I have been describing, it also makes available for comparison a different historical archive. In glossing the status of the *Vision* as a prophecy, I adduced three late fourteenth- and early fifteenth-century alliterative verse prophecies, five other post-1450 alliterative verse prophecies, sixteenth-century metacommentary on alliterative verse by Crowley and Puttenham, and an early seventeenth-century print collection of (alliterative and non-alliterative) verse prophecies. The period before 1350 also contains items relevant to study of the *Vision* because they form part of the same continuous history of form and style. A more extensive study of the position of the *Vision* in verse history might take notice of the following: Lawman's *Brut*, which contains several prophetic set-pieces not found in Lawman's source text, Wace's *Roman de Brut* (ca. 1155); the couplet of alliterative verse on St. Kenelm's body said to have been sent from God to the Pope, the English text of which (*NIMEV* 1477.5) is alluded to (and occasionally given in manuscript glosses) in the Latin *Vita Kenelmi* (1045–1075) and quoted directly in the Kenelm episode in the *South English Legendary* (late thirteenth c.) and later English and Anglo-Latin histories; the poetics of *knowe* "generation" (<OE *cneo*), a rare poetic word used in the *Vision* (though misunderstood by a scribe) and in several prior alliterative poems from *Genesis A* to the *Conflict of Wit and Will*; the evolving texts of multiply attested Middle English alliterative poems, such as the *First Scottish Prophecy*, as evidence of scribal participation in metrical tradition; and the meter of the other seven post-1450 alliterative poems, including the two not classifiable as political prophecies (William Dunbar's *Tretis of the Tua Mariit Wemen and the Wedo*, ca. 1500, and *Scottish Field*, 1515-47). This list is suggestive rather than exhaustive. Few surviving alliterative poems date after 1450, and the period 1100–1350 is scarcely more fortunate. The paucity of primary evidence heightens the need to integrate

methodologies from several fields of inquiry, including literary criticism, metrics, textual criticism, codicology, and historical linguistics.

A key assumption of Russom's research into alliterative meter is that verse form must be intelligible to poets and audiences "at the speed of performance."[56] Accordingly, Russom has sought to articulate a metrical theory that is psychologically plausible. This is an attractive goal for metrics, especially if "performance" is understood to cover both mental and aural events. Before the deselection of alliterative meter from the repertoire of English verse forms ca. 1550, well-versed practitioners will have versified and scanned alliterative meter at speed. Verse history represents a methodology for inquiring into the formal competencies that made scansion possible, as well as the cultural knowledge that made scansion meaningful. The *Vision of William Banastre*, of considerable literary interest in itself, is even more valuable as an exhibit of late alliterative style. Much work remains to be done on this intriguing poem. In this preliminary study, I hope to have shown how meter, literary history, and literary culture intersect and illuminate one another in and through a particular poetic composition.

NOTES

[1] Julia Boffey and A. S. G. Edwards, *A New Index of Middle English Verse* (London: British Library, 2005). Thanks are due to Lindy Brady, Ian Cornelius, A. S. G. Edwards, Daniel Helbert, and M. J. Toswell for commenting on earlier versions of this chapter, to Barbara A. Shailor and Ralph Hanna for advice on paleographical matters, and to Jessica Brantley for help in capturing digital images of Oxford, Bodleian Library, MS Hatton 56.

[2] **H** described in Falconer Madan, et al., *A Summary Catalogue of Western Manuscripts in the Bodleian Library at Oxford* (7 vols. in 8) (Oxford: Oxford University Press, 1895–1953), vol. 2 pt. 2, pp. 821–22; **R** described in William D. Macray, *Catalogi Manuscriptorum Bibliothecæ Bodleianæ Partis Quintæ*, 5 vols. (Oxford: Clarendon, 1862–1900), vol. 2, pp. 415–20. On **H** see also Lesley A. Coote, *Prophecy and Public Affairs in Later Medieval England* (York: York Medieval Press, 2000), pp. 201–211 and 276–77; on the second compilation in **R**, see Sharon L. Jansen Jaech, "'The Marvels of Merlin' and the Authority of Tradition," *Studies in Medieval and Renaissance History* 8 (1985): 35–73, at pp. 48–9.

[3] *The Welles Anthology: MS. Rawlinson C. 813: A Critical Edition*, edited by Sharon L. Jansen and Kathleen H. Jordan (Binghamton: State University of New York, 1991).

[4] A. S. G. Edwards, "Editing and Manuscript Form: Middle English Verse as Prose," *English Studies in Canada* 27 (2001), pp. 15–28, and Eric Weiskott,

"Lawman, the Last Old English Poet and the First Middle English Poet," in *Laȝamon's* Brut *and Other Medieval Chronicles: 14 Essays*, edited by Marie-Françoise Alamichel (Paris: L'Harmattan, 2013), pp. 11–57, at pp. 41–2.

[5] Apart from the *Vision*, these are: the *Ireland Prophecy*, another political prophecy containing coded references to the Wars of the Roses; the *Prophecie of Beid*, *Prophecie of Bertlington*, *Prophecie of Waldhaue*, and *Prophesie of Gildas*, all found in the printed *Whole Prophesie of Scotland, &c.* (first published 1603), and containing coded references to significant post-1450 dates or events; the Scottish author William Dunbar's *Tretis of the Tua Mariit Wemen and the Wedo* (ca. 1500); and *Scottish Field*, a poem on the Battle of Flodden (1513). On the *Ireland Prophecy* see Eric Weiskott, "*The Ireland Prophecy*: Text and Metrical Context," *Studies in Philology* (forthcoming).

[6] See A. S. G. Edwards, "A Verse Chronicle of the House of Percy," *Studies in Philology* 105 (2008): 226–44, "Books Owned by Medieval Members of the Percy Family," in *Tributes to Kathleen L. Scott: English Medieval Manuscripts: Readers, Makers, and Illuminators*, edited by Marlene Villalobos Hennessy (Turnhout: Brepols, 2009), pp. 73–82, and "Recording a Dynasty: Verse Chronicles of the House of Percy," in *Recording Medieval Lives*, edited by Julia Boffey and Virginia Davis (Donington: Shaun Tyas, 2009), pp. 74–84. BL MS Cotton Vespasian E.vii (1460–1480), containing numerous political prophecies, was owned by a member of the Percy family: Coote, *Prophecy*, pp. 225–26.

[7] For a handlist of similar Middle English poems, see Robbins, "Poems Dealing with Contemporary Conditions," in *A Manual of the Writings in Middle English*, edited by Albert E. Hartung, 10 vols. (New Haven: Connecticut Academy of Arts and Sciences, 1967–1998), vol. 5, pp. 1385–1536. On late medieval and early modern English political prophecy see esp. Rupert Taylor, *The Political Prophecy in England* (New York: Columbia University Press, 1911); Sharon L. Jansen, *Political Protest and Prophecy under Henry VIII* (Woodbridge, Suffolk: Boydell & Brewer, 1991); Karen R. Moranski, "The *Prophetie Merlini*, Animal Symbolism, and the Development of Political Prophecy in Late Medieval England and Scotland," *Arthuriana* 8 (1998): 56–68; and Tim Thornton, *Prophecy, Politics, and the People in Early Modern England* (Woodbridge, Suffolk: Boydell & Brewer, 2006).

[8] T. M. Smallwood, "*The Prophecy of the Six Kings*," *Speculum* 60 (1985): 571–92. On the "first revised version," see Smallwood, "*Prophecy of the Six Kings*," pp. 572–73 and n. 10.

[9] Numbering and quotations of *Piers Plowman* are from *Piers Plowman: The B Version*, edited by George Kane and E. Talbot Donaldson (London: Athlone, 1975). To the play on *bale* and *bote* in the *Vision* cp. *Piers Plowman* B.4.92–3 and B.11.122.

[10] *First-Line Index of English Poetry 1500–1800 in Manuscripts of the Bodleian Library Oxford*, edited by Margaret Crum, 2 vols. (Oxford, 1969), A1272. See Eric Weiskott, "Prophetic *Piers Plowman*: New Sixteenth-Century Excerpts," *RES* 67

(2016): 21–41. For other excerpts of the same two passages in other sixteenth-century manuscripts see Sharon L. Jansen, "Politics, Protest, and a New *Piers Plowman* Fragment: The Voice of the Past in Tudor England," *RES* 40 (1989): 93–9, and Lawrence Warner, *The Myth of* Piers Plowman: *Constructing a Medieval Literary Archive* (Cambridge: Cambridge University Press, 2014), pp. 72–5. For an alliterating poem echoing both passages and printed in the mid sixteenth century, see Wendy Scase, "*Dauy Dycars Dreame* and Robert Crowley's Prints of *Piers Plowman*," *Yearbook of Langland Studies* 21 (2007): 171–98. For a copy of *Piers Plowman* titled "The Prophecies of Piers Plowman" and including annotations and cross-references for, among others, both of the passages in question, see Bryan P. Davis, "The Prophecies of *Piers Plowman* in Cambridge University Library MS Gg.4.31," *Journal of the Early Book Society* 5 (2002): 15–36.

[11] Thomas Grey, *Scalacronica*, edited by Joseph Stevenson (Edinburgh: Maitland Club, 1836), p. 317; *Bernardus de cura rei famuliaris with some Early Scottish Prophecies*, edited by J. Rawson Lumby. Early English Text Society o.s. 42 (London: Oxford University Press, 1870), pp. 19 and 22 (ll. 54 and 136); Coote, *Prophecy*, p. 208; Sharon L. Jansen Jaech, "British Library MS Sloane 2578 and Popular Unrest in England, 1554–1556," *Manuscripta* 29 (1985): 30–41, at pp. 35 and 41; and John Leland, *De rebus Brittanicis collectanea*, edited by Thomas Hearne, 2nd ed., 6 vols. (London, 1774), vol. 2, pp. 509–10.

[12] Possibly a reference to Edward IV's ineffectual siege of Harlech Castle, Gwynedd, in northwest Wales (4a *westward*), to which Margaret of Anjou fled after the Battle of Northampton in 1460. Edward did not take Harlech until 1468.

[13] Conceivably a reference to the rebellion of Richard Neville against Edward IV in 1469.

[14] H *the whiles* and R *the whiell* show a conjunctive phrase meaning "while, during the time that" (*MED* Online, "whīles (n.)," c and "whīle (n.)," 1b(a)), but an adverb is required by the future tense of 22a. Cf. 10a.

[15] The speech tag *said William* is extra-metrical (hence **H** omits it). Other extra-metrical speech tags are 28a *"Lord," said William*; 30a and 39a *William*; and 54a *lord*. Cf. *Finnsburgh Fragment* 24a "Sigeferþ is min nama (cweð he)" and *Piers Plowman* B.1.85a "Whan alle tresors arn tried (quod she)." See W. W. Skeat, "An Essay on Alliterative Poetry," in *Bishop Percy's Folio Manuscript*, edited by John W. Hales and Frederick J. Furnivall, 3 vols. (London: Trübner, 1867–1868), vol. 3, pp. xi–xxxix, at pp. xxxv–xxxvi.

[16] The sense is "tell this (prediction) for me to (the) good men," with *me* representing an ethical dative and *men* the dative plural. **H** simplifies the syntax, omitting *me* with reinterpretation of *þis* as a form of "these."

[17] *Vision*, ll. 41–2 = *First Scottish Prophecy*, ll. 5–6. A similar succession of images, including the bugle, occurs in the roughly contemporary *Marvels of Merlin*, ll. 5–7 (*NIMEV* 1260 and 2613.5). See Jansen Jaech, "'Marvels,'" p. 37.

[18] "That guards the corner" or possibly "embrasure (of a castle)" (*MED* Online, "corner (n.(2))"). The emendation improves the meter, maintains parallelism with

the other two items in the list, and makes good poetic syntax (cf. 46b). A scribe overlooked *þat* in an unexpected syntactical position. **R** omits this line.

[19] **H** *trent andres* could have arisen from misprision of *u* as *n* and *l* as *d*, perhaps buttressed by misprision of *trent* as a complete word with the same meaning (*MED* Online, "trent"). **R** omits this line.

[20] The a-verse means "I shall give over (the place) to him" (*MED* Online, "keie (n.(1))," 1b(b)). Cf. *First Scottish Prophecy* 39, "And þe comoynis of kynt | sall kast hime key" and the alliterative *Prophecies of St. Thomas of Canterbury*, l. 172. A text of the *Prophecies of St. Thomas* occurs in **H** (partially edited by Taylor, *Political Prophecy*, p. 165). The b-verse means "who keeps a curlew" (*MED* Online, "yēmen," 2c).

[21] To ll. 56–8 cf. *NLW* MS 441C (*olim* Williams 219) (sixteenth c.), p. 16: "At som*er* aft*er* at Sandyefoorde is more care/ for eu*er* of Mawdelyens day aft*er*"; and BL MS Sloane 2578, fol. 73v (a rhyming verse prophecy copied as prose): "a wyndy som*er*, a whyte harvest, before this said shalbe. a wtry wynter w*ith* wakinge knight*es*. a blody lenton after shalbe. haue good day I goo my waye. & of my foo I make my frend. & aft*er*ward by magdelen day. all warres at an ende," with notes in the same hand above the underlined portions, "a white midsom*er*, a wyndy harveste. a windy som*er*, a wett harveste" and "great blud dovne shall wynd."

[22] Margaret of Anjou, making Edward IV the *floure* (l. 61b) and Henry VI the *brodel* (l. 62a), with reference to Henry's reinstatement late in 1470?

[23] The syntax is difficult. Line 64 is a relative clause following 63b *knyghtes* without relative pronoun. "... and the arrival of knights (who) are just journeying around and wandering out of sorrow."

[24] A coat of arms, including a lion (*lion leopardé*), a label, and in the sinister a helmet. I have not been able to identify the intended personage, if any. *Prophecies of St. Thomas*, ll. 194–96, depict lions and a label on the coat of arms of a valiant, identified as Edward the Black Prince by Coote, *Prophecy*, pp. 131–32.

[25] The Despenser family were royal favorites opposed by the Marcher Lords, including Roger de Mortimer, earl of March, in the Despenser War (1321–1322). The reference, however, may include more contemporary rivalries. Richard Neville married into the Despenser inheritance, while the Percies descended from Elizabeth Mortimer, daughter of Edmund Mortimer, earl of March. The House of York could claim Mortimer ancestry through Edmund's granddaughter Anne de Mortimer. Jack Cade took the pseudonym "Mortimer" during his 1450 rebellion in an attempt to connect himself with Richard, duke of York.

[26] **H** *Landesbury* would be Londesborough, Yorkshire, far from other places named in the poem and of little significance in the Wars. Cf. **R** *Lanseburg*. Perhaps the place meant is Lesbury, Northumberland, a small coastal village and a Percy manor. Glanton, twelve miles west, was the site of the Battle of Hedgeley Moor (1464). *Bannbury* (*Banbury* in **R**) is probably not Banbury, Oxfordshire, but an alternate spelling or corruption of *bambury*, Bamburgh, Northumberland, another Percy manor. Bamburgh lies seventeen miles north of Lesbury. Cf. *First*

Scottish Prophecy 114a *bambrwgh*. Bamburgh Castle could be "þe eldest burgh | þat euer was biggid" (l. 82): the castle was renowned as Din Guarie, capital of Yr Hen Ogledd "The Old North." Henry VI fled there several times between 1462 and 1464. Warwick successfully besieged the castle by artillery (a first) in 1464. The b-verse is a *locus desperatus*: has another place-name dropped out after *on*?

[27] *Bale Hill* is Bale Hill, Cumbria, lying between Warcop and Brough. Barnard Castle, a Warwick manor, lies eighteen miles east. Middleham Castle, Warwick's residence, lies 33 miles southeast. In the b-verse the poet imagines the complement to Bale Hill as the personification of evil, playing on *bale* "evil-doing" <OE *bealu*. The alliterating phrase *bote of bale* means "redemption" (*MED* Online, "bāle (n.(1))," 3 and 4) and had been in use already in OE (cf. *Beowulf*, ll. 281 and 909).

[28] Misrecognized by a scribe as "known," meaningless in context. This would be by far the latest attestation of *MED* Online, "knē," 3.

[29] *Vision*, l. 109 = *Prophecy of the Six Kings* (couplets) 171, "He sal whet his tuskes on Pariss ȝates," quoted fr. *The Poems of Laurence Minot*, edited by Joseph Hall (Oxford: Clarendon, 1887), pp. 97–105. King Arthur was said to have besieged Paris: Geoffrey of Monmouth, *The History of the Kings of Britain*, edited by Michael D. Reeve and translated by Neil Wright (Woodbridge, Suffolk: Boydell & Brewer, 2007), p. 206.

[30] The reference is to the reputed relics of the Three Magi housed at Cologne Cathedral since 1164. Cf. the prose *Prophecy of the Six Kings* in the Middle English *Brut*: "This Boor [...] shal bene enterede at Coloigne," quoted fr. *The Brut; or, The Chronicles of England*, edited by Friedrich W. D. Brie, 2 vols. Early English Text Society o.s. 131 and 136 (London: Oxford University Press, 1906–08), 1.75; *Prophecy of the Six Kings* (couplets) 188: "And for his nobilles be grauen bitwen kinges thre"; and *Marvels of Merlin*, l. 97. On the Middle English prose legend *Three Kings of Cologne*, see Julia Boffey, "'Many grete myraclys ... in divers contreys of the eest': The Reading and Circulation of the Middle English Prose *Three Kings of Cologne*," in *Medieval Women: Texts and Contexts in Late Medieval Britain: Essays in Honour of Felicity Riddy*, edited by Jocelyn Wogan-Browne, et al. (Turnhout: Brepols, 2000), pp. 35–47. On the use of Cologne in late medieval English political prophecy, see Victoria Flood, "*Wynnere and Wastoure* and the Influence of Political Prophecy," *Chaucer Review* 49 (2015): 427–48, at pp. 432–36 and 447–48.

[31] Overviews include Thomas Cable, "Progress in Middle English Alliterative Metrics," *Yearbook of Langland Studies* 23 (2009): 243–64; Kristin Lynn Cole, "*The Destruction of Troy*'s Different Rules: The Alliterative Revival and the Alliterative Tradition," *Journal of English and Germanic Philology* 109 (2010): 162–76, at pp. 162–64; and Eric Weiskott, "Phantom Syllables in the English Alliterative Tradition," *Modern Philology* 110 (2013): 441–58.

[32] Geoffrey Russom, "The Evolution of Middle English Alliterative Meter," in *Studies in the History of the English Language II: Unfolding Conversations*, edited

by Anne Curzan and Kimberly Emmons (Berlin: Mouton de Gruyter, 2004), pp. 279–304; Nicolay Yakovlev, "The Development of Alliterative Metre from Old to Middle English" (PhD diss., University of Oxford, 2008); and Cable, "Progress," p. 264 (quotation). See also Weiskott, "Lawman," and "Phantom Syllables," pp. 448–58.

[33] Geoffrey Russom, "Evolution of the A-Verse in English Alliterative Meter," in *Studies in the History of the English Language III: Managing Chaos: Strategies for Identifying Change in English*, edited by Christopher M. Cain and Russom (Berlin: Mouton de Gruyter, 2007), pp. 63–87, and "Some Unnoticed Constraints on the A-Verse in *Sir Gawain and the Green Knight*," in *Approaches to the Metres of Alliterative Verse*, edited by Judith A. Jefferson and Ad Putter (Leeds: Leeds Studies in English, 2009), pp. 41–57.

[34] Hoyt N. Duggan, "The Shape of the B-Verse in Middle English Alliterative Poetry," *Speculum* 61 (1986): 564–92, and Thomas Cable, *The English Alliterative Tradition* (Philadelphia: University of Pennsylvania Press, 1991), pp. 85–113.

[35] Nicolay Yakovlev, "Prosodic Restrictions on the Short Dip in Late Middle English Alliterative Verse," *Yearbook of Langland Studies* 23 (2009): 217–42. See also Yakovlev, "Development," pp. 142–54.

[36] Hoyt N. Duggan, "Stress Assignment in Middle English Alliterative Poetry," *Journal of English and Germanic Philology* 89 (1990): 309–29, and Cable, *English Alliterative Tradition*, p. 80. For the hypothesis that Middle English alliterative poetry employed the same mix of phrasal and rhythmic stress assignment as syllabic verse, see Ad Putter, Judith Jefferson, and Myra Stokes, *Studies in the Metre of Alliterative Verse* (Oxford: Society for the Study of Medieval Languages and Literature, 2007), pp. 145–216. Ian Cornelius, "The Accentual Paradigm in Early English Metrics," *Journal of English and Germanic Philology* 114 (2015): 459–81, points out that Putter, Jefferson, and Stokes's view is implausible with respect to the longer history of the alliterative verse form. An engaging attempt to reconcile the two explanations is Ad Putter, "A Prototype Theory of Metrical Stress: Lexical Categories and Ictus in Langland, the *Gawain*-poet and Other Alliterative Poets," in *The Use and Development of Middle English*, edited by Richard Dance and Laura Wright (Frankfurt: Peter Lang, 2013), pp. 281–98.

[37] Russom, "Some Unnoticed Constraints," p. 48.

[38] Cable, *English Alliterative Tradition*, pp. 78–9; Nicolay Yakovlev, "On Final *-e* in the B-Verses of *Sir Gawain and the Green Knight*," in *Approaches*, ed. Jefferson and Putter, pp. 135–57; and Putter, Jefferson, and Stokes, *Studies*, pp. 19–117.

[39] Hoyt N. Duggan, "The End of the Line," in *Medieval Alliterative Poetry: Essays in Honour of Thorlac Turville-Petre*, edited by John A. Burrow and Duggan (Dublin: Four Courts, 2010), pp. 67–79, at p. 76.

[40] Geoffrey Russom, *Old English Meter and Linguistic Theory* (New York: Cambridge University Press, 1987), pp. 39–44, and Beowulf *and Old Germanic Metre* (Cambridge: Cambridge University Press, 1998), pp. 60–63.

[41] On metrical licenses accorded to monosyllables in alliterative meter and other meters, see Donka Minkova, "Diagnostics of Metricality in Middle English Alliterative Verse," in *Approaches*, ed. Jefferson and Putter, pp. 77–113, at pp. 94–7 ("The Monosyllable Rule").

[42] The *Conflict* is found uniquely in a manuscript copied in "the middle or the second quarter of the fourteenth century": A. I. Doyle, "The Manuscripts," in *Middle English Alliterative Poetry and Its Literary Background: Seven Essays*, edited by David Lawton (Cambridge, D. S. Brewer, 1982), pp. 82–100, at p. 91. For a desperate suggestion for emendation of *Gawain* 13b, see the note *ad loc.* in *Sir Gawain and the Green Knight*, edited by J. R. R. Tolkien and E. V. Gordon, revised by Norman Davis, 2nd ed. (Oxford: Oxford University Press, 1967).

[43] Cable, *English Alliterative Tradition*, p. 86.

[44] For two-lift scansion of a-verses like *Gawain* 2a, see esp. Marie Borroff, Sir Gawain and the Green Knight*: A Stylistic and Metrical Study* (New Haven: Yale University Press, 1962), pp. 190–210; Joan Turville-Petre, "The Metre of *Sir Gawain and the Green Knight*," *English Studies* 57 (1976): 310–28; Noriko Inoue, "A New Theory of Alliterative A-Verses," *Yearbook of Langland Studies* 18 (2004): 107–32; Putter, Jefferson, and Stokes, *Studies*, pp. 217–54; and Inoue and Myra Stokes, "The Caesura and the Rhythmic Shape of the A-Verse in the Poems of the Alliterative Revival," *Leeds Studies in English* 40 (2009): 1–26. For three-lift scansion see esp. Hoyt N. Duggan, "Extended A-Verses in Middle English Alliterative Poetry," *Parergon* 18 (2000): 53–76; Kristin Lynn Cole, "Rum, Ram, Ruf, and Rym: Middle English Alliterative Meters" (PhD diss., University of Texas at Austin, 2007), pp. 62–73; Yakovlev, "Development," pp. 172–80; and Cornelius, "Accentual Paradigm."

[45] Noriko Inoue and Myra Stokes, "Restrictions on Dip Length in the Alliterative Line: The A-Verse and the B-Verse," *Yearbook of Langland Studies* 26 (2012): 231–60.

[46] Yakovlev, "Development," pp. 163–67.

[47] Old English: Cable, *English Alliterative Tradition*, p. 16; Early Middle English: Yakovlev, "Development," p. 249: "Polysyllabic final dips do not occur in either two- or three-lift a-verses," of Lawman.

[48] I assume synaeresis in *William* at 3a, 27a, 35a, 55a, and 60a and loss of final *-e* in the adverbial suffix of 20a *frekely* <OE *freclice* and 109a *boldly* <OE *bealdlice*.

[49] Russom, "Evolution of Middle English Alliterative Meter," p. 279, "Evolution of the A-Verse," p. 63, and "Some Unnoticed Constraints," p. 41.

[50] Weiskott, "Lawman" and "Phantom Syllables."

[51] Geoffrey Russom, "Dating Criteria for Old English Poems," in *Studies in the History of the English Language: A Millennial Perspective*, edited by Donka Minkova and Robert P. Stockwell (Berlin: Mouton de Gruyter, 2002), pp. 245–66, at pp. 246–47. Cf. Thomas A. Bredehoft, *Early English Metre* (Toronto: University of Toronto Press, 2005), pp. 6–8.

[52] Quoted fr. *The Riverside Chaucer*, edited by Larry D. Benson, 3rd ed. (Boston: Houghton Mifflin, 1987).

[53] John Scattergood, *The Lost Tradition: Essays on Middle English Alliterative Poetry* (Dublin: Four Courts, 2000); Christine Chism, *Alliterative Revivals* (Philadelphia: University of Pennsylvania Press, 2002); and Alex Mueller, *Translating Troy: Provincial Politics in Alliterative Romance* (Columbus: Ohio State University Press, 2013). See also along these lines Elizabeth Salter, *English and International: Studies in the Literature, Art, and Patronage of Medieval England* (Cambridge: Cambridge University Press, 1988); Patricia Clare Ingham, *Sovereign Fantasies: Arthurian Romance and the Making of Britain* (Philadelphia: University of Pennsylvania Press, 2001); and Randy P. Schiff, *Revivalist Fantasy: Alliterative Verse and Nationalist Literary History* (Columbus: Ohio State University Press, 2011). For a contrasting view of Schiff's topic see Ian Cornelius, "Alliterative Revival: Retrospect and Prospect," *Yearbook of Langland Studies* 26 (2012): 261–76.

[54] Derek Pearsall, *Old English and Middle English Poetry* (London: Routledge & Kegan Paul, 1977), p. 150.

[55] For three passages in Middle English alliterative poetry often taken as reflexive statements on meter but better interpreted otherwise, see Pearsall, *Old English and Middle English*, pp. 153–54. For a fourth, see Cornelius, "Alliterative Revival," pp. 270–71.

[56] Russom, Beowulf *and Old Germanic Metre*, p. 4, and "Evolution of the A-Verse," p. 63.

Publications of Geoffrey Richard Russom

Professor Emeritus, Department of English, Brown University;
Nicholas Brown Professor of Oratory and Belles Lettres, Emeritus

Books / Monographs

Collaboration on the late George Anderson's *Saga of the Volsungs.* East Brunswick, DE: University of Delaware Press, 1982.

Old English Meter and Linguistic Theory. Cambridge: Cambridge University Press, 1987. Paperback edition by Cambridge University Press, 2010.

Beowulf and Old Germanic Metre. Cambridge Studies in Anglo-Saxon England, vol. 23. Cambridge: Cambridge University Press, 1998. Electronic republication by Cambridge University Press, 2002. Paperback edition by Cambridge University Press, 2008.

Managing Chaos: Strategies for Identifying Change in English. Ed. Christopher M. Cain and Geoffrey Russom. Topics in English Linguistics [TiEL], volume 53. Berlin: Mouton de Gruyter, 2007.

Evolution of Verse Structure in Old and Middle English Poetry. Forthcoming.

Articles, Book Chapters, and Commissioned Pieces

"A Syntactic Key to a Number of *Pearl*-group Cruxes." *Journal of English Linguistics* 10 (1976): 21–9.

"Exeter Riddle 47: A Moth Laid Waste to Fame." *Philological Quarterly* 56 (1977): 129–36.

"A Germanic Concept of Nobility in *The Gifts of Men* and *Beowulf.*" *Speculum* 53 (1978): 1–15.

"Artful Avoidance of the Useful Phrase in *Beowulf, The Battle of Maldon,* and *Fates of the Apostles.*" *Studies in Philology* 75 (1978): 371–90.

"Verse Translations and the Question of Literacy in Beowulf." In John Miles Foley, ed., *Comparative Research on Oral Traditions: A Memorial for Milman Parry,* 567–80. Columbus, OH: Slavica, 1987.

"Word and Foot in *Beowulf.*" *Style* 21 (1987): 387–99.

"The Drink of Death in Old English and Germanic Literature." In Daniel G. Calder and T. Craig Christy, eds., *Germania: Comparative Studies in the Old Germanic Languages and Literatures,* 175–89. Woodbridge: Boydell & Brewer, 1988.

"A New Kind of Metrical Evidence in Old English Poetry." In *Papers from the 5th International Conference on English Historical Linguistics,* vol. 65 of *Current*

Issues in Linguistic Theory, 435–57. Amsterdam: John Benjamins, 1990.

Reprint of "Artful Avoidance of the Useful Phrase in *Beowulf, The Battle of Maldon,* and *Fates of the Apostles.*" In *Interpretations of Beowulf: A Critical Anthology,* ed. R. D. Fulk, 206–18. Bloomington, IN: Indiana University Press, 1991.

Entries: (1) iprottir; (2) Old Norse Eddic meters. In *Medieval Scandinavia: An Encyclopedia,* ed. Phillip Pulsiano, *et al.* New York: Garland, 1993, 148–9, 337.

"Constraints on Resolution in Beowulf." In *Prosody and Poetics in the Early Middle Ages,* ed. M. J. Toswell, 147–63. Toronto: University of Toronto Press, 1995.

"Purely Metrical Replacements for Kuhn's Laws." In *English Historical Metrics,* ed. C. B. McCully and John J. Anderson, 30–41. Cambridge: Cambridge University Press, 1996.

"Tolkien's Versecraft in *The Hobbit* and *Lord of the Rings.*" In *J. R. R. Tolkien and his Literary Resonances,* ed. George Clark and Daniel Timmons, 53–69. Westport, CT: Greenwood Press, 2000.

"Metrical Evidence for Subordinate Stress in Old English." *Journal of Germanic Linguistics* 13.1. (2001): 39–64.

"A Bard's-Eye View of the Germanic Syllable." *Journal of English and Germanic Philology* (2002): 305–28.

"Dating Criteria for Old English Poems." In *Studies in the History of the English Language: A Millenial Perspective,* ed. Donka Minkova and Robert Stockwell. Topics in English Linguistics 39, 245–65. Berlin: Mouton de Gruyter, 2002.

"The Evolution of Middle English Alliterative Meter." In *Studies in the History of the English Language II: Unfolding Conversations,* ed. Anne Curzan and Kimberly Emmons. Topics in English Linguistics 45, 279–304. Berlin: Mouton de Gruyter, 2004. In the same volume (pp. 313–14), A brief response to Robert D. Fulk, "Old English Poetry and the Alliterative Revival: On Geoffrey Russom's 'The Evolution of Middle English Meter,'" (pp. 305–12).

"At the Center of *Beowulf.*" In *Myth in Early Northwest Europe,* ed. Stephen Glosecki. Medieval and Renaissance Texts and Studies, 225–40. Tempe, AZ: Arizona Center for Medieval and Renaissance Studies, 2007.

"Evolution of the A-verse in English Alliterative Meter." In *Managing Chaos: Strategies for Identifying Change in English,* ed. Christopher M. Cain and Geoffrey Russom. Topics in English Linguistics [TiEL], volume 53. Berlin: Mouton de Gruyter, 2007, 63–87.

"Literary Form as an Independent Domain of Validation in History of the English Language Pedagogy." Special Issue: Rethinking History of the English Language Pedagogy and Teaching, *Studies in Medieval and Renaissance Teaching* 14.1 (2007): 1–9.

"History of English Prosody." In *A Companion to the History of the English Language,* ed. Haruko Momma and Michael Matto, 81–7. Oxford: Blackwell, 2008.

"Historicity and Anachronism in *Beowulf.*" In *Epic and History,* ed. David Konstan and Kurt A. Raaflaub, 243–61. Oxford: Wiley-Blackwell, 2009.

"On the Distribution of Verse Types in Old English Poetry." In *Form and Order in the Anglo-Saxon World* (Anglo-Saxon Studies in Archaeology and History 16), ed. Sally Crawford and Helena Hamerow with Leslie Webster, 108–18. Oxford: Oxford University School of Archaeology, 2009.

"Some Unnoticed Constraints on the A-verse in *Sir Gawain and the Green Knight.*" In *Approaches to the Metres of Alliterative Verse,* ed. Judith Jefferson and Ad Putter, Leeds Texts and Monographs, 41–57. Leeds: Leeds Studies in English, 2009.

"Why There are Three Eddic Meters." In *Anglo-Saxons and the North,* ed. Matti Kilpiö, Leena Kahlas-Tarkka, Jane Roberts, and Olga Timofeeva, 69–88. Tempe, AZ: Arizona Center for Medieval and Renaissance Studies, 2009.

"Aesthetic Criteria in Old English Heroic Style." In *On the Aesthetics of Beowulf and Other Old English Poems,* ed. John Hill, 64–80. Toronto: University of Toronto Press, 2010.

"Word Patterns and Phrase Patterns in Universalist Metrics." In *Frontiers in Comparative Prosody,* ed. Mihhail Lotman and Maria Kristiina Lotman, 337–73. Bern: Peter Lang, 2011.

"What Explanatory Metrics Has to Say about the History of English Function Words." In *Analysing Older English,* ed. David Denison, Ricardo Bermúdez-Otero, Christopher McCully, and Emma Moore, with the assistance of Ayumi Miura, 15–27. Cambridge: Cambridge University Press, 2012.

Book Reviews

David Yerkes, *The Two Versions of Waerferth's Translation of Gregory's Dialogues: An Old English Thesaurus*. *Speculum* 55 (1980): 878–9.

Alexandra Hennessey Olsen, *Guthlac of Croyland: A Study of Heroic Hagiography*. *Speculum* 58 (1983): 519–21.

James E. Cross and Thomas D. Hill, eds., *The Prose Solomon and Saturn and Adrian and Ritheus*. *Speculum* 59 (1984): 388–90.

Marian C. Bean, *The Development of Word Order Patterns in Old English*. *Journal of English and Germanic Philology* 74 (1985): 117–18.

An Eleventh-Century Anglo-Saxon Illustrated Miscellany, ed. P. McGurk, D. N. Dumville, M. R. Godden, and Ann Knock. *Modern Language Studies* 16 (1986): 356–7.

Stephen O. Glosecki, *Shamanism and Old English Poetry*. *Speculum* 66 (1991): 637–9.

Nicholas Howe, *Migration and Mythmaking in Anglo-Saxon England*. *Speculum* 66 (1991): 893–5.

Calvin B. Kendall, *The Metrical Grammar of "Beowulf." ANQ* 5.2–3 (1992): 165–8.

The Cambridge History of the English Language. Vol. I: *The Beginnings to 1066*, ed. Richard M. Hogg. *Journal of English and Germanic Philology* 93.3 (1994): 407–9.

Hans Sauer, *Nominalkomposita im Fruemittelenglischen mit Ausblicken auf die Geschichte der englischen Nominalkomposition*. *Speculum* 71 (1996): 209–11.

John Miles Foley, *The Singer of Tales in Performance*. *Speculum* 72 (1997): 468–9.

Seiichi Suzuki, *The Metrical Orgnization of "Beowulf":Prototype and Isomorphism*. *Speculum* 73 (1998): 269–71.

B. R. Hutcheson, *Old English Poetic Metre*. *Anglia* 116 (1998): 404–6.

Susan Deskis, *"Beowulf" and the Medieval Proverb Tradition*. *Journal of English and Germanic Philology* (1999): 246–48.

Haruko Momma, *The Composition of Old English Poetry*. *Speculum* 75 (2000): 224–6.

Catherine E. Karkov, *Text and Picture in Anglo-Saxon England*. *Speculum* 78 (2003): 224–6.

Earl R. Anderson, *Folk-Taxonomies in Early English*. *Speculum* 80 (2005): 820–22.

Donka Minkova, *Alliteration and Sound Change in Early English*. *Language* 81 (2005): 745–48.

Seiichi Suzuki, *The Metre of Old Saxon Poetry: The Remaking of Alliterative Tradition*. *Anglia* 123 (2005): 702–5.

Andrew Wawn, ed. *Constructing Nations, Reconstructing Myth*. *Journal of English and Germanic Philology* 109 (2010): 219–21.

Typeset in Garamond Premier Pro
Composed by Martine Maguire-Weltecke

Medieval Institute Publications
College of Arts and Sciences
Western Michigan University
1903 W. Michigan Avenue
Kalamazoo, MI 49008-5432
http:/ /www.wmich.edu/medieval/mip

WESTERN MICHIGAN UNIVERSITY